From Identity to Politics

*The Lesbian and Gay Movements
in the United States*

In the series

QUEER POLITICS, QUEER THEORIES

edited by Shane Phelan

From Identity to Politics

The Lesbian and Gay Movements in the United States

CRAIG A. RIMMERMAN

TEMPLE UNIVERSITY PRESS
Philadelphia

Temple University Press, Philadelphia 19122
Copyright © 2002 by Temple University
All rights reserved
Published 2002
Printed in the United States of America

⊛ The paper used in this publication meets the requirements of the American
National Standard for Information Sciences—Permanence of Paper for Printed
Library Materials, ANSI Z39.48-1984.

Library of Congress Cataloging-in-Publication Data

Rimmerman, Craig A.
    From identity to politics : the lesbian and gay movements in the United States /
Craig A. Rimmerman.
    p. cm. — (Queer politics, queer theories)
  Includes bibliographical references and index.
    ISBN 1-56639-904-1 (cl. : alk. paper) — ISBN 1-56639-905-X (pbk.)
    1. Gay liberation movement—United States. 2. Gay rights—United States.
  3. United States—Social policy. 4. United States—Politics and government.
  I. Title. II. Series.

  HQ76.8.U+
  305.9'0664–dc21   2001027644

This book is dedicated to
Eleanor Taylor Rimmerman.
May she grow up in a more decent,
just, and humane world.

Contents

Acknowledgments

GIVEN THAT liberal democracy has provided a certain measure of lesbian and gay rights, what are its limits? Is it possible for the lesbian and gay movements to link identity concerns with a progressive coalition for political, social, and economic change, one that takes into account race, class, and gender inequities? What are the barriers to doing so? What might such a strategy look like in practice? These are the questions at the heart of this book and that have informed my thinking over the past five years. They are not easy questions and there are few easy answers. But these questions are important, especially for political scientists, because they address issues of power, marginalization, and difference.

In attempting to do justice to such important questions, I draw upon the work of an increasing body of interdisciplinary scholarship and journalism that explores various aspects of the lesbian and gay movements. My analysis draws on a number of personal interviews that I have conducted over the past eight years in Washington, D.C., and New York City, not to mention the many informal conversations about these issues that I have had with activists, scholars, and journalists. I acknowledge the pioneering work of these committed people, who have provided me and other teachers and scholars with a wealth of material on which to draw. This book is also informed by my American Political Science Association Congressional Fellowship, which I enjoyed during the 1992–93 academic year, working in the offices of Senator Tom Daschle (D–South Dakota) and former Representative Barbara Kennelly (D-Connecticut). I watched the first eight months of the Clinton administration unfold from my privileged position as a staffer on Capitol Hill, and this book has very much benefited from the discussions that I had with many of my co-workers and other American Political Science Association Congressional Fellows, and from my own observations in the corridors of Congress.

I wish to thank the leaders of a number of national movement organizations, who generously provided material for this book through a series of personal interviews. Because I promised them anonymity I cannot thank them by name here, but I remain grateful for the invaluable assistance they provided.

I also acknowledge conversations with students in my Sexual Minority Movements and Public Policy course at Hobart and William Smith

ix

Colleges, conversations that have convinced me that a book like this needed to be written. All of my students have inspired me to celebrate the joys of teaching and my life's work as a teacher. A number of my colleagues continually remind me of the crucial connection between quality teaching and scholarship in a liberal arts setting. I thank Betty Bayer, Chip Capraro, Jodi Dean, Manisha Desai, Robert Gross, Chris Gunn, Susan Henking, Steven Lee, Derek Linton, Dunbar Moodie, Ilene Nicholas, David Ost, Eric Patterson, Lee Quinby, Don Spector, Deborah Tall, and David Weiss for their longstanding encouragement, support, and generosity. David Ost suggested the title for this book, and words cannot express all that he has been and done for me over the years. I also appreciate the support and encouragement of friends Mary Caponegro, Carola Frege, and Aida Hozic, three wonderful human beings, whose friendship and wisdom I cherish.

Dan Mulvey, Hobart and William Smith's fine interlibrary-loan librarian, helped me locate various books and articles that have informed this project in so many ways. I am very grateful to Bill Crumlish and to his staff for all of their excellent research resources and professionalism over the years. And as always, I appreciate the generous support of Pat Cool, Dawn Feligno, Melody Joyce, and Kelly Switzer, whose various administrative contributions on Hobart and William Smith's campus are clearly undervalued and, more importantly, underpaid. Thank you for your good cheer and encouragement over the past fifteen years.

A special thanks goes to Patricia Cain, who very generously reviewed the entire manuscript and offered detailed comments on Chapter 3. An anonymous reviewer for Temple University Press offered a most thoughtful and beautifully written response to the completed first draft. The efforts of these two reviewers remind me that I am indeed privileged to be part of a profession where colleagues whom I do not even know are generous with their time and expertise.

I have been particularly fortunate to have had Doris Braendel as my editor at Temple University Press. Not only is Doris a superb editor, one who represents the publishing business in the best of ways, but she is a generous, decent, and gentle human being. I thank Shane Phelan, the original editor of Temple's "Queer Politics, Queer Theories" series, who supported this project from its inception some five years ago. Margaret Weinstein, Jennifer French, and Shamell Roberts of Temple University Press helped usher the book into its published form, and Janet Greenwood made sure that the project maintained a timely production schedule. Elizabeth Johns applied her considerable copyediting skills to the manuscript. I know that the finished project is much more clearly written as a result of her incredible hard work and dedication to her craft.

All writers need pleasant diversions from the task at hand. Mine come in the form of reading contemporary fiction and listening to classical music. I am fortunate to have two fine independent bookstores here in Ithaca, New York—the Bookery and Borealis Books. Thanks to Jack Goldman and his staff at the Bookery and Ellen Kline and her staff at Borealis for responding to my various requests for books. And a special thanks, as well, to Ted Richards, Eliot Sternfeld, and Jim Tenney of Olsson's Books and Records in Washington, D.C. Ted, Eliot, and Jim have provided a treasure trove of reading and music recommendations over the years.

This book is addressed to several different audiences. First and foremost, I hope that it is taught to and read by undergraduates in colleges and universities. It is written with that goal in mind. Second, I trust that lesbian, gay, bisexual, and transgendered activists might read part or all of this book and interrogate some of the ideas presented here. I have enormous respect for the many scholars and activists who have preceded me, and any criticisms that appear in the pages of this book are not meant to diminish their accomplishments in any way. Indeed, their courageous work has made my life as a teacher, scholar, and activist much easier. Third, I believe that this book makes a qualitative contribution to political science. Those who look for a tight empirical analysis of the lesbian and gay movements will be disappointed. But those political scientists who are interested in connecting theory and practice, thus linking our work to the practical world of politics, may find something of interest here.

This book is dedicated to my five-year-old niece, Eleanor Taylor Rimmerman. She is named after my late mother, who died at sixty-four on June 20, 1991, after a courageous but ultimately losing battle against breast cancer. In a just world, my mother would be alive to see the publication of this book and to watch her granddaughter develop into a young woman. In dedicating this book to Eleanor, I acknowledge the crucial importance of educating the young about the challenging issues that pervade this book. May she grow up in a more tolerant, decent, just, and humane world.

From Identity to Politics

The Lesbian and Gay Movements
in the United States

1 Perspectives on the Lesbian and Gay Movements

We forget that all significant political change, and this is going to be the case for gays more than anyone, doesn't just need a wide spectrum of styles and strategies—it depends on a wide range of styles and strategies.

—Franklin Kameny, veteran Washington, D.C., activist

FRANKLIN KAMENY'S observation captures both the limitations and the possibilities of the contemporary lesbian and gay movements. He reminds us that, like most other contemporary social movements, they have made progress by embracing an array of approaches to political, social, and economic change. Indeed, to talk about "the movement" essentializes the rich number of communities, approaches, and debates that have contributed to the lengthy struggle for lesbian, gay, transgendered, and bisexual rights in this country.[1]

Yet regardless of how we conceptualize "the movement," lesbians and gay men can celebrate progress.[2] Over the past twenty-five years, the lesbian and gay movements have achieved greater visibility and more legal protections (Bronski 1998). How has this progress been manifested? There are open communities of lesbians and gay men in urban areas throughout the United States. In addition, openly gay men and lesbians have been successful in the electoral arena, as they have been elected to city councils, state legislatures, and the United States Congress. Community organizations and businesses exist that appeal directly to the needs of the lesbian and gay population (Escoffier 1998, 33). Lesbians and gay men have infiltrated mainstream culture in television, film, and music. The 1998 Pulitzer Prize for fiction was awarded to Michael Cunningham, an openly gay man, for his powerful novel, *The Hours*.

But for all of the so-called "progress," lesbians and gay men remain second-class citizens in vital ways. Fewer than one-tenth of one percent of all elected officials in the United States are openly lesbian, gay, or bisexual. Lesbians and gay men are forbidden to marry, to teach in many public schools, to adopt children, to provide foster care, to serve in the armed forces, National Guard, reserves, or the ROTC. If evicted from their homes, expelled from their schools, fired from their jobs, or refused public lodging, they usually are not able to seek legal redress. The topic of homosexuality is often deemed inappropriate for discussion in public schools, including in sex education courses. Many public school libraries refuse to own some of the many books that address the issue in important ways. Lesbians and gays are often reviled by the church and barred from membership in the clergy. They are the victims of hate crimes and targets of verbal abuse. Their parents reject them, and many gay youth have either attempted or contemplated suicide. Indeed, one political scientist concludes that "no other group of persons in American society today, having been convicted of no crime, is subject to the number and severity of legally imposed disabilities as are persons of same-sex orientation" (Hertzog 1996, 6).

Like all other social movements, the lesbian and gay rights movements have often been divided over approaches to political, social, and cultural change. In one major approach, the assimilationists typically embrace a rights-based perspective and work within the broader framework of liberal, pluralist democracy, fighting for a seat at the table. Theirs is a "work within the system" approach to political and social change. Typically, they espouse a "let us in" approach to political activism, rather than the "let us show you a new way of conceiving the world" style associated with lesbian and gay liberation.[3] Assimilationists are more likely to accept that progress will have to be incremental, and that slow, gradual change is built into the very framework of our government. A second approach, the liberationist perspective, favors more radical, cultural change, change that is transformational in nature and that often arises from outside the political mainstream. Much of the conflict within the lesbian and gay movements concerning political and social strategy has reflected disagreements over assimilation and liberation. It is far too facile to reduce this conflict to a simple dualism. However, the assimilation and liberation categories are useful for understanding the dominant strains within the lesbian and gay movements in the United States over the past fifty years. Liberationists argue that there is a considerable gap between access and power, and that it is not enough simply to have a seat at the table. For many liberationists, what is required is a strategy that embraces both structural political and cultural change, often through "outsider" political tactics. The political and cultural approaches are not mutually exclusive.

The ability of assimilationists and liberationists to work with one another at various times has helped to achieve important progress for lesbians and gays, as will be suggested throughout this book. Yet this strength is also a weakness. The movements have been characterized by a deep ambiguity over what should be their goals, as recent debates over integration of the military, lesbian and gay marriage, and the Millennium

March suggest. Such differences among movement leaders have had negative practical consequences in terms of public policy outcomes, especially when the Christian Right has enormous resources at its disposal for fighting any advances for lesbians and gays.

This book addresses the following questions in light of the themes I have just stated: Given that it has afforded lesbians and gays a certain measure of rights, what are the limits of liberal democracy? To the extent that the lesbian and gay movements continue to work within the framework of "interest-group liberalism," will they merely pursue a reformist strategy embracing a narrow form of identity politics? Is it possible for the movements to link identity concerns within a progressive coalition for political, social, and economic change, one that takes into account race, class, and gender inequities? What are the barriers to doing so? What might such a strategy look like in practice? Can such change be accomplished working within the broader confines of liberal democracy?

In recent years, the mainstream lesbian and gay movements have largely been based on a fundamentally flawed conception of American politics. It is one that reinforces a narrow form of identity politics rooted in a top-down, state-centered approach and that embraces the language and framework of liberal democratic institutions, interest-group liberalism, and pluralist democracy. This book proposes to evaluate that approach critically and to evaluate how well it has succeeded in advancing the status of lesbians and gays in the political, social, and economic spheres. This is an appropriate time to assess the strategies and overall direction of the lesbian and gay movements, especially since American politics and political discourse have become much more conservative over the past twenty years. Before we can accomplish these goals, we must first provide a brief overview of each of the key concepts that are central elements of the overall analysis.

LIBERAL DEMOCRACY, INTEREST-GROUP LIBERALISM, AND PLURALISM

Liberal democracy is the political and economic framework that has guided the American political system since its founding well over two hundred years ago. It rejects excessive interference from the federal government in the private sphere and promotes the right of individuals to pursue their own interests in the economic marketplace. Liberal democracy works in tandem with classical liberalism to promote values that are central to the American ideology: individualism, equality of opportunity, liberty and freedom, the rule of law, and limited government. Those who embrace liberal democratic principles generally believe that the principal decision makers should be political elites chosen by the citizenry in periodic elections. Citizens play a passive role in the political system to the extent that their participation consists merely of periodic voting. And if citizens choose not to vote, then many proponents of liberal democracy contend that they are generally satisfied with the existing state of affairs.[4] As James Scott has suggested, "for the pluralists, the absence of significant protest or radical opposition in relatively open political systems must be taken as a sign of satisfaction or, at least, insufficient dissatisfaction to warrant the time and trouble of political mobilization" (Scott 1990, 72).

Political scientists have embraced the pluralist model to describe the institutionalized politics associated with a healthy liberal democracy. Yet as Doug McAdam has pointed out, "the model is important for what it implies about organized political activity that takes place outside the political system" (McAdam 1982, 5). The central tenet of pluralist theory is that power is not concentrated in the hands of any one element in society; it is widely distributed among a host of competing groups. Robert Dahl explains how pluralist theory works in the United States: "Political power is pluralistic in the sense that there exist many different sets of leaders; each set has somewhat different objectives from the others, each has access to its own political resources, each is relatively independent of the others. There does not exist a single set of all-powerful leaders who are wholly agreed on their major goals and who have enough power to achieve their major goals" (quoted in McAdam 1982, 5). This broad distribution of power means that the political system is open and responsive to a wide array of competing claims. Because of the open nature of liberal democracy, as conceptualized in this way, there is no need for individuals to embrace any form of unconventional politics—that is, one that requires participants to go outside the formal channels of the American political system (voting, interest-group politics) to resort to the politics of protest and mass involvement. Those lesbians and gays who endorse an assimilationist, insider-politics strategy are choosing to work within this broader pluralist framework, which also accepts the dictates of interest-group liberalism.

The central feature of interest-group liberalism "is the adjudication through compromise of competing interests" (Phelan 1994, 105). Theodore Lowi, whose classic work *The End of Liberalism* remains the most important analysis of interest-group liberalism, is worth quoting at length:

> It is liberalism because it is optimistic about government, expects to use government in a positive and expansive role, is motivated by the highest sentiments, and possesses a strong faith that what is good for government is good for the society. It is interest-group liberalism because it sees as both necessary and good a policy agenda that is accessible to all organized interests and makes no independent judgment of their claims. It is interest group

liberalism because it defines the public interest as a result of the amalgamation of various claims. (Lowi 1979, 51)

Lowi then makes the important connection between interest-group liberalism and pluralism:

A brief sketch of the working model of interest-group liberalism turns out to be a vulgarized version of the pluralist model of modern political science: (1) Organized interests are homogeneous and easy to define. Any duly elected representative of any interest is taken as an accurate representative of each and every member. (2) Organized interests emerge in every sector of our lives and adequately represent most of those sectors, so that one organized group can be found effectively answering and checking some other organized group as it seeks to prosecute its claims against society. And (3) the role of government is one of insuring access to the most effectively organized, and of ratifying the agreements and adjustments worked out among the competing leaders. (Lowi 1979, 51)

This hierarchical, top-down model of American institutional politics is one that nicely dovetails with liberal democracy.

But what if the political process is not nearly as open and responsive to minority groups as the pluralists and the proponents of interest-group liberalism suggest? The roots of this question explain why social movements have historically been a vital part of the American political system. Over time, lesbians and gays have been largely unrepresented in the political process and have faced numerous structural and cultural barriers as they attempt to secure their rights politically. Supreme Court Justice William Brennan, dissenting from denial of certiorari in the case of *Rowland v. Mad River Local School District* (1985), stated the problem well: "Because of the immediate and severe opprobrium often manifested against homosexuals once so identified publicly, members of this group are particularly powerless to pursue their rights openly in the political arena" (cited in Wachtell, Lipton, Rosen, and Katz 1993, 19). From the vantage point of many lesbians and gays, the pluralist political process is hardly responsive at all. But if the pluralist model is accurate, why do we even need social movements? It is to a brief discussion of these questions, which underlie this entire book, that we now turn.

SOCIAL MOVEMENTS AND MARGINALIZATION THEORY

Anti-pluralists have pointed out that social movements arise because the political and economic system is less open than pluralists believe. Over time, social movements have become an integral part of the American political landscape. How are they different from parties, interest groups, and protests? Three factors distinguish them: (1) they grow out of "a mass base of individuals, groups, and organizations linked by social interaction"; (2) they also "organize around a mix of political and cultural goals"; and (3) they "rely on a shared collective identity that is the basis of mobilization and participation" (Wald 2000, 5). Social movements are also decentralized and made up of an array of organizations. Social movements are often confused with political movements, but there are key differences between them, as Table 1.1 suggests.

Unlike political movements, which tend to represent middle-class interests, social movements represent those at the margins of American society, as defined by class, race, gender, and/or sexual orientation. Political movements are also often identified with a single leader and her or his organization, while social movements are generally much more decentralized and sometimes have no real leader per se. Finally, social movements develop a comprehensive ideology, while political movements most often focus on narrow political objectives such as handgun control or the nuclear freeze. Social movements push for political change at the same time that they often seek structural change in the social, cultural, economic, and private spheres as well (Baer and Bositis, 1993). The lesbian and gay movements certainly meet the criteria for an existing social movement. Lesbians, gays, bisexuals, and transgendered people have persistently occupied a place at the margins of American society.

The vulnerability of groups at the margins of American society[5] permits elites to create serious obstacles to political participation and to control the political agenda (Scott 1990, 72). In response to their structural and cultural marginalization, groups outside the mainstream identify strategies that they perceive will meet their needs while challenging structures that constrain their life choices. These strategies commonly include developing alternative resources, constructing different ideological frame-

TABLE 1.1. Social and Political Movements Compared

Social Movements	Political Movements
Ideology	Lifestyle
Multiple Leaders	Single Leader Entrepreneur
Social and Political Spheres	Political Spheres Only
Have-Nots	Haves
Social Group Identity	Diverse Social Groups
Group Consciousness	Issue Positions

Source: Denise L. Baer and David A. Bositis, *Politics and Linkage in a Democratic Society* (Englewood Cliffs: Prentice-Hall, 1993), 166. © 1993. Reprinted by permission of Prentice-Hall, Inc., Upper Saddle River, NJ.

works, and creating oppositional organizations and institutions. Such structures are most often "grounded in the indigenous or communal relationships of marginal groups" (Cohen 1999, 48). This is especially true for the lesbian and gay movements.[6]

From the vantage point of marginalized groups, then, social movements are seen as a vehicle for organization, education, and resistance. Social movements include those activities that comprise, as Darnovsky, Epstein, and Flacks explain it, "persistent, patterned, and widely distributed collective challenges to the status quo." They encompass a wide array of strategies and approaches to political and social change; in this way, they "appear to be simultaneously spontaneous and strategic, expressive (of emotion and need) and instrumental (seeking some concrete ends), unruly and organized, political and cultural" (Darnovsky, Epstein, and Flacks 1995, vii). Under what circumstances do social movements form, survive over time, and influence public policy? Several factors have been identified by students of social-movement theory: a mature communications network, media attention, a series of crises or more general social change, movement resources, movement activity, and supportive public opinion (Haider-Markel 1999, 243). One of the most important activities that social movements engage in is creating "issue frames." The framing of issues and grievances is crucial for movement members and supporters alike, as they devise political and social strategies for challenging policy elites to respond to their concerns. Issue frames change as social-movement members alter their conceptions of what can and needs to be accomplished in terms of strategy and public policy. Donald Haider-Markel provides a succinct statement of what constitutes successful framing: "Successfully constructed frames usually appeal to widely held values and are, therefore, more likely to invoke government response and mobilize potential participants" (ibid., 245).[7]

Students of social-movement behavior have pointed out that the contradictory nature of movement activity has challenged both political and social systems, as well as analytic categories and explanatory frameworks. These complications have certainly arisen in the context of the lesbian and gay movements over the years. For that reason, this book does not embrace one approach to understanding the movements. Instead, it borrows from the resource-mobilization, political-process, and new-social-movement theory approaches. Much of the conflict among social movements is over who controls access to power, a concept that is of particular interest to political scientists. Ultimately, this book is concerned with the nature and distribution of power in the United States, and conflicts over power, as reflected in how the lesbian and gay movements have intersected with political and public-policy processes at all levels of government.[8]

RESOURCE-MOBILIZATION AND POLITICAL-PROCESS APPROACHES TO SOCIAL MOVEMENTS

The resource-mobilization and political-process perspectives on social movements de-emphasize the specifics of group grievances and focus instead on macrolevel external political processes, as well as the internal characteristics of organizations that have consequences for both the development and the daily work of movements (Taylor and Whittier 1992, 104). Of central interest to the resource-mobilization approach are the resources available to the group. What resources determine the success or failure of a social movement? Leadership, organizational capacity, and wealth are such qualities, and they are generally associated with groups that have established extensive social ties and well-developed structures for internal communication and social interaction. In their study of the battles over local gay-rights initiatives, James Button, Barbara Rienzo, and Kenneth Wald (1997) conclude that groups possessing an abundance of these resources and qualities are much more likely to succeed. They found that certain characteristics were particularly important in determining the outcome of campaigns on behalf of gay and lesbian concerns: the level of social and political organization, gay leaders' skills, and "the gay community's" financial resources (pp. 16–17).

The organizational structure of the movement is crucial to resource-mobilization theorists. They also view the activities of collective actors in terms of tactics and strategy. This permits them to "examine movements and countermovements as engaged in a rational game to achieve specific interests, much like pluralist competition among interest groups in political analysis" (Johnston, Larana, and Gusfield 1994, 5). The key here is that movements can be understood not as spontaneous and formless phenomena but as deliberate and patterned frameworks of collective action that operate to achieve specific movement goals. The broad goal of resource-mobilization theory is to understand the conditions that promote both movement growth and political effectiveness (Darnovsky, Epstein, and Flacks 1995, xii).

The central contribution of the resource-mobilization approach is the recognition that social movements are "shaped more by opportunities available to members for expression and action than by the ideologies they profess to represent" (Darnovsky, Epstein, and Flacks 1995, xii). Their actions are then connected in a formal way to practical accomplishments, such as a short-term impact on public policy. The resource-mobilization approach is also useful for understanding the established, "work within the system" gay and lesbian organizations that embrace insider, elite-centered, pluralist politics. Yet an uncritical acceptance of the pluralist, interest-group, liberal model of political change is also a central weakness of any systematic attempt to use the resource-mobilization approach to analyze the lesbian and gay movements. It cannot account for groups that embrace unconventional politics, such as ACT UP,[9] Queer Nation, and the Lesbian Avengers. For this and other reasons, the resource-mobilization model is insufficient for understanding the lesbian and gay movements, as Noël Sturgeon suggests:

> While based on an elite model of politics, resource mobilization thus reveals a repressed pluralist belief system: that "out" groups can be included in the political system without major structural change. Resource mobilization cannot thoroughly account for movements that attempt political change through direct changes in what are seen as "private" social relations, or through a complex contestation with various other social forces over the discursive construction of a range of political and economic developments whose political implications are ambiguous. (Sturgeon 1995, 38)

In this sense, then, the resource-mobilization approach, by itself, is unconvincing as an analytical tool for understanding social movements. Recognizing these limitations, social-movement theorists have developed alternative approaches to understanding social movements. It is to a discussion of the political-process and new-social-movement approaches that we now turn.

Like the resource-mobilization approach, the political-process approach also focuses on movement resources. But the political-process perspective focuses more attention on the external resources of the political system, rather than the internal resources of movement organizations. Doug McAdam's 1982 study of the civil rights movement, which traced the development of the movement to political, organizational, and consciousness change, synthesized various political-process approaches into a full-fledged model.[10]

As McAdam points out, theories of social movements cannot be separated from a more general conception of institutionalized power. Like the resource-mobilization model, the political-process model is also consistent with the elite model of the political system. The core assumption is that wealth and power in the United States are concentrated in the hands of the very few. As a result, most people have little control over the large political decisions that impinge on their lives. Both the resource-mobilization and political-process models view social movements "as rational attempts by excluded groups to mobilize sufficient political leverage to advance collective interests through noninstitutionalized means" (McAdam 1982, 36–37). The political-process approach denies the omnipotence of centralized elite rule while also recognizing that the inequality in power between the elite and excluded groups is substantial. Unlike the resource-mobilization approach, the political-process approach is rooted in the notion that the elite will generally exercise power in ways that will enable them to protect their privileged positions in society. Proponents of the resource-mobilization approach believe that some elites will actually encourage social insurgency on behalf of excluded groups, whereas those who adhere to the political-process model think that such elite activity is very unlikely (ibid., 38–39).

To those who subscribe to the political-process model, "movements develop in response to an ongoing process of action between movement groups and the larger sociopolitical environment they seek to change" (McAdam 1982, 40). The model describes insurgency as a response to factors both internal and external to the movement. McAdam identifies three sets of factors that shape insurgency: "the confluence of expanding political opportunities, indigenous organizational strength, and the presence of certain shared cognitions within the minority community" (ibid., 58–59). In support of this third factor, the development of a collective identity, shared values, and shared demands is essential if groups are to acquire "the capacity for exercising effective political power" (Sherrill 1993, 112). Like most political and social movements, the lesbian and gay movements have endured fissures and splits over what strategies to adopt, and these disagreements have been an obstacle to combating the considerable resources of the Christian Right. These three factors will be used to evaluate insurgency in the lesbian and gay movements. Each concept will be developed more fully at relevant points along the way. The political-process approach to studying social movements does not fully capture the intricacies of movements that organize at least partially around identity politics. With that in mind, it is important to integrate new-social-movement theory in our approach to understanding lesbian and gay movements.

NEW-SOCIAL-MOVEMENT THEORY

The resource-mobilization and political-process perspectives have dominated most of the social-movement theoretical work in the United States. What this has meant in practice is that organizational, political, and structural aspects of social movements have been privileged over "the more cultural or ideational dimensions of collective action" (McAdam 1994, 36).

The underlying principles of new-social-movement theory were developed in Western Europe during the late 1980s and early 1990s. New-social-movement theorists typically embrace social protest that attempts to transform societies in fundamental and emancipatory ways. The focus is on broad structural and social change as opposed to the attitudinal and organizational studies generally associated with American resource-mobilization theory. The central goal of new-social-movement theory is to address the "why" rather than the "how" of social movements. As it does so, it attempts to link social movements to large-scale cultural or structural change. Such linkages include the connections among the structural sources of social movements, their relation to the culture of advanced capitalist society, and their ideologies (Mayer and Roth 1995, 300). At its core, new-social-movement theory emphasizes the importance of understanding identity in everyday life. As applied to lesbian and gay movements and other identity-based movements, new-social-movement theory suggests "that large-scale social change is accomplished in face-to-face relations, at the level of personal identity and consciousness, in the household and neighborhood, whether or not such change is enunciated in public policy and macro-level power relations" (Darnovsky, Epstein, and Flacks 1995, xiii–xiv). Such views of identity have been associated with the "queer politics" that emerged in the United States during the late 1980s. Queer theorists reject essentialist notions of identity—the belief that identity is fixed. Embracing the social-constructionist perspective, queer theorists have challenged those studying the gay and lesbian movements in important ways.[11] For example, how are politics even possible when relevant actors champion the fluidity of identity and resist categorization? And just what is the relationship between culture and politics in so-called "new" movements? What should it be?

New-social-movement theory has done less well in answering these questions and in addressing issues of class, power, and policy in meaningful ways. By itself, then, it is an inadequate framework for understanding the contemporary lesbian and gay "movements,"[12] which often go beyond mere identity politics. But used in combination with elements of the resource-mobilization and political-process approaches, new-social-movement theory is a useful explanatory framework. This book attempts to build on these approaches by placing the factors that shape insurgency—political opportunities, indigenous organizational strength, and views shared by members of the gay and lesbian community—within the broader context of class, power, policy, and identity politics.

THE ASSIMILATIONIST, RIGHTS-BASED STRATEGY

The quest for equal rights is at the core of the contemporary lesbian and gay rights movements' strategy. As we will soon see, this rights-based approach has dominated mainstream movement thinking from the early years of the homophile movement to today's debates over the military-service ban and same-sex marriage. Over time, this rights-based strategy has pivoted on the state's relationship to lesbians and gay men. Lesbians and gays have fought for the right to live their personal lives as fully and freely as possible from negative state intervention. At the same time, they have asked the state to intervene more positively to protect their ability to meet basic daily needs. How have these issues manifested themselves politically? The movements have organized to abolish laws that restrict the right of individuals to engage in private, consensual sexual relations. In addition, they have fought against discrimination in employment, housing, and public accommodation and for equal legal protection. This claim of equal legal rights has led to the further demand that lesbians and gays should be entitled to have their intimate relationships "recognized legally, institutionally, and socially" (Blasius 1994, 132). This demand, if transformed by the state into a right, would enable lesbians and gays to enjoy the same privileges that are currently the province of heterosexuals. Finally, in light of the AIDS crisis, the movements have demanded that the state provide lesbians and gays with distributive justice in their right to pursue their sexual health, free from stigma and discrimination.[13] These are the central elements of the rights-based strategy, which has largely been unquestioned and unchallenged by the contemporary lesbian and gay movements. In the pages that follow, I examine what this assimilationist, rights-based strategy has accomplished over the years, suggesting that it has proved far too narrow and ultimately limited.

METHODOLOGICAL CHALLENGES

A central goal of this book is to identify the political strategies that will best promote the social, economic, cultural, and political changes that lesbians, gays, bisexuals, and transgendered people need in order to achieve much more than a "place at the table" or "virtual equality."[14] In his fine comparative analysis of the contemporary lesbian and gay movements in Canada, the United States, and the United Kingdom, David Rayside cautions that scholars writing on social movements in general, and the lesbian and gay movements more specifically, are often guilty of two serious mistakes: we romanticize the movement under study "and imagine that all failings are a result of factors external to it," and we tend to treat mainstream movement activists as "unwitting dupes easily assimilated and drawn into unprincipled compromise" (Rayside 1998, xiv). Social-movement politics are conflictual, messy, and complicated; they defy easy generalizations and often even explanations for various behaviors and strategies. I hope that the analysis that follows captures some of this complexity as it pertains to the lesbian and gay movements. My goal has certainly been to avoid the problems that Rayside so clearly describes.

The AIDS policy and activist arena, discussed in detail in Chapter 4, is one that reveals the often-complicated relationship between lesbians and gay men. These complications cannot be separated from the privileges of power, status, and wealth that men have always enjoyed, relative to women, in American society. We will see in Chapter 2 that lesbians have played courageous and integral roles in the development of the broader lesbian and gay movements over time. Beth E. Schneider and Nancy E. Stoller have argued that "sustained attention to the social relations of race, class, sexuality, and culture" deserve considerable attention (Schneider and Stoller 1995, 4). This book examines these social relations within the context of inequalities in resources that impinge on the ability of women to engage in political organizing at all levels of the American political system.

The AIDS policy narrative, which has largely and understandably been offered by gay men, and then replicated by elements of the larger society, has generally understated the crucial roles played by women during the epidemic. Nancy Stoller reminds us of the importance of considering an alternative narrative:

> Although AIDS has struck men in higher numbers than women, women have been among the ill since the beginning. They have also been involved as caretakers, educators, physicians, public health officials, and community activists. As a diverse group linked by gender in an epidemic where gender and sexuality are key, women and lesbians in particular have played powerful symbolic, sexual, and social roles. (Stoller 1995, 275)

This alternative narrative has received little attention in most of the scholarly work on AIDS policy and activism. But it is an important one, especially in a society that regards health care as a privilege or "benefit" rather than as a right. It is also important to consider this narrative as we attempt to examine the many challenges and debates facing the lesbian and gay movements with regard to political organizing and policy strategy. One of those challenges is to highlight the importance of breast cancer education, prevention, and treatment for lesbians, in particular, and women more generally. Just as lesbians played a crucial role in organizing around AIDS in the 1980s and 1990s, gay men should play an integral role in insuring that the health care service delivery system is more responsive to the specific needs of women. These issues are examined more fully in Chapter 6.

THE PLAN OF THE BOOK

Chapter 2 examines electoral and interest-group politics within the context of changing political opportunities, and it emphasizes the limitations of a top-down, insider approach to political, social, and cultural change. This reformist approach has been practiced by an array of national lesbian and gay organizations, including the Human Rights Campaign, the National Gay and Lesbian Task Force, the Gay and Lesbian Victory Fund, and the Lambda Legal Defense and Education Fund. The goals and policies of these organizations are outlined in both contemporary and historical context.[15] The discussion here is meant to lay the groundwork for a discussion of the role of national organizations in key policy areas, including the military-service ban, lesbian and gay marriage, and AIDS. In doing so, Chapter 2 examines indigenous organizational strength and shared views within the lesbian and gay community, two of the crucial components of movement insurgency.

Some attention is also devoted in Chapter 2 to the advantages of having openly lesbian and gay officials serve at all levels of government. The chapter addresses these questions: In what ways does their election further the lesbian and gay movements? What can we expect them to accomplish, given the limitations of working within the liberal democratic framework? To what extent do they merely reinforce a narrow form of lesbian and gay identity politics? Finally, Chapter 2 explores the advantages and disadvantages of working within the framework of liberal democratic principles and considers whether having access to those in power will further the lesbian and gay movements' desire for greater equality at all levels of society. A key goal of this book is to examine the complicated relationship between a top-down approach to political change and the grassroots organizing and mobilizing strategies that are integral to any political and social movement.

If an electoral and interest-group-based strategy will not allow the movements to transcend assimilationist goals, then perhaps a legal-rights strategy will do so. Chapter 3 outlines the basic elements of a legal-rights strategy and identifies the limitations and possibilities of such an approach. This strategy has been championed by many within the lesbian and gay movements because they believe that the law reflects societal prejudices and fears. As a result, it needs to be altered to take into account the basic rights of lesbians and gays. Those who criticize a legal-rights strategy view it as another approach that reinforces liberal democratic, pluralist principles rooted in top-down, state-centered politics, one that focuses far too much attention on the individual.

The chapter explores the limitations and possibilities of a legal-rights strategy by considering three key policy areas: legal strategies challenging the "Don't Ask, Don't Tell" policy, the Supreme Court's *Bowers v. Hardwick* decision (1986), and same-sex marriage. Ultimately, the chapter addresses these questions: What have the movements accomplished when pursuing a legal-rights strategy? In what ways does such a strategy merely reinforce the basic principles of interest-group liberalism? Can such a strategy be pursued without merely reinforcing a narrowly based identity politics? If so, how?

Chapters 2 and 3 examine the lesbian and gay movements largely in terms of top-down, state-centered approaches. Chapter 4, however, explores the grassroots elements of these movements, by evaluating unconventional politics as practiced by groups such as ACT UP, Queer Nation, and the Lesbian Avengers. Unconventional, direct-action politics as practiced in the lesbian and gay movements are placed within their proper historical and theoretical context. The chapter examines AIDS policy at the federal level during the Reagan, Bush, and Clinton administrations, thus providing a context for examining the direct-action, unconventional politics that arose in response to the federal government's neglect of the 1980s and early 1990s. The chapter also explores the tensions between those within the lesbian and gay movements who embrace unconventional politics and those who champion mainstream electoral, interest-group politics.

The consequences of unconventional politics are explored by examining the role played by ACT UP in AIDS policy making. The following questions are addressed: What have been the results of ACT UP's organizing for AIDS policy? What has been the relationship between ACT UP and mainstream AIDS organizations, such as the AIDS Action Council? Are these organizations merely an embodiment of a radical form of nationalistic, identity politics? In what ways have such organizations challenged the underlying presuppositions of liberal democratic, pluralist politics? Discussion of these issues is set in the context of the social-movement theoretical synthesis outlined earlier. Finally, the chapter examines the apparent decline in grassroots activism within the lesbian and gay movements since the early 1990s and attempts to account for this development. One possible explanation is that lesbians and gay men have embraced a politics of privatism that privileges the economic individualism associated with markets in liberal democratic societies.

Chapter 5 explores the conflicts that have pervaded the American political scene over the past thirty years in response to the lesbian and gay movements. The argument here is that the Christian Right has reacted to the movements' gains by mobilizing and organizing at all levels of government. These conflicts are placed in historical context through a discussion of specific examples, such as the Briggs initiative and Anita Bryant's organizing in the late 1970s, the actions of Jesse Helms, Jerry Falwell, William Dannemeyer, and their supporters in response to AIDS, and the various state and local referendums of the 1970s 1980s, and

1990s. The chapter investigates the Christian Right's actions in thwarting federal, state, and local government responses to AIDS, and the ways the lesbian and gay movements have responded to these efforts. Finally, the chapter concludes by discussing the Christian Right's mobilization in response to Bill Clinton's plan to overturn the ban on lesbians and gays in the military through executive order, and over the issue of lesbian and gay marriage. It also explores how the Christian Right has used radio programming and organized around local school curricular issues to pursue its conservative agenda.

A central purpose of this chapter is to explore the sources of the Christian Right's antagonism toward lesbians and gays. In doing so, it analyzes the relationship between these movements over time. In addition, the chapter devotes considerable attention to the electoral, legislative, and grassroots strategies embraced by the Christian Right in response to the lesbian and gay movements' attempts to achieve greater equality. Finally, Chapter 5 examines how the latter have responded to the Christian Right's organizing efforts over the years. The entire discussion is grounded in the social-movement theoretical synthesis guiding this book.

Chapter 6 outlines a political strategy for the lesbian and gay movements in light of the analysis presented throughout the book. It builds connections between the positive moral dimensions of the black civil rights movement and the quest for substantive equality that should be a central goal of the lesbian and gay civil rights movement. At the same time, it eschews mere rights-based strategies as far too limiting. It attempts to develop a political language that can move the lesbian and gay movements beyond an unquestioning acceptance of liberal democratic principles and link identity politics to broader class, race, and gender concerns, all on behalf of fundamental and progressive political, social, cultural, and economic change. As it develops these ideas, Chapter 6 considers how coalitions might be built with other groups on the American political landscape. (For example, coalitions can surely be built across a variety of interest groups favoring national health insurance in the United States.) This progressive challenge will embrace participatory democratic principles rather than the top-down, state-centered approach that characterizes interest-group liberalism. By its very nature, such an approach must also challenge the economic class, gender, and race-based hierarchies that are reinforced in the lesbian and gay community. The ultimate goal is to question the naturalness and superiority of the heterosexual paradigm. Chapter 6 also explores the barriers to the proposed political strategy and asks how these might be overcome. As we will see throughout this book, the barriers are significant but should not be treated as insurmountable.

Ultimately, our goal must be to build a political and social movement that attempts to weaken hierarchies, challenge prejudices, and end inequalities in political, social, and cultural life. The challenge is to do so in a way that rises above people's sexual identities at the same time that it respects those identities. That is a central challenge of this book.

2 The Assimilationist Strategy

Electoral Politics and Interest-Group Liberalism

If we are to transform our state of virtual equality, evident in pervasive discrimination, ambivalent public opinion, and the persistence of the closet, we must begin with ourselves—both individually and as a movement. Coming out is the one step each gay, lesbian, or bisexual person can take to shatter virtual equality and move closer to the genuine equality with heterosexuals that is our birthright as moral human beings. Our challenge as a movement requires an examination of the strategies that have brought us to this troubling juncture.

—Urvashi Vaid

WHAT ARE THE advantages and possibilities of embracing a top-down, insider-politics approach to political, social, and cultural change? This reformist approach has been practiced largely by the contemporary national lesbian and gay movements, despite an array of structural impediments. Lesbian and gay groups that are organized around sexual-orientation issues face several structural and institutional disadvantages as they enter into mainstream political processes. They often lack the resources of the interest groups with whom they are competing. Kenneth Sherrill argues persuasively that "gay people are saddled with the burdens of cumulative inequalities." As a result, the mainstream political process "is far more likely to deprive [lesbian/gay/bisexual] people of our rights than to protect those rights" (Sherrill 1996, 469).

Some have argued that the practical impact of federal-government policy toward lesbians and gays has more symbolic than substantive value (Gertsmann 1999, 64). If this is true, the movements should devote more of their resources to the state and local level, rather than squandering invaluable, limited resources at the national level. But this argument is far too simple and ignores the important relationship that can and should be fostered between insider, assimilationist politics often practiced in the national-policy arena and the outsider, grassroots, liberationist politics often embraced at the state and local levels. While this chapter focuses on the national-level political process, chapters 4, 5, and 6 address politics at the state and local levels from a number of different strategic and public-policy perspectives. One political scientist has suggested that a number of variables affect the

18

kind of public policies that are formulated at the national level: "1) the permeability of the institutional settings in which activists work; 2) the constellation of partisan forces; 3) the political leanings of governing parties; 4) the receptivity of the media; 5) the range of allies; 6) the beliefs of the general public" (Rayside 1998, 282–83). These factors are often enormous barriers for the lesbian and gay movements to overcome. In addition, it is difficult to foster and maintain a relationship between the mainstream, assimilationist lesbian and gay movement and outsider, grassroots activist organizations. Yet this relationship is a crucial one, one that needs to be celebrated and encouraged, as the case studies discussed later in this book—the military-service ban, lesbian and gay marriage, and AIDS—make clear.

The analysis begins by placing the contemporary lesbian and gay movements within their proper historical context. As we do so, the tensions between assimilationist and liberationist perspectives are developed. Much of the work of the national lesbian and gay organizations has relied on an insider, assimilationist strategy, one that strives for access to those in power and is rooted in an interest-group and legislative-lobbying approach to political change. The strategy is centered on civil rights, legal reform, political access, visibility, and legitimation. It is an approach that reinforces the existing political and economic framework that is associated with classical liberalism. As Donald Haider-Markel suggests, this strategy "has resulted in congressional activity driven more by gay interest groups and the opposition than by changes in public opinion, or grassroots resources" (Haider-Markel 1997, iii–iv). For those who embrace a liberationist approach, the assimilationist perspective is far too narrow. As Urvashi Vaid has argued, the assimilationist perspective is far too rooted in "virtual equality—a state of conditional equality based more on the appearance of acceptance of straight America than on genuine civic parity" (Vaid 1995, xvi). Liberationists challenge "virtual equality" and emphasize the goals of cultural acceptance, social transformation, understanding, and liberation (ibid., p. 106).

Assimilationist and Liberationist Political Strategies in Historical Context

Popular lore has it that the contemporary lesbian and gay movements began with the Stonewall Rebellion of 1969. Thanks to a number of scholars, we now know that this is not the case. The historian George Chauncey has written of the extensive gay network that developed in the streets, apartments, saloons, and cafeterias of New York City in the late nineteenth and early twentieth centuries.[1] When laws were enacted that prohibited them from gathering in any state-licensed public place, as a part of the virulent New York City crackdown of the 1930s, lesbians and gays fought for their rights in courageous ways—a precursor to the organized political resistance of the Daughters of Bilitis and Mattachine Society of the 1950s. Allan Bérubé's pathbreaking work on lesbians and gays in the military during World War II found that the discriminatory treatment accorded them did not lead to an organized resistance movement per se, but it did inspire many lesbians and gay men to develop an all-important group identity.[2]

John D'Emilio's important historical work chronicles the early years of the Mattachine Society and the Daughters of Bilitis, organizations that developed at the height of the McCarthy Era in the 1950s.[3] And Barry Adam's study of the lesbian and gay movement focuses considerable attention on the rise of the homophile movement in the United States during the 1950s and the connections between that movement and the movements growing out of the Stonewall Rebellion of 1969.[4] These connections are explored more fully later in this chapter.

THE BIRTH OF THE HOMOPHILE MOVEMENT

The homophile movement arose within the context of a prevailing ideology that regarded lesbians and gays "as perverts, psychopaths, deviates, and the like" (D'Emilio 1983, 53). Lesbians and gays internalized these negative labels, which ultimately became stereotypes. As John D'Emilio points out, "whether seen from the vantage point of religion, medicine, or the law, the homosexual or lesbian was a flawed individual, not a victim of injustice. For many, the gay world was reduced to a setting where they shared an affliction" (ibid.).

In its early manifestations, the homophile movement embraced liberationist principles through the Mattachine Society,[5] founded in Los Angeles in 1951. Based on an idea by Harry Hay, then working at the Los Angeles People's Education Center as a music teacher, the Mattachine Society was founded by Hay and several of his Education Center colleagues—Rudi Gernreich, Bob Hull, Dale Jennings, and Chuck Rowland. Hay and his co-organizers built the Mattachine Society based on Communist principles of organizing and social change (Adam 1995, 67–68), a model that would soon lead to considerable controversy within the organization. Mattachine's founding statement of "Missions and Purposes" articulated the intended purposes of the new organization:

- "To unify" those homosexuals "isolated from their own kind . . ."
- "To educate" homosexuals and heterosexuals toward "an ethical homosexual culture . . . paralleling the emerging cultures of our fellow-minorities—the Negro, Mexican, and Jewish Peoples. . . ."

- "To lead"; the "more . . . socially conscious homosexuals [are to] provide leadership to the whole mass of social deviates" and also
- To assist "our people who are victimized daily as a result of our oppression." (quoted in Adam 1995, 68)

As the above principles suggest, the organizers wished to galvanize a large gay constituency, one that was cohesive and capable of militant activity (D'Emilio 1983, 63).

In its early years, the Mattachine Society secured the acquittal of Dale Jennings, who was charged with a sex violation through police entrapment. It also held discussion groups where "group members speculated on causes of homosexuality, reasons for social hostility to it, and whether sexual 'deviants' could lead well-adjusted lives" (D'Emilio 1983, 67). The discussion groups had the impact that the Mattachine founders had intended, as many participants experienced a transformation in consciousness and came "to see themselves as members of a minority group with a need to act collectively" (ibid., 68). Mattachine emerged as the first effective gay political organization in the United States, one that in its early years devoted itself to challenging and repealing repressive legislation and altering public opinion. Out of a Mattachine discussion group emerged One, the first publicly distributed American homophile magazine. The U.S. Post Office placed a ban on One in 1954 but was overruled in 1958 by the Supreme Court, which stated that the ban violated free-speech protections guaranteed by the First Amendment (Adam 1995, 68). This incident serves as a sobering reminder of the repressive nature of the times.

In 1953 the organizational structure and militant ideology of the Mattachine Society was challenged by rank and file organization members. A Los Angeles Daily Mirror columnist had identified Frank Snyder as the lawyer for the organization. Snyder had been an uncooperative witness when called to testify before the House Un-American Activities Committee. Given the repressive political and cultural climate associated with the McCarthy era, it is no surprise that rank and file Mattachine members grew increasingly concerned with the organization's possible association with communism (Hunt 1999, 129). The split that ultimately occurred between the organization's founders and its newer members reflected serious disagreements over assimilation and liberation, conflicts that have plagued the movements over the years. The Mattachine founders envisioned a separate homosexual culture while other members worried that such a strategy would only increase the hostile social climate. Instead, they called for integration into mainstream society (D'Emilio 1983, 81). In the end, Harry Hay was expelled from the Mattachine Society in 1953, at the height of the McCarthy era, due to his Communist Party background and his unwavering support for more radical principles.

Hay's successors—Hal Call, Marilyn Reiger, and David Finn—and Phyllis Lyon and Del Martin, two lesbian activists who founded the Daughters of Bilitis in 1955,[6] all embraced an assimilationist and accommodationist approach to political and social change. In practice this meant the two groups sought to open a productive dialogue with an array of professionals or "experts" who had expressed views concerning homosexuality. Their strategy was to present themselves as reasonable, well-adjusted people, hoping that these heterosexual arbiters of public opinion would rethink their assumptions regarding homosexuality. This approach, rooted in dialogue, emphasized conformity and attempted to minimize any differences between heterosexuality and homosexuality. The activists hoped to de-emphasize sex, since the act of sex itself was the source of so much anger and fear directed at homosexuals. Ultimately, the architects of this assimilationist, accommodationist strategy hoped to reduce social hostility as a necessary precursor to the changes desired in both law and public policy (D'Emilio 1983, 109). They attempted to frame issues in ways that would accomplish this important goal. The Mattachine Society, the Daughters of Bilitis, and the magazine *One* were the central organized elements of the homophile movement until the 1969 Stonewall riots.

The assimilationist, accommodationist strategy prevailed within the broader movement until Stonewall. During the 1960s, the movements experienced slow and incremental growth. The homophile movement witnessed the ascendancy of the medical model of homosexuality, which equated homosexuality with mental illness, a model that was successfully challenged in 1974, when the American Psychiatric Association eliminated homosexuality from its list of recognized disorders (Cruikshank 1992, 68, 105). But there were challenges to the more mainstream homophile, assimilationist strategy by such activists as Barbara Gittings and Franklin Kameny.

In 1965 small numbers of militant homophiles embraced unconventional politics and picketed for basic rights and human dignity. Franklin Kameny was among the demonstrators.[7] Kameny expressed the ideological foundations of the 1960s homophile movement by arguing that homosexuals did not suffer from mental illness, they constituted 10 percent of the population at large, they did not need medical experts to speak on their behalf, and they had a right to live their lives free from discrimination (Clendinen and Nagourney 1999, 114). Several years later he commented on the appropriate use of various political tactics in light of the Stonewall Rebellion:

> I don't believe in picketing until you've tried negotiation and gotten nowhere and then tried picketing and gotten nowhere, then . . . I'm perfectly willing

to go along to the next step—which is probably some sort of confrontation that possibly mildly oversteps the bounds of the law. If that doesn't serve, I'm willing to go further, although I do draw the line at violence. (Teal 1995, 73–74)

Kameny's endorsement of a more radical political strategy, with precedent in the African-American civil rights movement, reflects some of the tensions that would soon be felt within the homophile movement, as it came under increased criticism and scrutiny from more radically minded lesbian and gay activists, who called for liberatory change in light of Stonewall. Such tensions have continued to pervade the movements until today.

By the time of Stonewall, some concrete gains had been made. The Supreme Court had affirmed the legality of lesbian and gay publications. State court rulings in a number of states afforded gay bars more security, and the homophile movement had won constraints on police harassment of lesbians and gays in New York and San Francisco. In employment discrimination cases, the federal court provided the first victories. A dialogue was established with members of the scientific community regarding whether homosexuality should be classified as a mental illness. The movements had begun to achieve occasional media visibility, largely as a result of the shift to public protest. At the time of the Stonewall riots, there were some fifty lesbian and gay organizations nationwide. Finally, and perhaps most importantly, the notion that lesbians and gays were a persecuted minority had not only infiltrated the lesbian and gay subculture but also the larger society (D'Emilio 1992, 238–39).

Despite these accomplishments, the mainstream homophile organizations were thrown on the defensive in wake of Stonewall, as a new style of political organizing and leadership was demanded by newly energized lesbian and gay activists, many of whom were veterans of the various social and political movements of the 1960s. This more confrontational, liberationist approach embraced unconventional politics associated with the antiwar, women's liberation, and civil rights movements. What was the connection between the latter and the lesbian and gay movements? Grant Gallup, a priest who was active in the African-American civil rights movement, makes the connection well: "Many of us who went south to work with Dr. King in the sixties were gay. A lot of gay people who could not come out for their own liberation could invest the same energies in the liberation of black people" (Kaiser 1997, 136). Indeed, as early as 1966, gay activists adopted a symbol of the civil rights movement—a black and white civil rights lapel button with an equals sign on a lavender background (ibid.).

Yet the rights-based strategy associated with the civil rights, women's, and homophile movements came under increased scrutiny and criticism in light of Stonewall. The modern gay liberation movement was soon born, built on some of the same ideas that undergirded the original Mattachine Society almost twenty years earlier. For those who embraced gay liberation, a rights-based strategy was far too limited. In their view, the goal should be to remake society, not merely reform it (Loughery 1998, 323).

It is in this broad context that the Gay Liberation Front (GLF) was founded in late 1969. Toby Marotta captured the essence of the organization in its first few weeks of existence: "Radicals and revolutionaries shared the conviction that since every dimension of the existing system was bankrupt, a total transformation of society was desirable, and that to effect such change, it was necessary to unite all oppressed minorities into a broad-based movement" (Loughery 1998, 324).

As it attempted to build the coalitions necessary for this movement, the GLF championed a broad New Left platform. It attacked the consumer culture, militarism, racism, sexism, and homophobia. In challenging the latter, the GLF devoted considerable energy to how lesbians and gays were represented in the larger culture through language. With this in mind, the more widespread but clinical term "homosexual" was replaced by "gay," "pride" became an important feature of liberation consciousness, and "coming out" was a crucial element of the liberatory experience (Loughery 1998, 321). Those who embraced the importance of "coming out" perceived that "if every gay and lesbian person in the United States could be persuaded to come out, our lives would be different because heterosexuals would have to recognize how very many of us there were and grant us our rights" (Jay 1999, 89). Ultimately, "coming out" was seen as a political act, one that reinforced the feminist idea that the personal is, indeed, political. The distinction between the public and the private had become blurred. In a variety of important ways, the feminist movement informed lesbian and gay life and politics. Many lesbians involved in the GLF had already done extensive political organizing in the women's movement.

Within one year of the group's founding in New York, Gay Liberation Front organizations were born throughout the United States, including in Atlanta, Boston, Chicago, Iowa City, Los Angeles, Milwaukee, Portland, San Francisco, Seattle, and Washington, D.C. College students organized many local groups on their campuses (Loughery 1998, 325). Meetings were run according to participatory principles, and hierarchy was eschewed as much as possible. Thanks to the courage and hard work of lesbian and gay activists around the country, an impressive amount of organizing was done in a short period of time, confirming the liberationist message about the importance of coalition building and the historical context of the times.

Yet as several invaluable histories of this period suggest, there was considerable disagreement within the broader organization over its purpose (should it focus only on gay liberation, or should it be part of a larger political movement for progressive change?), its organizational structure, and the role of women and minorities. The euphoria and sense of unity that accompanied the birth of GLF were short-lived as the post-Stonewall lesbian and gay movements faced the internal conflicts that beset many political and social movements in the late 1960s. The role of women in GLF was a particularly difficult issue since many of the women who wished to participate encountered serious sexism. In her memoir, *Tales of the Lavender Menace,* Karla Jay reveals the sexism she faced:

> Despite the push toward a gynandrous center, the sexism of some of the men was—for me, at least—the biggest obstacle toward immediately and completely immersing myself in GLF. A number of the men were more oppressive to women than any heterosexual guy I had known. A few of the men looked at me with such unveiled contempt that I started to give credence to the old adage that some men were gay because they hated or feared women. I'm sure that these guys would have preferred for the women to leave so that the GLF would become an all-men's group, sort of like a political bathhouse, where they could get naked with one another. If we were going to be there, however, a few men thought we might as well make ourselves useful by baking some cookies and making coffee. Some of the other women and I were constantly correcting men who called us "girls." "I'm a woman, not a 'girl.' How would [you] like me to call you 'boy'?" we'd remind them over and over. (Jay 1999, 82)

Disagreements over the treatment of women and other issues undermined the overall effectiveness of the GLF, led to its ultimate destruction, and paved the way for another, less radical organization born out of the Stonewall Rebellion—the Gay Activists Alliance.

Founded by former GLF members Jim Owles and Marty Robinson in New York City in December 1969, the GAA attempted to focus on the single issue of gay rights, without the issue fragmentation and anarchic organizational style that characterized the GLF. The GAA founders had become increasingly disenchanted with the GLF's inability to plan effectively and to temper revolutionary New Left doctrine in an effort to address the daily discrimination faced by lesbians and gays (Adam 1995, 86). They were particularly concerned with the GLF's affiliation with other elements of the political left, including the Black Panthers and the antiwar movement. To the critics of the GLF, such affiliations "drained energy from the homosexual rights cause," and some of the affiliated groups were also clearly antigay (Hunt 1999, 81).

The GAA membership thought that meaningful reform would occur only if lesbians and gays organized politically and exercised their political muscle to force positive legislative change. Their involvement in electoral politics set the stage for a strategy that has come to dominate the contemporary mainstream lesbian and gay rights movements. Candidates for election were questioned extensively concerning their views regarding issues of interest to lesbians and gays.

The GAA also embraced direct action in the form of "zaps," which were direct confrontations in public meetings, on city streets, and in offices. Such nonviolent civil disobedience captured occasional media attention, disrupted the normal patterns of people's lives, and set the stage for the kind of political organizing associated with ACT UP in the late 1980s. In this way, the GAA's tactics were much closer to the GLF's than the Mattachine Society and Daughters of Bilitis pickets at the White House in the 1960s.[8] This kind of unconventional politics, as a deliberate political strategy, will be explored more fully in Chapter 4.

Five demands were at the heart of GAA politics:

1. the repeal of New York State's sodomy and solicitation laws;
2. an end to police entrapment of gay men;
3. an end to police harassment of gay bars and an investigation into corruption in the New York State Liquor Authority;
4. a law protecting gays and lesbians against discrimination in employment; and
5. an end to the bonding company practice of denying bonds to gays and lesbians. (By refusing to bond gays and lesbians, bonding companies had the power to exclude them from jobs requiring bonding.) (Hunt 1999, 82)

An early GAA statement, "What is GAA?" stressed the organization's commitment "to a militant but nonviolent homosexual civil rights struggle and a membership open to all who shared this approach and objective." Bob Kohler, a veteran GLF organizer, responded to the more assimilationist GAA approach by calling it "well-mannered conformist shit," while Kay Tobin, one of just a handful of women involved in the early years of GAA's existence, claimed that it was "an exciting place for a range of us who weren't out-and-out revolutionaries" (Loughery 1998, 329). Most acknowledge that the GAA was even less responsive to women and people of color than the GLF had been. GAA members were charged with tokenism when it came to dealing with issues of race and feminism (ibid., 331).

The GAA adopted an institutional structure that it found lacking in the GLF, one built around committees and elected leadership. As Barry

Adam points out, "the movement was facing a transition experienced by so many others before it, when charisma and chiliasm give way to structure and institution" (Adam 1995, 86). Like many other students of social movement organizations, Adam believes that the GAA was much more effective because it established institutional structures that proved to be more long lasting. Indeed, many of these institutional structures have been embraced by an array of lesbian and gay organizations operating at the national level today. The GAA ceased formal operations in 1974, soon after its community center suffered a catastrophic fire, but many of the organization's activists founded the National Gay Task Force, which today is the National Gay and Lesbian Task Force (Hunt 1999, 82).

William Eskridge describes the long-term effects of the Stonewall Rebellion: "Literally overnight, the Stonewall riots transformed the *homophile reform movement* of several dozen homosexuals into a *gay liberation movement* populated by thousands of lesbians, gay men, and bisexuals who formed hundreds of organizations demanding radical changes in the way gay people were treated by the state" (Eskridge 1999, 99; emphasis in original). The movement introduced four key ideas into the existing homophile movement that remain relevant even now. First, the importance of "coming out" as a crucial personal and political statement is integral to movement politics today. Second, it was thought that a more visible lesbian and gay presence would challenge traditional notions of the family, gender roles, and sexism. Third, Stonewall and its aftermath created a lesbian and gay counterculture, which helped to establish lesbian and gay identity, thus providing a foundation for the identity-politics strain in the movements today. (This counterculture has been assailed by conservatives, and the progressive left has taken issue with identity politics.) Finally, the politics of the late 1960s and early 1970s emphasized that the lesbian and gay movements could not be divorced from movements addressing broader economic concerns, gender, and race. A mere rights-based agenda was far too narrow. This principle remains as controversial now as it was when the GLF introduced it to the existing homophile movement almost thirty years ago. Should the movements embrace a single-issue politics, or attempt to build coalitions with other aggrieved groups to foster more progressive social change? This question continues to tear at the fabric of the movements and is an important question underlying this book.[9]

These issues and conflicts over political strategy and organizing have pervaded the contemporary political movements in all sorts of powerful ways. To get a better understanding of these conflicts, we turn now to a discussion of the national lesbian and gay organizations.

THE NATIONAL ORGANIZATIONS
AND ASSIMILATIONIST STRATEGIES

In the decade of the 1980s, lesbian and gay activists became much more actively involved in mainstream politics at the national level. As David Rayside points out, this shift in emphasis is rooted in several factors. Prior to the 1980s, many activists did not believe that the federal government would be responsive to lesbian and gay concerns. As we have seen in our discussion of the GAA, there were exceptions, but for the most part, lesbian and gay activists concentrated their reform efforts at the local level. But with the Republican ascendancy in national politics, which threatened previous movements' accomplishments and coincided with the spread of the AIDS epidemic, lesbian and gay activists recognized the importance of having a presence in the national-level, mainstream political process. Indeed, the AIDS epidemic made that national presence essential (Rayside 1998, 284–85). It is important to recognize, however, that the local and state organizing activities discussed earlier in this chapter helped to pave the way for the creation of nationally based organizations. While the focus in this chapter is largely on the national organizations, we cannot forget that considerable local and state movement organizing continues far removed from Washington, D.C.

These developments led to the creation of new national organizations and the growth of already existing ones, all of which embraced mainstream politics to a certain extent. Rayside describes the consequences of this growth:

> The six largest groups went from a combined budget of $3.2 million in 1987 to $8.8 million in early 1991, reflecting both the development of resources within gay and lesbian communities and the opening up of opportunities for activist entry into national politics. To some extent, organizational growth was accompanied by specialization in each of the primary channels of mainstream activism: the instigation of legal challenges through the courts; the lobbying of legislators and officials; the promotion of lesbian and gay electoral candidates; and the participation in partisan networks. (Rayside 1998, 285)

The national organizations discussed here have been chosen for their diversity, for their overall commitment to lobbying and/or public education, and for their support of the mainstream electoral process. Organizations that pursue a litigation strategy will be discussed more fully in Chapter 3, when the legal-rights approach to political and social change is assessed.

For now, it is important to recognize that all of these organizations believe that any viable lesbian and gay political strategy must access insider politics (to some extent) at the national level. In this way, all of the following organizations embrace, in one way or another, an assimilationist strategy that celebrates the importance of achieving a seat at the table.

Human Rights Campaign (HRC)

Founded in 1980, the Human Rights Campaign Fund (HRCF) has developed into an aggressive lobbying and education-based organization, one that largely works in the mainstream, national political and policy process. HRCF grew out of the earlier work of the Gay Rights National Lobby, an organization created in 1978 to lobby Congress and organize a national network of lobbyists at the local level.

HRCF's period of greatest growth occurred during the late 1980s and early 1990s. In early 1991 HRCF had a budget of $4.5 million, the result of a five-fold budgetary increase and a three-fold staff increase following the 1987 March on Washington. It was among the fifty largest Washington, D.C., political action committees (PACs) as of mid-1992. By the 1996 elections, HRCF had changed its name to Human Rights Campaign (HRC) after marketing surveys indicated that potential contributors would think more highly of the organization if "Fund" was dropped from its title. The organization raises much of its funding through highly publicized and visible dinners in over twenty cities throughout the United States. Some of these attract over a thousand people, each of whom contribute at least $150 in order to attend (Rayside 1998, 287).

The organization became even more aggressive in its fundraising, membership recruitment, and overall visibility when former Apple Computers associate Elizabeth Birch replaced Tim McFeeley as executive director in 1995. Birch had also been affiliated with the National Gay and Lesbian Task Force and brought several of her associates with her. Under Birch's leadership, HRC not only changed its name but also developed a new website, moved into sleek, new Washington, D.C., headquarters reminiscent of corporate America, and issued a glossy magazine.

HRC's central activities include lobbying the federal government on lesbian, gay, and AIDS concerns, participating in election campaigns, educating the general public, organizing volunteers, and offering expertise and training at the state and local level. The latter activities produced direct benefits in 1994, when HRC's Americans Against Discrimination project assisted states and communities across the United States that had been targeted for antigay initiatives sponsored by the Christian Right. The project, which was co-chaired by former Oregon Governor Barbara Roberts and retired Arizona Senator Barry Goldwater, was particularly helpful in defeating antigay initiatives in Idaho and Oregon in 1994. HRC's political action committee offers financial and in-kind contributions to

Democratic, Republican, and independent candidates for federal office. It also offers expertise in organizing, fund raising, and outreach to the lesbian, gay, and bisexual community. To this end, HRC contributed more than $1 million to lesbian and gay-friendly candidates, political parties, and other PACs during the 1995–96 election cycle.

Its $10 million budget, sixty full-time staffers, and 175,000 members led the Washington *Blade* in 1996 to characterize HRC as "the largest— and most influential—national Gay political organization" (Freiberg 1996, 1). David Mixner, a longtime gay political consultant and activist, believes that "there's not a question that they have evolved dramatically over the last five years to a more influential player in Washington. There's still room for growth, but Elizabeth Birch is taken very seriously by major political players in the city" (Freiberg 1996, 1). To lesbian activist Mandy Carter, who worked for HRC for three and a half years, much of HRC's strength comes from the organization's recognition that the movement needs both electoral politics and street politics in order to be successful. She believes that HRC "got it a long time ago . . . our presence in Washington is necessary" (ibid.). One long-time gay activist added, "Elizabeth Birch has moved HRC in the direction of being more than a PAC, and has aggressively used the financial clout of the [lesbian and gay] community to get a seat at the table" (personal interview, February 19, 1997).

With this kind of success also come greater scrutiny and criticism. The organization is often charged with being elitist and catering largely to upper-class lesbian and gay concerns. Critics say that HRC spends too little time on political activity and is more concerned with hosting fancy dinners for wealthy contributors and potential contributors (Haider-Markel 1997, 129). In addition, HRC attracted considerable criticism for endorsing incumbent Senator Alfonse D'Amato (R–New York), who sought reelection against Democratic challenger Charles Schumer in the 1998 New York Senate race. HRC defended its endorsement by arguing that it seeks to support incumbents who have generally voted in favor of lesbian and gay rights initiatives. D'Amato's voting record in the Senate reflected consistent support for narrowly circumscribed lesbian and gay concerns. But critics identified this endorsement as further evidence that HRC was out of touch with the grassroots.[10] When Schumer handily defeated D'Amato, HRC was in the embarrassing position of having endorsed a losing and largely popular candidate in the lesbian and gay communities. HRC also received considerable criticism for its hierarchical planning of the 2000 Millennium March. These criticisms and HRC's response are developed more fully in Chapter 4, when we consider unconventional politics.

Of all the national organizations, HRC may well be the most hierarchical, as it has no local affiliates. HRC does have field directors in each region of the country, who attempt to coordinate the group's activities. From the vantage point of those movement activists who wish to see a more decentralized structure, the central problem is that "the executive board makes all decisions for the organization and individual members do not have a formal means of communicating issues or concerns to HRC leaders" (Haider-Markel 1997, 129). However, HRC has begun to respond to these criticisms in tangible ways. It has selected coordinators in more than a dozen states and fifty congressional districts in an effort to galvanize grassroots support. In doing so, it has also increasingly attempted to strengthen its ties to local lesbian and gay organizations (ibid., 130).

Like many other organizations, HRC recognizes the importance of getting people to come out of the closet. With this in mind, it sponsors the National Coming Out Project, which encourages lesbians and gays to inform others about who they are. HRC also sponsors a five-thousand-member Field Action Network, which trains and organizes grassroots volunteers. These volunteers are often recruited by HRC staff to assist in local Congressional or Senate campaigns. HRC staff also assist candidates by providing campaign advice. In addition, HRC has organized "Speak Out Action Grams," a direct-mail organizing campaign designed to pressure members of Congress (Haider-Markel 1997, 130).

In recent years the organization has fought for the passage of the Employment Non-Discrimination Act (ENDA), which would ban sexual-orientation discrimination in employment as part of federal law, and it has continued to advance awareness, funding, and education on HIV. In addition, it has tried to promote the acceptance of lesbian and gay marriage at the federal level. Finally, it was generally quite supportive of former president Bill Clinton. In the words of one HRC strategist, "Clinton has transformed this country for the better on gay and lesbian issues" (personal interview, February 5, 1997).

HRC's recent efforts reveal both the value and limitations of an insider, largely hierarchical, nationally based political strategy. As Urvashi Vaid has pointed out, HRC thrives on access to politicians and has consistently taken "a safe, middle-of-the-road approach to political change" (Vaid 1995, 92). To gain an understanding of another approach to political and social change—one that embraces both an assimilationist and liberationist political strategy—we turn to a discussion of the National Gay and Lesbian Task Force (NGLTF).

National Gay and Lesbian Task Force

Founded in November 1973 to "fill the void where no national work was being done on behalf of gays" (personal interview, February 6, 1997), the National Gay Task Force was the nation's leading gay political group at that time. The organization was formed by New Yorkers who had been associated with the Gay Activists Alliance. In his engaging cultural and political history of the lesbian and gay movements, John Loughery describes the circumstances related to the organization's founding:

> The lack of a centralized gay leadership or organization worried some observers, who looked to the black civil rights movement and saw (or, more accurately, thought they saw) a cohesive structure and a unified philosophy for achieving racial equality. The National Gay Task Force in New York was one answer to this perceived need. (Loughery 1998, 344)

Those involved at the founding were New York City Health Administrator Harold Brown (who had recently come out publicly), Professor Martin Duberman, publicist Ronald Gold, longtime activist Franklin Kameny, and New York physician Dr. Bruce Voeller. The organization's initial goals were to bring "gay liberation into the mainstream of American civil rights" and to "focus on broad national issues" (Thompson 1994, 82). In its early years, the Task Force enjoyed several major accomplishments:

a. it convinced the American Psychiatric Association to end its classification of homosexuality as a mental illness;
b. it challenged the media's portrayal of gays;
c. it persuaded then U.S. Rep. Bella Abzug (D-NY) to introduce the first gay civil rights bill in Congress;
d. it initiated the first meeting in the White House between gay leaders and a top presidential advisor in the administration of President Jimmy Carter. (*Washington Blade* 1997, 23)

In addition, the Task Force provided advice to local groups and served as a clearinghouse for information. At this point in its history, however, it was an elite organization; it had a narrow membership base and was cautious in its choices of strategy. In the late 1970s and early 1980s, the group experienced organizational and financial problems. Its annual budget for 1980 was only $260,000, reflecting the organization's small size. The Task Force moved to Washington, D.C., in 1986 and also changed its name to the National Gay and Lesbian Task Force. The catalyst for the organization's growth was the October 1987 March on Washington for Lesbian and Gay Rights. At this point in the organization's history, the Task Force focused on issues of violence, privacy, and AIDS (Rayside 1998, 285). During the late 1980s and through the mid-1990s, the Task Force sponsored the Gay and Lesbian Violence Project, which issued annual reports on the numbers of lesbians and gays who were victims of gay-bias crimes.

At the end of the 1980s, the Task Force devoted more attention to the ban on lesbians and gays in the military as well as to family issues. The latter included adoption, foster care, reproductive rights, and questions of relationship and recognition. The organization diversified its national leadership considerably, as lesbians such as Urvashi Vaid (who served as executive director from 1989–1993), Peri Jude Radicec, and Tanya Domi played major roles. Virginia Apuzzo had been executive director of the Task Force from 1982 to 1986. The racial composition of the organization's staff also became much more diverse in the late 1980s, and there was a much greater emphasis on the intersection of race with lesbian and gay politics. By late summer 1996, the organization had 40,000 members, a yearly budget of $2.4 million, and twenty-two full-time staff.

Today the organization addresses a range of issues, including antigay ballot initiatives, violence against lesbians and gays, general homophobia, sodomy laws, anti-discrimination policies for lesbians and gays, legal protections for lesbian and gay families, and AIDS research funding. The overall goals and strategy are decided within the Washington, D.C., national office. The Task Force is not constituted as a federation of local chapters, but the group's literature contends that it is building a grassroots movement. Since the Task Force has no local chapters or committees, it galvanizes grassroots support in other ways. It "holds an annual Creating Change Conference, started its Youth Leadership Training program in 1993, has built partnerships with more than 120 local groups through its Cooperating Organization program, and coordinates the activities of local and state groups through its 'activist alert' network" (Haider-Markel 1997, 126).

In the years since its founding, the Task Force has practiced both insider, mainstream politics as well as more radical, direct-action politics, often at the grassroots. As one staffer pointed out, "NGLTF has been on the inside and outside from time to time" (personal interview, February 6, 1997). Unlike HRC, which has pursued a more focused and well-defined political and policy agenda, NGLTF has embraced various political strategies over the course of the past seventeen years. This has led some to ask what role the Task Force is playing in the larger lesbian and gay movements.[11] Torie Osborn, who followed Vaid as executive director, argues that there is a "gap between the reality and the potential" at the Task Force. Osborn believes that the organization could become a "mobilizing force" by organizing around cutting-edge lesbian and gay rights issues. But the Task Force has failed to fulfill this potential because, as Osborn suggests, "they're an organization without a vision" (Moss 1996, 45). However, most would agree that the Task Force has occupied a niche on the progressive left of the political and ideological spectrum. The organization's progressive political leanings have led to tensions between itself and other national groups, notably the Human Rights Campaign, which occupies a more centrist position.

The Task Force continues to devote more attention to statewide organizing. The assumption here, in the words of one staffer, is that "state-level politics are far more important than politics at the national level over the next four years and there are opportunities to move forward incrementally at the state level" (personal interview, February 6, 1997). The Task Force Policy Institute, which was founded by historian and activist John D'Emilio in 1995, has also embraced this state-level focus to a large extent. The Institute "is a think tank dedicated to research, policy analysis and strategic projects that advance equality for GLBT people" ("Task Force Report," Summer 1998, p. 3). It has been involved in a number of strategic projects, including the March 1999 "Equality Begins at Home Campaign," a week-long organizing effort consisting of more than 250 rallies, lobby days, caravans, town meetings, and other grassroots actions on behalf of lesbians and gays in all fifty states, the District of Columbia, and Puerto Rico. This project "was proposed to the Federation of Statewide GLBT Political Organizations to increase visibility and capacity of state organizations through coordinated national days of action" (ibid.). This important mobilization campaign was ultimately organized by the Federation of GLBT Statewide Political Organizations and coordinated by the Task Force.

Of all the national organizations, perhaps the Task Force is the one most committed to grassroots political and social change. Yet like HRC, the Task Force also embraces the hierarchical model of decision making to the extent that its national office is in Washington, D.C., and a board of directors ultimately governs its day-to-day operations. When the Task Force moved from New York to Washington in 1986, it was acknowledging the importance of having a serious lobbying presence. The move was largely prompted by the AIDS crisis. Indeed, Urvashi Vaid argues that "there is no question that AIDS forced the gay and lesbian movement to institutionalize, nationalize, and aggressively pursue the mainstream" (Vaid 1995, 74). Indeed, AIDS has had consequences for all of the national organizations. To see how it and other lesbian and gay issues have intersected with race, we turn now to a discussion of the National Black Lesbian and Gay Leadership Forum.

The National Black Lesbian and Gay Leadership Forum

The National Black Lesbian and Gay Leadership Forum was originally founded in 1988 by veteran civil rights activists Ruth Waters and Phill Wilson as a Los Angeles–based local organization. Its goal was to address issues facing the black lesbian and gay community as well as to focus on racial concerns that had not been satisfactorily addressed by national groups such as the Human Rights Campaign Fund, the National Gay and Lesbian

Task Force, and the Lambda Legal Defense and Education Fund (*Washington Blade* 1997, 22). The Leadership Forum's first conference took place in 1988 and was very well attended by people from all over the country. The conference addressed racism in the gay community and homophobia in the straight black community. As one organization official said, "The good turnout reflected a growing desire for black lesbians and gays to come together to organize" (personal interview, February 28, 1997).

Since 1995 the Leadership Forum has restructured itself as a national organization. In his book *One More River to Cross: Black and Gay in America*, Keith Boykin, the former executive director (1995–98), writes of his dismay in the early 1990s upon visiting the Washington, D.C., offices of such groups as the National Lesbian and Gay Journalists Association (NLGJA), HRC, and NGLTF and finding very little or no representation of people of color. Boykin argues that separate national organizations that address the concerns of black lesbians and gays are needed because of the inability of other national organizations to represent their concerns adequately. He quotes Tim McFeeley's comments on HRC's efforts to promote diversity and greater representation of blacks, shortly after McFeeley completed his five-year tenure as executive director: "I think we've done a good job, and I think it needs to always be examined and the question needs to be raised. . . . I think HRC is clearly defined as a white person's organization. HRC will not be as comfortable a place to black gay people as their own" (Boykin 1996, 230). Boykin believes that McFeeley's attitude is shared by other national leaders as well, providing a clear justification for the existence of organizations such as the National Black Lesbian and Gay Leadership Forum.

Today, the Leadership Forum hosts a yearly national conference, which has become an important source of income and publicity, as well as an occasion for networking. One of its first major projects was the creation of a Los Angeles–based AIDS Prevention Team, designed to offer services to African American gay and bisexual men locally. Since the late 1980s, the Leadership Forum has extended its AIDS-prevention programs to the national level through grants from the U.S. Centers for Disease Control and Prevention (*Washington Blade* 1997, 22).

The organization's Washington, D.C., headquarters were opened in 1995 and the Leadership Forum's budget nearly doubled from $450,000 in 1996 to $850,000 in 1997, reflecting increased fundraising activity. Today it advocates on behalf of black lesbians and gays before Congress and the White House, the news media, universities, and churches. Other recent efforts include the development of a Women's Health Program and the creation of a black gay community center at the Leadership Forum's Washington office, which houses a diverse collection of materials and records pertaining to black lesbian and gay history. The Leadership Forum has also addressed the needs of young people by creating its first national youth council. When asked by the *Washington Blade* to identify its top priorities for the coming year the Leadership Forum said: (1) "working with the black church to help transform attitudes within the black community;" and (2) "working with the mainstream media to encourage 'fair and accurate' representation of black Gay people" (*Washington Blade* 1997, 22–23).

The Leadership Forum's major operating and staffing decisions are made by a seventeen-member board of directors, composed of members from throughout the United States. Keith Boykin has justifiably received credit for his leadership and fundraising activities. But he also recognizes that the Leadership Forum cannot depend on the efforts of one individual if it is to be successful. The organization needs a committed grassroots base of supporters. At its February 1998 annual meeting, Boykin told members gathered for a plenary session: "It's time to stand up. It's time to dare to be powerful. I don't want the organization to fall by the wayside because of one individual" (Smith 1998a, 1). At the same meeting, the Leadership Forum announced that Jubi Headley, Jr., formerly an executive assistant and press secretary to Kenneth Reeves, the openly gay mayor of Cambridge, Massachusetts, would replace Boykin as executive director. But Headley's tenure lasted less than four months; he resigned on June 5, 1998, apparently over the Leadership Forum's developing serious financial problems and its inability to pay his salary in a timely manner. In announcing his resignation, Headley also said that the Leadership Forum needed to restructure if it wished to remain viable in the future. This restructuring meant that the executive director's position would be eliminated and a five-person management team would be created. The ultimate goal of this organizational change was to devote considerable attention to program delivery (Smith 1998b, 1).

The organization relocated its office in January 2000, moving from Washington, D.C., to Oakland, California, and it restructured its board of directors in order to cut operating costs and to streamline operations. It secured the services of a new, volunteer executive director, Alvan Quamina. And it pledged at its February 2000 annual meeting in Chicago to gets its fiscal house in order before embarking on expensive initiatives. The goal is to rebuild the organization as much as possible from the grassroots and to retire a fifty-thousand-dollar debt and deal with unpaid taxes. These serious financial problems raise questions about the continued viability of the organization.[12]

But despite these practical concerns, the Leadership Forum has played an invaluable role in the mainstream political and policy process by insuring that black lesbians and gays are represented when the movement's national organizations meet to coordinate strategy. Like all of the other organizations discussed thus far, the Leadership Forum can be criticized for focusing too heavily on national-level politics. But like the Task Force, the Leadership Forum is attempting to make progress at the grassroots as well. However, the organization faces considerable difficulties so long as its finances and organizational structure remain problematic. Perhaps the greatest accomplishment that the Leadership Forum might make in the immediate future is to inspire black lesbians and gays to kick the closet doors down, recognize that they are not alone, and realize that they have an organization working on their behalf. In addition, the mere existence of this organization is a reminder to white lesbians and gays that the broader movements have still not adequately addressed race concerns some thirty years after the same charge was leveled against the Gay Liberation Front and the Gay Activists Alliance.

Log Cabin Republicans

Founded in 1993, the Log Cabin Republicans are a national group that represents lesbian and gay Republicans. Much of its organizing work is done by more than fifty chapters located throughout the United States, some of them formed long before the national organization was created (*Washington Blade* 1997, 22). Indeed, the earliest such club was formed in California in 1978 as a response to the Briggs initiative, which would have required schools to terminate the contract of any teacher who even mentioned homosexuality in positive terms in the classroom (personal interview, February 10, 1997).

All the local clubs joined together as the Log Cabin Federation in 1990. Over the course of the next two years, Rich Tafel, the new head of the federation, and veteran conservative organizer Marvin Liebman gained considerable media attention. The federation's third annual meeting at the 1992 Republican National Convention in Houston brought together fifteen clubs from ten different states. However, Log Cabin activists were still outsiders in a party largely dominated by the Christian Right.

In early 1993, a small group of individuals formed a Washington, D.C.–based organization, which acted as a lobbying group and served as a clearinghouse for information about legislators and legislation. Within two years, it merged with the Log Cabin Federation (Rayside 1998, 291). Kevin Ivers, who had been an organizer of the Capital Area Log Cabin Club, and who serves as the director of public affairs for the Log Cabin Republicans today, cited the 1992 Republican National Convention in Houston as an important factor in the creation of the national organization. More specifically, Ivers pointed to Pat Buchanan's convention speech:

Houston was horrific. Pat Buchanan, who loyal Bush supporters fought against in every Republican primary, was given a prime-time slot to speak. . . . That speech, full of lurid and violent references to an emerging "cultural war" in America, left me feeling sick. My sense of patriotism had been wounded. He meandered from one deeply disturbing image to the next, painting a picture of a nation on the verge of civil war over an insolent refusal to tolerate difference. (Tafel 1999, 118)

It is no surprise, then, that one of the central goals of the organization has been "to convey the idea that gay rights and the party's philosophy [are] not inimical" (Bull and Gallagher 1996, 79). The organization's first major political success was the election of Governor William Weld in Massachusetts. Weld appointed lesbians and gays to visible positions throughout his administration and confronted challenging issues such as gay teen suicide rates (ibid., 80). In many ways, he has been one of the most pro-gay governors in the United States to date.

Rich Tafel was appointed to a post in the Weld administration, and subsequently became executive director of the Log Cabin Republicans. Since 1993 he has presided over the growth of the organization and has guided it through its greatest political controversy—whether to endorse Bob Dole for President in 1996. By early 1997, Log Cabin Republicans had a budget totaling seven hundred thousand dollars, a staff of six, and a membership of ten thousand (personal interview, February 10, 1997).

The Log Cabin Political Action Committee, an arm of the Log Cabin Republicans, raises money for Republican candidates who support gay and AIDS issues. It contributed half a million dollars to national, state, and local candidates in the 2000 elections.

Until June 1998, the Log Cabin Republicans were the only national gay organization that was affiliated with one of the two major political parties in the United States. Obviously influenced by their success, Rep. Barney Frank (D-Massachusetts) announced the creation of the National Stonewall Democratic Federation, a nationally based organization with direct ties to the Democratic Party.

The Log Cabin Republicans received considerable media attention when it was revealed by openly lesbian reporter Deb Price that in August 1995 then-presidential-candidate Bob Dole returned a thousand-dollar contribution from the group. Dole and his campaign were widely criticized for this rebuff, and the mainstream press wondered "whether Dole had hurt his overall chances of winning the presidency by appearing to be 'pandering' to the religious right faction of the Republican party" (Chibbaro 1995a, 1). Eventually, he accepted the donation, blamed the returned check on his staff, and accepted a Log Cabin endorsement.

The Dole incident produced considerable turmoil within the organization, especially since the Log Cabin Republicans ultimately decided to endorse his presidential candidacy. Turmoil erupted again during the 2000 presidential campaign, when candidate George W. Bush, Jr., was asked on NBC's *Meet the Press* whether he would meet with the Log Cabin Republicans if elected President. In reply, Bush said, "Oh, probably not. It creates a huge political scene." After he was assured his party's nomination, Bush did meet with representatives of the organization, but they were people that he and his staff personally approved. Some Log Cabin members understandably rejected this meeting as a Bush publicity stunt designed to win the support of gay Republican voters without appearing to endorse the organization or lesbian and gay rights more generally. Perhaps most importantly, Bush changed no policy positions as a result of the meeting.[13] This episode suggests that the Log Cabin Republicans have considerable work to do in forcing the Republican Party even to acknowledge lesbian and gay concerns. The organization has plenty of opportunities to do so with George W. Bush in the White House. In the aftermath of the 2000 presidential elections, the Log Cabin Republicans were understandably excited to have a Republican president. How the organization interacts with Bush's Christian Right advisors and supporters will be a significant challenge in the years ahead.

At the same time, the Log Cabin Republicans have an important role to play in supporting lesbian and gay Republican candidates at the national, state, and local levels. HRC has supported a limited number of Republican lawmakers, such as Rep. Nancy Johnson (R-Connecticut), Rep. Christopher Shays (R-Connecticut), and former Republican Senator James Jeffords (I-Vermont). They will also continue to lobby on AIDS and the Employment Non-Discrimination Act. But perhaps most important of all, they can potentially use their political mainstreaming strategy and their decentralized organizational structure in various state and local chapters throughout the United States to educate about lesbian and gay concerns.

Gay and Lesbian Victory Fund

Since its creation in 1991, the primary goal of the Gay and Lesbian Victory Fund (GLVF) has been to elect openly lesbian and gay officials to all levels of government. The organization's book, *Out for Office*, argued that "gay men and lesbians are the most underrepresented group in electoral politics," and it posed this question: "If we don't support our own, who will be there for us?" (DeBold 1994, xiii).

Political scientists have also identified a number of reasons why the election of openly lesbian and gay officials is crucial if the goal is to increase the movements' political power. One important reason often cited is that "merely increasing the public's exposure to gay men and lesbians through the high-profile visibility of openly lesbian and gay candidates and officials should contribute to the breakdown of negative stereotypes and prejudices, thereby reducing their pernicious consequences in the form of discrimination, hate crimes, and political and social intolerance of gays and lesbians" (Golebiowska and Thomsen 1999, 192–93). In other words, the public will develop a greater understanding and respect for difference if openly lesbian and gay candidates run for office and are ultimately elected. A second argument suggests that lesbian and gay elected officials will likely champion legislation that protects the rights of lesbians and gays. Third, openly lesbian and gay elected officials could serve as role models for lesbian and gay youth, who are particularly vulnerable to the negative consequences of discrimination, harassment, and stigmatization (ibid.). The Victory Fund embraces all of these arguments in its fundraising and organizing efforts on behalf of openly lesbian and gay candidates.

The founder and first director of the Victory Fund, William Waybourn, had been influenced by the success of Emily's List, a Washington, D.C.-based PAC that helped Ann Richards defeat Clayton Williams in the 1990 Texas governor's race. As a native Texan, Waybourn was well aware that Richards credited Emily's List for providing crucial financial support at an early phase of her campaign. Waybourn thought that lesbians and gays needed a similar organization at the national level. He contacted Vic Basile, who had once been executive director of the Human Rights Campaign Fund, to see if Basile would be interested in joining forces with Waybourn. Basile agreed, and the two began working to secure the support of lesbian and gay donors throughout the United States. Their efforts produced the Victory Fund's first board of directors, composed of individuals with considerable political and fundraising experience. More importantly, each had pledged ten thousand dollars to support the creation of the Victory Fund (Rimmerman 1994, 215).

Unlike the other nationally based lesbian and gay organizations discussed in this chapter, the Victory Fund exists solely to recruit and elect openly lesbian and gay candidates to public office. As David Rayside points out, "the Victory Fund is a peculiarly American formation, one that illustrates the prominence of money in United States elections and the need for candidates to raise funds outside party channels" (Rayside 1998, 287). Given that there are some five hundred thousand elected offices at all levels of government in the United States, the Victory Fund has a chance to play an important role in assisting openly lesbian and gay candidates for public office.

The organization's board of directors plays the central role in deciding which candidates will get Victory Fund support. Board members, who are generally wealthy individuals with strong political connections, reside in all areas of the United States and have likely contributed significant financial support to the Victory Fund in the past. Ultimately, the board is responsible for hiring the executive director and for serving as the organization's conduit to the political world (Rimmerman 1999).

In deciding which candidates to support, the board engages in a thorough and rigorous process that has remained largely the same since the organization's founding. In the early stages of its decision-making process, the Victory Fund relies on an outside consulting firm to provide independent evaluations of the races in question. After carefully reviewing the evidence, the Victory Fund staff makes recommendations to the board of directors about which candidates to support. Spirited debate and discussion often follow, after which the board decides which candidates merit Victory Fund support. Candidates must meet the fund's published criteria. They:

1. must be openly lesbian or gay;
2. must endorse the Federal Gay/Lesbian Civil Rights Bill in a public manner, as well as similar state and local anti-discrimination laws or legislation;
3. must advocate aggressive public policies and positions relevant to AIDS education, treatment, and research, as well as lesbian and gay health and wellness;
4. must have a strong supportive base outside of the lesbian and gay community;
5. must be strongly pro-choice;
6. must demonstrate the ability to organize and to raise money;
7. must have a viable candidacy (i.e. a legitimate chance to win). (Rimmerman 1999; personal interview, February 26, 1997)

During the 1996 election cycle, some 180 candidates contacted the organization requesting support. The Victory Fund decided to support 32 of these candidates, 22 of whom won. These numbers represent considerable progress on behalf of the organization. By way of comparison, during the 1992 election cycle, some 72 candidates for office at all levels of government contacted the Victory Fund asking for its support, and the organization responded by giving half a million dollars to 13 candidates (Rimmerman 1999). In the 1994 off-year elections, the Victory Fund backed 27 candidates with some eight hundred thousand dollars in contributions, and 14 of those won. Perhaps its greatest success was during the 1997 off-year elections, when 10 of the 15 openly lesbian and gay candidates backed by the Victory Fund achieved electoral victories and another 3 forced runoff elections (*Washington Blade* 1997, 21). The Victory Fund endorsed 50 candidates who ran for offices at the local, state, and federal levels during the 2000 election cycle. Out of those, 29 won, giving the organization an overall win rate of 58 percent for that election (Josh Siegel, email communication, May 22, 2001).

The Victory Fund's success and the resulting publicity have had positive consequences for membership numbers as well. In 1991 the fund had only 181 members, but by 1994, there were some 3,500 members; by 1996 members had contributed more than $1.3 million. During the 1996 election cycle the organization ranked as the fifteenth largest independent PAC in the United States and gave more than $400,000 to candidates (Haider-Markel 1997, 132).

The Gay and Lesbian Victory Fund has had three executive directors during its brief existence—William Waybourn (1992–95), David Clarenbach (1996–97), and Brian Bond (1997–present). As a former Democratic National Committee official, Bond brings with him significant political organizing expertise, but his partisan background concerns some members of other national organizations, given that the Victory Fund supports candidates of any party who meet the organization's published criteria. The executive director of the Victory Fund is responsible for the day-to-day running of the Washington-based organization and coordinates its political and fundraising strategies.

As the organization heads into the next election cycle, it faces a number of important issues. Campaign finance reform has become a prominent issue, and any reforms enacted by Congress could mean an end to bundling, the primary way that the Victory Fund receives contributions and distributes money to its chosen candidates. Nonconnected ideological PACs,[14] such as the Victory Fund, are able to avoid the five thousand dollar spending limit for any single candidate in a national primary of general election by requiring their members to earmark their contributions for candidates who have been identified by the Victory Fund for support. In practice this means that Victory Fund contributors will write their checks, for example, to "Barney Frank for Congress," and the checks are then gathered and "bundled" (forwarded to the Frank campaign) every two days, helping to supply the cash flow it needs throughout the campaign (Rimmerman 1994, 219). One Victory Fund official defended bundling when he argued "that there is nothing more grassroots and democratic than bundling. Campaign finance reform should not take away democratic forms of contributions" (personal interview, February 26, 1997).

Besides their concerns over campaign-finance reform, organization leaders worry that they do not have the financial base needed to support all the candidates who deserve their attention. In addition, they wish to aggressively help those candidates who are already in office, and who seek election to higher office (personal interview, February 26, 1997). The fact that the Victory Fund has these worries is a testimony to its accomplishments during its brief existence and to the real progress that has been made in encouraging openly lesbian and gay officials to run for public office. But the fact remains that there are only two openly gay representatives in the entire U.S. Congress. Questions remain, as well, about what elected officials can actually accomplish working within mainstream political structures to bring about necessary political, social, and cultural change. Perhaps the movements would be better off to pursue a legal-rights strategy modeled on the approach used by the mainstream elements of the African-American civil rights movement of the 1950s and 1960s. Chapter 3 explores the strengths and weaknesses of such a strategy for change.

CONCLUSION AND IMPLICATIONS

This chapter has placed the contemporary lesbian and gay movements in historical context. In addition, it has described the rights-based strategy that has dominated movement politics for the past fifty years. The central strain has been a pluralist, insider-politics approach to change, one that celebrates having access to those in positions of power, thus endorsing a political system that has largely excluded lesbians and gays from meaningful participation in American politics. Theorists of pluralist democracy have argued over time that as competing interests struggle for political power, they will have meaningful access to some resources as they attempt to advance or block proposals related to their various causes (Sherrill 1996, 469). But the analysis presented here suggests that lesbians and gays are largely excluded from resources that are available to other groups within a pluralist system.

How can lesbians and gays protect their interests in a political and economic system that regards them with negative stereotypes and prejudice? The contemporary national organizations discussed here largely rely on hierarchical, pluralist models of organizing, although the National Gay and Lesbian Task Force has pursued aggressive local and statewide policy and organizing efforts in recent years. Grassroots strategies are now being recognized as important by other organizations as well—the Human Rights Campaign, the National Black Lesbian and Gay Leadership Forum, and the Log Cabin Republicans. But the Christian Right has been much more successful in organizing at the grass roots, while the lesbian and gay movements lag behind in this crucial area. They remain focused on channels to power in our nation's capital, although this situation may finally be changing. The discussion in the next chapter of the broader movements' interactions with the Clinton presidency points out the serious weaknesses in this strategy.

Finally, with the occasional exception of the National Gay and Lesbian Task Force, all of the organizations discussed here embrace the basic tenets of liberal democracy and ignore important class-based issues that could allow them to build important coalitions with one another and with other groups committed to meaningful political, social, and structural change. Indeed, the leaders of these organizations are constrained by the very institutional structures in which they operate. These constraints manifest themselves in terms of policy options, legislative action, and class-based economic distribution.[15] As a result, most of the radical goals of the earlier lesbian and gay liberation movements have been diluted considerably or discarded altogether. There is little discussion of entrenched structural privilege of the kind associated with class, ethnic, gender, and racial discrimination.[16] Instead, the focus is on what John D'Emilio calls "the track of liberal reform: it [the movement] had identified a particular problem, proposed a limited solution, formed organizations to work for change, and employed a range of tactics to win redress of grievances" (D'Emilio 1992, 247). The fight for comprehensive health care is one arena that might be particularly ripe for a more broad-based kind of organizing and coalition building at all levels of the political system. At the same time, however, such a coalition cannot and will not be built unless the national organizations transcend a mere rights-based organizational strategy rooted in a narrow form of identity politics.

What does all of this mean for social-movement theory and how it might inform our understanding of the contemporary lesbian and gay movements? First and foremost, the above analysis suggests that there is considerable disagreement among the various national organizations concerning political strategy and overall movement goals, though admittedly a "rights-based" strategy is the dominant paradigm for the movements, as it has been over time. Such a strategy also pervades state and local organizing efforts, as recent fights over local discrimination laws suggest. But there is little consensus over which rights should be emphasized within the broader movements. In this sense, the movements are quite fragmented, as they have always been, around issues of strategy and substance, such as race, class, and gender. This fragmentation, then, limits the utility of the resource-mobilization model to the extent that it depends largely on a shared consensus of overall movement goals, a consensus that, for the most part, simply does not exist. This model of social action also falls short because it largely embraces and reinforces an uncritical acceptance of the pluralist, interest-group, liberal model of political change.

3　The Legal Rights Strategy

Strategic concerns are critical for the lesbian and gay civil rights movement, but they include choosing where as well as what battles are fought. . . . Strategically, gay people have found far more success in the courts than in Congress.

—Kevin M. Carthcart

Scarcely any political question arises in the United States that is not resolved, sooner or later, into a judicial question.

—Alexis de Tocqueville

SHOULD LESBIAN and gay movements look to the legal system for change? If so, why? What kind of change might be expected? And what are the barriers and limitations to such change? What have the movements accomplished when pursuing a legal-rights strategy? How effective are courts at fostering social change? What might be criteria for effectiveness? These questions are central to the analysis in this chapter.

But in order to address these important questions of movement strategy, we must place our discussion in historical and theoretical context. For example, it is important to know that the lesbian and gay movements had produced a number of notable gains by the early 1980s, many of which involved litigation. As legal scholar William Eskridge summarizes, they included legislative repeal or judicial nullification "of laws criminalizing consensual sodomy in most jurisdictions, of almost all state criminal laws targeting same-sex intimacy and municipal cross-dressing ordinances, of the immigration and citizenship exclusions, of all censorship laws targeting same-sex eroticism, of almost all laws or regulations prohibiting bars from becoming congregating places for gay people, and of exclusions of gay people from public employment in most jurisdictions" (Eskridge 1999, 139). Since the early 1980s a number of states and cities have adopted laws that recognize gay families as domestic partnerships, allow second-parent adoption by a parent's same-sex partner, and affirmatively protect gay people against violence and private discrimination (ibid.).

Yet, as Eskridge points out, lesbians and gays remain second-class citizens in important areas, in no small part due to discriminatory governmental policies. For example, all states refuse to grant same-sex couples the civil marriage licenses that are routinely issued to different-sex couples. Legal efforts to extend such rights have incurred significant opposition in Alaska, Hawaii, and Vermont, although the Vermont Supreme Court's December 1999 landmark decision, which required the Vermont state legislature to grant lesbian and gay couples the protections and benefits that heterosexuals enjoy, and the subsequent Vermont law legalizing civil unions as of July 1, 2000, have given marriage-rights advocates cause to celebrate. At the same time, however, thirty-two states have adopted statutes that ban the recognition of same-sex marriages in their jurisdictions. As Eskridge points out, "the [federal] Defense of Marriage Act (DOMA) exempts these statutes from challenge under the full faith and credit clause and directs that 1,049 federal statutes adverting to spousehood or marriage never include same-sex couples" (Eskridge 1999, 140).

Governmental policies directly discriminate against lesbians and gays in other ways. For example, seventeen states continue to criminalize sodomy, with five of them targeting only same-sex sodomy (O'Bryan 2001, 1). In some of the states that have decriminalized sodomy, it is still "illegal to solicit for deviate sexual intercourse" ("A Sodomy Law's Last Stand" 2000, 13). A number of state policies discriminate against "lesbian or gay male parents when former spouses desire custody, and other states have effectively the same approach because they consider social prejudice when determining the best 'interests of the child'" (ibid.). At least three states have passed laws that prevent gay people from adopting. In the area of employment, some state and local governments exclude gay people from working as police officers, firefighters, and teachers. In addition, the U.S. armed forces exclude "out" lesbians and gays, along with anyone who commits a homosexual act and cannot prove that he or she is heterosexual.

In the all-important area of education, a number of states recommend or even require that their schools teach that homosexuality and/or same-sex intimacy are unacceptable in their states. Such "no promo homo" (no promotion of homosexuality) dictates are regularly proposed for inclusion in antigay legislation at the federal level as well. Finally, the federal government has ignored discrimination faced by lesbians and gays in the workplace. It has yet to pass new laws, or interpret existing laws, in ways that protect lesbian or gay employees who are discriminated against by homophobic straight employees. This problem exists at the state level as well, since only eleven states and the District of Columbia have laws that protect lesbians and gays from harassment in the workplace. This gap at the federal level is particularly disconcerting because federal laws do exist that "prohibit discrimination because of sex in private as well as public schools and workplaces" (Eskridge 1999, 140). These laws protect straight males and females, but not anyone who fails to conform to accepted gender behavior, thus excluding lesbians, gay men, bisexuals, transsexuals, and transvestites. Finally, lesbians and gays are not eligible for estate tax benefits, regardless of how long they have lived together. As we know, these discriminatory legal practices do not even begin to encompass the array of informal ways that lesbians and gays encounter discrimination in their daily lives (Eskridge 1999, 140–41).

This all raises important questions about whether a legal-rights framework can ever adequately address the structural sources of both de facto and de jure forms of discrimination, or whether a broader political and cultural strategy is needed, one that transcends mere rights-based organizing. This chapter assesses the legal-rights perspective critically by placing it in historical context[1] and then discussing two contemporary policy areas that have involved judicial challenges—lesbians and gays in the military and same-sex marriage. These conflicts are discussed in the broader context of battles and strategies that have preceded them. The goal is to evaluate the limitations and possibilities of a legal-rights strategy.

THE LEGAL RIGHTS STRATEGY IN HISTORICAL CONTEXT

Pre-Stonewall Legal Strategy

What are the central elements of a legal-rights strategy? In their narrowest form, "legal challenges are short-term strategies that provide relief in emergency situations or give redress to people persecuted by unfair policies, because laws are subject to repeal and or nullification" (Vaid 1995, 130–31). A goal of this more limited legal-reform strategy might be to win concrete benefits, such as those that would accrue from the legal recognition of same-sex marriage or from an official redefinition of "spouse" that encompassed lesbian and gay identity, and would thereby allow for welfare, health care, property, and taxation benefits. But from the outset, lesbian and gay rights movements have engaged in legal struggle in hopes of achieving victories at a more general and symbolic level. The courtroom becomes a vehicle for forcing themselves into the mainstream. They often argue that meaningful legal reform signals to bigots that discriminatory behavior is unacceptable. In its most idealistic form, the goal is to create a supportive and affirming environment for previously closeted lesbians and gays to "come out," in the assurance that the law can provide safety and security (Herman 1994, 4). The focus is clearly on individual rights and liberties. In this way, the legal-rights strategy is connected to the central elements of classical liberalism.[2]

Groups that pursue a litigation strategy that targets the Supreme Court file amicus curiae briefs in key cases where they are not a direct party, directly sponsor test cases, and, most often, embrace some combination of both tactics. Amicus curiae briefs are "friend of the court" briefs that are introduced by individuals or groups who are not parties to a lawsuit, but who can influence or aid the court in reaching its decision (Plano and Greenberg 1986, 298). When interest groups choose to file an amicus curiae brief in cases that are already in the legal pipeline, they embrace a litigation strategy that obviously limits their control over the issues. On the other hand, the direct sponsorship of cases enables organizations to control the management of the litigation. Following this strategy, they establish the conditions of a case, thereby initiating those events that serve as an impetus to a legal action test-case strategy (Salokar 1997, 393). In addition, "interest groups sponsor cases or file amicus briefs either urging the Court to hear a case or asking it to refuse to hear a case, a procedure called a 'denial of a writ of certiorari'" (Brewer, Kaib, and O'Connor 2000, 378). Most cases arrive at the U.S. Supreme Court as a result of the writ of certiorari, which was authorized by the Judiciary Act of 1925. Plano and Greenberg (1986) explain that, "The writ is issued at the discretion of the Court when at least four of the nine justices feel that the case should be reviewed" (p. 302). Once the Supreme Court has decided to hear a case, groups will very often file amicus curiae briefs. Legal organizations advocating on behalf of lesbian and gay rights, such as the Lambda Legal Defense and Education Fund, use all of the above strategies. Unfortunately, lesbian and gay activists have also often found themselves turning to the legal system in a reactive mode, seeking to preserve "the few rights they succeeded in gaining through legislative enactments and municipal ordinances" (Salokar 1997, 398).

Since World War II, the legal system has increasingly inserted itself in the political arena, prompting Urvashi Vaid to argue that "splitting the gay and lesbian legal movement from a political or legislative movement represents a false dichotomy: politics, lawmaking, and litigation are intimately connected" (Vaid 1995, 132). Students of legal history recall the efforts of Thurgood Marshall and lawyers for the National Association for the Advancement of Colored People (NAACP) in using the courts to end institutionalized forms of racial discrimination, such as racially segregated schools and local barriers to black voters in the South. Black civil rights activists determined that a legal challenge was the only avenue available for meaningful change (Toobin 1999, 5–6).

The success of this strategy in the early days of the civil rights movement paved the way for other marginalized groups to pursue legal change, even those with access to the ballot box. Throughout the 1950s, 1960s, and 1970s, environmentalists, feminists, and civil rights activists all pursued legal strategies. Lesbian and gay movements also pursued a similar strategy, although their effort was fragmented and disjointed.

With the adoption of a civil rights strategy as early as the creation of the Mattachine Society and the Daughters of Bilitis in the 1950s, lesbian and gay movements embraced a "minority rights" approach to political and social change. They framed specific issues by emphasizing the importance of equality for all human beings as they identified themselves as a distinct minority group. They presented lesbians and gays as ordinary people, eschewing an identity based on behavior. The civil rights, minority-group model worked to the extent that it won legislative and legal recognition that human beings should not suffer stigmatization as a result of their sexual orientations. Underlying this approach to framing was the appeal to the larger goal of "justice," a concept that has enabled lesbians and gays to make their concerns more meaningful to mainstream America (Vaid 1995, 181).

As we saw in Chapter 2, groups such as the Mattachine Society and the Daughters of Bilitis initially adopted a relatively low public profile and sought legitimacy in localized communities before seeking broader public acceptance. But when that broader acceptance became a more viable goal in the late 1950s and 1960s, the assimilationist, legal-rights framework was embraced successfully. The long-term goal was to eliminate laws that discriminated against lesbians and gays. The pre-Stonewall era was such a repressive political and social environment that many lesbians and gay men thought "of themselves as criminals just for being who they were" (Cain 1993, 1564). In the midst of police harassment and widespread repression during the McCarthy era of the 1950s, lesbians and gays won protections here and there in some courts. Compared to the police and the political system, the legal community might even be regarded as a bastion of moderation concerning lesbian and gay rights.

The earliest cases were not part of a coordinated legal strategy, although it is not surprising that they arose where local organizations such as the Mattachine Society, the East Coast Homophile Organization (ECHO), and the Society for Individual Rights were active. Such cases typically involved the dismissal of an individual from a government job, bars fighting for licenses that would allow them to serve lesbians and gays, lesbian and gay bar patrons who challenged police entrapment and harassment, and lesbian and gay publications that challenged existing obscenity laws (Vaid 1995, 131; Pacelle 1996, 199). The earliest bar case, *Stoumen v. Reilly*, was decided by the California Supreme Court in 1951 and may well have been the first successful American gay rights case. The case concerned whether the California Board of Equalization "could suspend the liquor license of the Black Cat restaurant solely because it catered to known homosexuals" (Cain 1993, 1567). In justifying the suspension, the state cited a provision in the Alcoholic Beverage Control Act that prohibited a licensed establishment from operating a "disorderly house." The court ruled in support of the right of lesbians and gay men to socialize in gay bars, thereby reinforcing the importance of the "bar scene" for lesbian and gay community building (ibid.).[3]

Despite this early legal victory, the harassment of patrons in gay bars continued in California and in other states throughout the 1950s and 1960s. In California the harassment was authorized by a subdivision of section 24200 of the Business and Professions Code, which had been enacted by the state legislature after the Stoumen decision. This subsection promised to revoke the liquor licenses of establishments that functioned as a "resort for illegal possessors or users of narcotics, prostitutes, pimps, panderers, or sexual perverts" (quoted in Cain 1993, 1569). The California Supreme Court finally declared this provision unconstitutional in a 1959 decision, *Vallegra v. Department of Alcoholic Beverage Control.* But as legal scholars have pointed out, the Vallegra decision was in many ways only a symbolic victory. The California court's ruling maintained the distinction between homosexual status and homosexual conduct by first citing "the Stoumen holding that catering to homosexuals was not sufficient 'good cause' for the revocation of a license. 'Something more' than the status of the patrons would be required to demonstrate good cause." In practice, the "something more" was the conduct of the patrons, a distinction that continues to be challenged by lesbian and gay rights litigation today, most notably in response to the "Don't Ask, Don't Tell" legislation proposed by President Clinton and modified and passed into law by Congress in 1993 (ibid., 1569–70).

Police entrapment and harassment were used successfully to crack down on the lesbian and gay community. Of course, the police in San Francisco and in other locales had a long history of harassing lesbian and gay bars, but the above court decisions insured that this new effort would be even more aggressive. Bill Plath, a San Francisco bar owner, described police entrapment in this way: "Police would send in plainclothesmen in tight pants, very handsome guys, and they'd go to work on some older number who was available for almost anything." Statistics suggest that the San Francisco campaign was quite effective. In the first six months of 1960 there were no felony convictions of gay men; they increased to twenty-nine in the following six months and to seventy-six during the first six months of 1961. Misdemeanor charges increased considerably as well, to an estimated forty to sixty a week (D'Emilio 1983, 183–84).

These statistics do not begin to suggest the environment of fear that pervaded the San Francisco bar scene as authorities used all means of deception to harass and entrap lesbians and gay men. This hostile climate for lesbian and gay life extended to most cities throughout the United

States. As John D'Emilio points out, "conditions were right to encourage a political response to the antigay campaign." Eventually, San Francisco lesbian and gay bar owners organized against the police crackdowns, but neither Mattachine nor the Daughters of Bilitis took up the issue. Like their counterparts in the East, the San Francisco chapters of both organizations continued to embrace an assimilationist, accommodationist strategy, one that eschewed the bar scene. As Chapter 2 pointed out, the existing lesbian and gay organizations emphasized "patiently educating the public, projecting a respectable middle-class image, seeking professional endorsement, and regenerating the individual lesbian and homosexual" (D'Emilio 1983, 185). An approach to political and social change that relied on fragmented, case-by-case litigation reinforced this accommodationist, gradualist perspective. In the end, the practical consequence of the Vallegra decision was to insure that illegal conduct, defined as " 'an offense to public morals' could be alleged to justify arrests and uphold convictions" (Pacelle 1996, 199).

Government dismissals constituted the second broad focus of gay rights legal activity in the pre-Stonewall era. Procedural safeguards were denied those working in the armed forces, whose jobs were terminated after they were charged with being lesbian or gay (Pacelle 1996, 199). Discriminatory government policies established the historical context for the current military ban on lesbians and gays.

Of particular interest is Franklin Kameny's 1957 dismissal from the U.S. Map Service after someone reported that he was gay. A government scientist, he not only lost his current job but faced the loss of any other kind of meaningful employment. His challenge to his dismissal went to the Supreme Court, but he lost the case when the Court denied a writ of certiorari. But Kameny refused to accept the pernicious discrimination that led to the loss of his livelihood, and within months of the Supreme Court's decision, he began to organize by founding the Washington, D.C., Mattachine Society. That organization lobbied politicians to end discrimination against lesbians and gays in government jobs, and it became actively involved in individual employment-discrimination cases brought forward by civil service employees. Such organizing efforts were surely needed given that early 1960s civil service regulations stated that one cause for disqualification from employment was "criminal, infamous, dishonest, immoral, or notoriously disgraceful conduct." At that time, consensual homosexual sodomy was regarded as a crime in the District of Columbia and in many states. In fact, any sort of homosexual conduct was viewed as immoral and constituted grounds for government dismissal (Cain 1993, 23). As might be expected, given the climate of the times, the legal system generally sustained the dismissals, but there were some victories.

For example, the legal challenge brought by the American Civil Liberties Union (ACLU) on behalf of Bruce Scott, the secretary of the Washington, D.C., Mattachine Society, provided the first gay rights legal victory in federal employment in *Scott v. Macy*. In that 1965 decision, "the Court of Appeals for the District of Columbia ruled that the dismissal of an employee for engaging in 'unspecified homosexual conduct' was improper" (Cain 1993, 1559). The same court issued important guidelines regarding the right of a federal employee to maintain her or his silence when questioned about homosexual conduct. The seeds of the modern lesbian and gay legal rights movement were planted in these litigation efforts that occurred in Washington, D.C.

In the area of obscenity law, the legal system had a mixed record in its response to lesbian and gay concerns. As discussed in Chapter 2, members of the Mattachine Society published the magazine *One* during the early years of the organization's existence. Subsequently, the magazine was taken over by One, Inc., an independent organization. Its stated purpose was to address the broad issue of homosexuality within a historical, scientific, and critical framework. Early editions of the magazine contained articles that challenged existing notions of heteronormativity, news reports of gay witch-hunts in Miami and Britain, an essay by Jim Kepner entitled "The Importance of Being Honest," and a lesbian-authored poem titled "Proud and Unashamed" (Cain 1993, 1559).

The Los Angeles postmaster confiscated the October 1954 issue and refused to mail it, claiming that it was "obscene, lewd, lascivious and filthy" (D'Emilio 1983, 115).[4] The editors contested the postmaster's decision by filing suit in federal court, claiming "First Amendment protection for its published speech, an abuse of discretion by the postmaster of Los Angeles, violation of equal protection, and a deprivation of property without due process" (Cain 1993, 1559). The postmaster's actions were sustained in 1956 by a federal district judge, and in 1957 an appeals court rejected *One*'s legal challenge, characterizing the publication as "cheap pornography." But One, Inc., and the larger lesbian and gay community achieved a major legal victory when the U. S. Supreme Court issued its 1957 *Roth v. United States* decision, which stated that the criteria for obscenity pivoted on whether something was "utterly without redeeming social importance."

Soon after the decision, the Court ruled that the lower court's opinion violated *Roth*. As a result, the original decision was reversed and Mattachine had the freedom to mail its magazine (Brewer, Caib, and O'Connor 2000, 380–81). The justices did not issue a written opinion, but lesbian and gay activists claimed that the Supreme Court's decision legitimated discussion of homosexuality. While this appeared to be a major legal victory for lesbians and gays, it was soon undermined by the actions of the postmaster in Alexandria, Virginia, as well as by the response of the legal system.

In 1960 the Alexandria, Virginia, postmaster confiscated hundreds of magazines and requested that the Post Office determine whether it was appropriate to mail them. The magazines' publishers cited the *Roth* decision and argued "that even if the magazines aroused the 'prurient interest of homosexuals,' they were not obscene under Roth's definition of obscenity, 'the so called average person in the community test.'" The District of Columbia Circuit Court of Appeals ruled that the magazines were obscene. On appeal, a closely divided Supreme Court reversed the lower court's 1962 decision in *Manual Enterprises v. Day.* Concurring with the majority and writing for himself and Justice Potter Stewart, Justice John Marshall Harlan argued "that the [embargoed] magazines could 'not be deemed so offensive on their face as to affront current community standards of decency.'" The remaining justices in the majority (Justices William Brennan, William O. Douglas, and Chief Justice Earl Warren) said that the Alexandria, Virginia, "postmaster had no independent legal authority to close the U.S. mails" (Brewer, Kaib, and O'Connor 2000, 381).

All of these examples suggest that lesbians and gays faced many obstacles in pursuing a legal-rights strategy through narrow, fragmented, case-by-case challenges. The cases discussed here were almost all narrowly circumscribed, and had few broader legal ramifications other than to indicate that the legal system could be open to lesbian and gay concerns. The discussion also suggests that perhaps meaningful legal change could come about only through a coordinated movement strategy, one that links legal challenges to the broader goals of the movements. But pursuing a comprehensive strategy requires that marginalized interests be able to marshal substantial resources.

Lesbian and gay rights activists turned to other established groups, recognizing that a more comprehensive legal-rights strategy would require resources and experience in legal proceedings they lacked. The ACLU had an established reputation and legal experience that could enable it to mount a coordinated effort on behalf of lesbians and gays. Further, it might help move litigation battles to the national level, giving them more visibility (Pacelle 1996, 201). Unfortunately, in the 1950s and into the 1960s, the ACLU was not supportive when lesbian and gay activists periodically approached it for legal assistance. For example, it refused to join Franklin Kameny in his fight against the ban on lesbians and gays in government employment. Richard Pacelle offers an insightful analysis of the ACLU's position and the negative repercussions of its lack of support:

> The national organization was primarily interested in expanding freedom
> of expression. In the minds of the leadership, prudence dictated moving
> slowly and concentrating its resources on direct First Amendment cases. The
> ACLU was willing to concede that the Court's distinction between pure
> speech (which would get the ultimate protection) and conduct (which could
> be regulated by the government) was reasonable. This construction had con-
> sequences for lesbian and gay rights. By drawing a line between speech and
> belief (which was protected) and sexual conduct (which was not constitu-
> tionally protected), the ACLU generally refused to handle lesbian and gay
> rights cases. This abdication had dramatic symbolic and practical conse-
> quences. Lesbians and gays were an easy target for McCarthyism. In the
> absence of support from the ACLU. there was no defense for lesbian and
> gay rights. Thus it was easy to codify laws that declared lesbian and gay
> individuals were security risks. Once sanctions had been placed into regu-
> lations, removing legal stigmas would be a laborious and costly task.
> (Pacelle 1996, 201)

The ACLU board of directors offered a national policy statement in January 1957, one that reinforced federal security regulations that denied
employment to lesbians and gay men and accepted the constitutionality
of existing sodomy statues. In the absence of a coordinated lesbian and
gays rights movement in the 1950s and 1960s, the ACLU's position was
not seriously challenged.

But with the changing composition of the ever more liberal Warren
Court of the early 1960s, Supreme Court decisions on First Amendment
issues were articulated in ways that supported the ACLU's positions. With
this changing political climate, the organization perceived that it could
focus on other issues and could "transplant favorable First Amendment
precedents to other areas of law" (Pacelle 1996, 202).

The Supreme Court's 1965 *Griswold v. Connecticut* decision provided
lawyers with the foundation required to challenge the criminalization of
homosexual conduct by recognizing the right to privacy within the context of marital sex (Cain 1993, 1581). This moment encouraged several
ACLU board members to insist that the organization embrace lesbian
and gay rights as a part of its overall agenda. After additional precedents
supported the Court's *Griswold* decision, the ACLU then argued "that
all private consensual conduct, heterosexual as well as lesbian or gay,
should be protected by the privacy rights recognized in Griswold" (Pacelle
1996, 202). This represented a major step forward in the organization's
support for a broader lesbian and gay legal-rights agenda.

What are the implications of the early legal decisions? First and foremost, they were often narrowly circumscribed and failed to provide precedents that could lead to further legal breakthroughs. Second, the early
legal victories established the principle that dominates lesbian and gay lit-

igation even today—the distinction between status and conduct. The courts provided some protection against discrimination solely on the basis of status and for conduct that was deemed totally private. Legal protections diminished, however, once conduct crossed into the public sphere (Cain 1993, 1579). Third, the largely fragmented and uncoordinated legal response by lesbian and gay activists suggests that a better coordinated, coherent, broader, and more sustained legal-rights strategy was necessary if the goal was to achieve both short- and long-term legal victories. As we will soon see, the 1969 Stonewall Rebellion provided the impetus for such a strategy.

Post-Stonewall Legal Strategy

Most importantly, the Stonewall riots offered the foundation for a radical challenge to a narrow, assimilationist claim to lesbian and gay rights. As Patricia Cain suggests, "no longer would the movement be primarily about obtaining the right, so long as lesbians and gay men looked and acted like heterosexuals, to be treated just like heterosexuals in public." Why? Because many of the individuals participating in the Stonewall riots—drag queens and nellies—provided a direct challenge to heteronormativity and signaled that the most unassimilated also needed to be represented as a part of the lesbian and gay movements (Cain 1993, 1581).

In the aftermath of Stonewall, two new organizations were created—the Gay Liberation Front and the Gay Activists Alliance. As we saw in Chapter 2, both of these organizations rejected the existing homophile movement and, inspired by the radical culture of the times, embraced an array of street protests. Neither organization turned immediately to the courts.

By the early 1970s, the two organizations went in divergent directions: the Gay Activists Alliance became much more structured and hierarchical, while the Gay Liberation Front embraced more radical forms of unconventional politics. Eventually the Alliance broke up and reconstituted itself as the National Gay Task Force in 1973.

The year 1973 also witnessed the formation of the Lambda Legal Defense and Education Fund, which was the first public law organization to be created and run by lesbians and gays. The central goal of Lambda has been to pursue greater equity for lesbians and gays through a mainstream legal-rights strategy. In its early days, advocates for lesbians and gays faced a challenging political and legal environment because older, more established public-interest groups—most notably the NAACP—had already been using a legal strategy for a number of years. The federal judiciary itself was hostile to Lambda's legal challenges throughout the 1970s and 1980s because the judicial system had been packed with judges whose social vision was generally conservative and who espoused both a narrow view of constitutional rights and a limited conception of judicial power (Pacelle 1996, 205). Today, the organization is one of four that work at the national level and attempt to promote legal rights for lesbians and gays. The others are the ACLU's Gay and Lesbian Rights Project, the National Center for Lesbian Rights, and the Service-members Legal Defense Network, which was formed in 1993 in an effort to assist military personnel faced with possible discharge (Rimmerman 2000, 69).

While the Lambda Legal Defense and Education Fund specializes in lesbian, gay, and AIDS-related cases, it generally accepts only those cases which, if successfully argued, may provide a breakthrough ruling, one that can benefit the largest number of lesbians, gays, and people with AIDS (Rimmerman 2000, 69). The organization follows a strategy used successfully by the NAACP. It acts as legal counsel or co-counsel for its clients or files amicus curiae briefs in those cases that could set legal precedent or alter current laws. In this way, Lambda has tried to transcend the "one-shot" approach to litigation that characterized the pre-Stonewall lesbian and gay legal-rights movement. Lambda's attorneys handle a wide diversity of cases, including those dealing with the right to marry, sodomy laws, job discrimination, child custody, and inheritance rights. Lambda's legal strategy is, first and foremost, rooted in protection and legal change for lesbians and gays. Once basic civil rights are guaranteed, then education can follow. The goal is for the government to treat everyone equally regardless of sexual orientation. Lambda served as the co-counsel for those opposing the anti-gay-rights ballot initiative in Colorado, which was ultimately struck down by the U.S. Supreme Court.

Working with the Gay and Lesbian Rights Project of the ACLU, Lambda has helped to shape lesbian and gay rights litigation throughout the United States. Both organizations joined together in 1977 to challenge the existing sodomy statute in New York State. At the time, the constitutionality of that statute was being considered by the New York Court of Appeals in *People v. Rice*. Ultimately, the court avoided the crucial constitutional issues and refused to issue a ruling "without a trial record and solely on the information filed" (Cain 1993, 1586). In doing so, the court refused "the defendants' motion to dismiss, without prejudice, and reserved review of the constitutional issues in the event the defendants were actually convicted" (ibid.). In the 1980 New York Court of Appeals decision in *People v. Onofre,* the state statute was ultimately ruled unconstitutional. At that time, the legal director of Lambda, Abby Rubenfeld, defended the organization's focus on challenging sodomy laws because "sodomy laws are the bedrock of legal discrimination against gay men and lesbians" (quoted in ibid., 1587). To be sure, earlier governmental action against lesbians and gay men had associated sodomy and criminal activity with homosexuals. For example, the 1950 Senate Committee recommended that all known homosexuals should be dismissed from government; this was because same-sex sexual conduct was deemed both immoral and criminal.

Gay bar raids were often justified because authorities linked criminal activity with the places where lesbians and gays congregated. Sodomy laws played the same important role in anti-lesbian and gay discrimination in the 1980s. Being labeled a criminal once one's sexual orientation became public was the central danger here, rather than the risk of being prosecuted for sodomy per se. If lesbians and gays were presumed to practice sodomy, then landlords could refuse to rent to, and employers could refuse to hire, "criminals" (Cain 1993, 1588). Given these ugly assumptions about consensual same-sex relationships, lesbian and gay activists recognized that sodomy laws themselves needed to be attacked at their core if discrimination was to be ameliorated. It is no surprise, then, that on November 20, 1983, the Gay and Lesbian Rights Project of the American Civil Liberties Union and Lambda hosted a national meeting of lesbian and gay legal organizations, with the avowed goal of developing a coherent and sustained national strategy for eliminating sodomy laws throughout the United States (ibid., 1586–87). What is surprising, however, is how in recent years the larger lesbian and gay movements appear to have de-emphasized overturning sodomy laws, though Lambda attorneys have continued to work on various state-level sodomy challenges, such as in Kentucky and Texas. But the broader movements have devoted far more attention and resources to the ban on military service and same-sex marriage, among other issues. This is particularly surprising given that seventeen states continue to criminalize sodomy and in only five of those is the prohibition limited to same-sex interactions.

There are at least three possible explanations for the mainstream movement's apparent unwillingness to emphasize the importance of challenging sodomy laws. One is that many of the states with sodomy laws do not enforce them, although there is always the chance that they might do so in individual cases. Second, the military ban and marriage issues were imposed on the larger movements by conservative actors and forces in the American political system. In other words, the movements had little control over when these high-profile battles would be fought on the national scene, but surely they had to respond at both the national and state levels within the broader context of a rights-based strategy for political, social, and legal change. But there is a third explanation that raises questions about the current state of the lesbian and gay movements. The failure to emphasize the importance of challenging sodomy laws in recent years may also suggest the pre-eminence of the assimilationist element of contemporary lesbian and gay movements. The campaign to eliminate sodomy laws has always been consistent with the goals of the broader lesbian and gay liberation movement, which have been to break down stereotypes and to celebrate sexual freedom. For those who associate themselves with liberation, the elimination of sodomy laws is an important concern. Giving the states ultimate "power to define good and bad sex was a barrier for those gay and lesbian individuals who sought to redefine themselves publicly as good, moral, and noncriminal" (Cain 1993, 1589). By refusing to challenge sodomy laws, contemporary lesbian and gay movements have implicitly and explicitly reinforced this state power.

The Lambda Legal Defense and Education Fund also appears to have de-emphasized the overturning of sodomy laws. In recent years, its major activities have been challenging the military ban and pursuing the necessary legal changes to insure same-sex marriage. The organization served as co-counsel in Margarethe Cammermeyer's successful suit against the United States Army, which attempted to discharge her after she publicly identified herself as a lesbian. One of its major accomplishments was a landmark decision rendered by a Wisconsin federal court, one that requires public schools to respond much more aggressively in protecting lesbian and gay students from harassment and assault (Rimmerman 2000, 69–70).

After Stonewall the ACLU also played an integral role in forming a more coherent and sustained legal-rights strategy. The ACLU advocated an "enclave theory," which argued that American society was composed of diverse groups whose members were systematically denied the protections associated with the Bill of Rights. The ACLU's purpose was to identify the groups in question and to expand their basic rights as much as possible. Their efforts received a boost from other political and social movements as well as from the rights consciousness that characterized the times (Pacelle 1996, 204–5).

The ACLU existed prior to Lambda, and it played both direct and indirect roles for a longer period of time in setting a lesbian and gay legal-rights agenda. First, when it finally agreed to take on cases involving lesbian and gay rights, the ACLU gave them a legitimacy that activists had desired for roughly twenty years. Second, the ACLU embraced cases that would have implications for lesbian and gay rights, even if they did not involve lesbians and gay men directly. Third, the organization established a Sexual Privacy Project, which contributed to the creation of an array of groups dedicated to litigation efforts and to supporting the extension of lesbian and gay rights. These new groups were often headed by former members of the ACLU; this factor also enhanced the role of the ACLU in the developing lesbian and gay legal-rights strategy (Pacelle 1996, 205). Fourth, the ACLU created a Lesbian and Gay Rights Project in the mid-1980s. The project enabled its attorneys to develop additional expertise and to use that expertise to help other lesbian and gay rights lawyers across the United States (Brewer, Kaib, and O'Connor 2000, 384). The ACLU's Lesbian and Gay Rights Project aided the larger lesbian and gay movements' efforts to overturn sodomy laws as the Supreme Court considered *Bowers v. Hardwick* in 1986.

Bowers v. Hardwick

The existence of sodomy laws represents a particular assault on the basic dignity and rights of lesbians and gay men, even if these laws are not generally enforced. The fact that they still exist in a number of states suggests how little progress has been made in eliminating structural discrimination and hatred directed toward a particular class of human beings. Sodomy laws clearly reflect societal discrimination against lesbians and gays, and for that reason alone should be overturned. Lesbian and gay rights advocates further argued in the 1970s and 1980s that such laws must be eliminated because of their practical consequences. The laws had countless negative spillover effects, including in such important areas as employment, housing, immigration, and the military. Opponents of lesbian and gay rights used these laws as the "quasi-legal basis for opposition" (Pacelle 1996, 207).

Lesbian and gay rights advocates perceived that these laws were vulnerable to serious constitutional challenge in light of a number of legal privacy decisions in the 1960s, 1970s, and early 1980s. Attorneys attempted to create a legal precedent rooted in the fundamental right to privacy as a strategy for overturning sodomy laws. The hope was that such a precedent would then be useful in challenging discrimination in employment, immigration, and the military. And if the issue were decided favorably, then the conduct/status distinction could finally be eliminated as well. Beginning in 1961 with Illinois, a number of states had already repealed their sodomy laws. But what this meant by the mid-1980s was that where one lived under our system of federalism really mattered; lesbians and gays who resided in one section of the United States had more rights than those living in other regions of the country (Pacelle 1996, 207).

Up until the mid-1980s, the Supreme Court had avoided ruling definitively on the issue of sodomy laws, despite numerous legal challenges in light of the *Griswold* decision.[5] Lesbian and gay legal-rights activists hoped that the Court would finally overturn all sodomy laws in a major test case, one that would establish new legal precedents in support of lesbian and gay rights.

This, then, was the background for the Supreme Court's 1986 five-to-four decision in *Bowers v. Hardwick*. This case originated when police in Atlanta, Georgia, arrested Michael Hardwick, a gay man, for having sex in his own bedroom and charged him with violating the Georgia law that states "a sexual act involving the sex organs of one person and the mouth or anus of another" is a felony that is punishable by a prison sentence of up to twenty years. The Court's decision concluded that individual states retained the "right to criminalize private sexual behavior between consenting adults" (Adam 1995, 135). William Eskridge argues that the decision is an "exemplar of legal homophobia" (Eskridge 1999, 150). That the decision came during the ascendancy of the AIDS crisis was a further blow to gay men. In addition, the case says something about organized litigation strategies and the potential pitfalls of relying on the legal system to advance lesbian and gay rights.

The *Bowers* decision did not invoke the Constitution's equal-protection clause. Instead, it focused on whether Georgia's anti-sodomy law violated the due-process clause of the Fourteenth Amendment. In its *Roe v. Wade* (1973) and *Griswold v. Connecticut* (1965) decisions, "the Court had previously held that the due process clause protects a somewhat vaguely defined 'right to privacy,' which is broad enough to encompass such things as the right to have an abortion and the right to use contraceptives" (Gertsmann 1999, 67). In *Bowers,* the Eleventh Circuit of the U.S. Court of Appeals found that Georgia's anti-sodomy law violated the due-process clause. The appeals court ruled that the "[Supreme] Court's prior cases had construed the Constitution to confer a right to privacy that extends to homosexual sodomy" (quoted in ibid.). The Supreme Court reversed the Court of Appeals after the state of Georgia sought a writ of certiorari.

Interestingly, the original Georgia statute prohibited both heterosexual and homosexual sodomy, but the Supreme Court ruling merely addressed whether the due-process clause protects homosexual sodomy. The Court's majority opinion, written by Justice Byron White, emphasized "that only two kinds of rights qualify for heightened judicial protection under the due process clause: (1) those rights 'implicit in the concept of ordered liberty' such that 'neither liberty nor justice would exist if [they] were sacrificed' and (2) rights that implicate liberties that are 'deeply rooted in this nation's history and tradition'" (Gertsmann 1999, 68).

Without discussion, the Court assumed that homosexual sodomy does not qualify under the first of these two formulations. With respect to the second formulation, the Court claimed that "proscriptions against [homosexual sodomy] have ancient roots" (quoted in Gertsmann 1999, 68). Additionally, the Court argued that the privacy of the home, when it is the setting for such acts, did not offer protection for them, pointing out that victimless crimes, such as adultery and incest, are also illegal, even when performed in the privacy of one's domicile (ibid.).

Lesbian and gay rights groups were understandably horrified by Chief Justice Warren Burger's language in his concurring opinion, when he identified homosexuality as " 'an offense of deeper malignancy' than rape, a heinous act 'the very mention of which is a disgrace to human nature,' and 'a crime not fit to be named' " (quoted in Brewer, Kaib, and O'Connor 2000, 392). Such language certainly did not bode well for the cases pertaining to lesbian and gay rights that were already in the legal-appeals process. And Burger's language, coming from the Chief Justice of the U.S. Supreme Court, did much to reinforce the worst kind of homophobia in the age of AIDS.[6]

What are the broader implications of the *Bowers* decision? The legal scholar Evan Gertsmann offers an important answer to that question:

> The holding of Bowers is quite narrow. It merely states that criminal prosecution of homosexual sodomy does not violate the due process clause. However, its implications have been enormous. Numerous federal courts have held that Bowers precludes them from treating gays and lesbians as a suspect or quasi-suspect class under the equal protection clause.[7] In each of these decisions the court has reasoned that, since homosexual sodomy is not constitutionally protected under the due process clause, those who practice it cannot receive enhanced judicial protection under the equal protection clause. (Gertsmann 1999, 68)

Despite the fact that Gertsmann and others argue that various courts' reliance on the *Bowers* decision is inappropriate, courts continue to do so, with continuing and enormous negative consequences for the lesbian and gay rights movements. In the end, the *Bowers* decision can only be understood as a major setback in the campaign to eliminate discrimination against lesbians and gay men.[8] It also raises serious questions regarding a legal test-case strategy for challenging discriminatory practices, a strategy that is at the core of the legal-rights movement.

LIMITATIONS OF A LEGAL-RIGHTS STRATEGY

Prior to the Supreme Court's ruling, lesbian and gay activists had viewed the *Bowers* case with cautious optimism. They saw the potential for a decision that would legitimate all forms of sexual conduct, thus eliminating government interference and recognizing the privacy rights of all people, including lesbians, gay men, bisexuals, and those who are transgendered. A positive decision on even the narrowest of issues, some legal observers believed, would open opportunities for further litigation that might expand sexual minority rights in other areas. Those who were even more optimistic thought that the Court's decision in the *Bowers* case might serve to place sexual minorities among those groups who are afforded specific, heightened protection under the Fourteenth Amendment's equal-protection clause (Salokar 1997, 394).

Some legal scholars have argued that it was wrong for the lesbian and gay movements to assume that *Bowers* could ever be an ideal test case, given the conservative composition of the Supreme Court at that time, not to mention the more conservative era ushered in by President Ronald Reagan's election in 1980. Since the early 1980s, the federal court system has been generally unwilling to expand the rights of minority group members. In addition, even some justices worried that an unfavorable decision would create a precedent that could have ugly repercussions for lesbian and gay rights in the years ahead. In fact, this is exactly what has happened.

There are additional reasons why the legal system has limited potential as an arena for major social reform. First, much reform occurs outside of the formal framework of the judicial system, and the courts lack the power to foster fundamental changes in people's attitudes and behavior. Courts also lack the tools needed for effective judicial implementation (Rosenberg 1991, 2). In our system of separation of powers, courts must rely on others to implement their legal decisions.[9] As we know from the nation's experience with school desegregation, this can take many years, and numerous structural obstacles at the state and local levels can undermine timely implementation.[10] Second, the legal system is a reactive branch of government and the Supreme Court only hears a small number of cases each year. Third, some judicial scholars believe that the legal system cannot construct coherent public policy, and groups that emphasize a legal-rights strategy may lose sight of larger movement goals by focusing on narrow legal victories. Further, any victories they may win will often energize their opponents, who then organize to block further gains in other arenas. Worse yet, as Pacelle points out, the symbolic value of a legal victory may be mistaken for real progress. In this way, the courts may simply lure "social movements to an institution that is structurally constrained from addressing their needs" (Pacelle 1996, 195–96).

It is important to recognize that courts simply cannot play *the* central role in a social movement's strategy, given the real constraints discussed above. Yet the early lesbian and gay movements were able to win some important symbolic victories through the legal system, victories that, while fragmented and often uncoordinated, did provide some momentum for the post-Stonewall lesbian and gay liberation movement. But having presidential and/or congressional support for a public policy is perhaps even more crucial than judicial endorsement. Having the support of the President and/or Congress carries more practical weight because the executive and legislative branches can provide tangible resources to implement the policies they favor (Pacelle 1996, 196).

Nevertheless, much of what occurs at the federal level has more symbolic than practical effect. For this reason, many favor state-based legal and political strategies. As Evan Gertsmann suggests, "state laws and regulations play a far greater role in constructing the legal and political environment of gays and lesbians." Sodomy statues reside with individual states, and the criminal proscription of conduct also occurs at the state level. The threat of prosecution informs lesbians' and gays' daily lives, even though such state-level laws are difficult to enforce (Gertsmann 1999, 64).

Yet lesbians and gays face serious legal disadvantages at the state level as well. Gertsmann documents these obstacles well:

> State courts have issued orders revoking a mother's custody of her child largely because she is a lesbian, imprisoning gays and lesbians for consensual private sexual acts, and placing restrictions on divorced gay fathers that effectively make visitation with their own children impossible. Meanwhile the federal courts at the highest level continue to tolerate overt job discrimination against gays and lesbians, even by public employers. In January 1998 the Supreme Court let stand an Eleventh Circuit decision upholding the right of Georgia's attorney general to rescind a job offer to a top-ranked Emory law school graduate solely because she planned to celebrate her commitment to her female partner in a Jewish ceremony performed by a rabbi. In 1985 the Supreme Court let stand a decision upholding a public school's right to suspend a guidance counselor solely because she had told some teachers she was bisexual, despite the jury's express finding that the counselor's statements did not "in any way interfere" with her job performance or the regular operation of the school. As these cases show, gays and lesbians are indeed members of a constitutional underclass. (Gertsmann 1999, 8)

Gertsmann's "constitutional underclass" argument is an important one, and if he is right, perhaps a state-based legal strategy is a waste of scarce movement resources that can better be used for other organizing purposes. But others have argued convincingly that a state-based legal approach can be an important component in a multi-pronged campaign for political and social change.[11] Such a strategy might well be called a "new judicial federalism," one that emphasizes state-based legal challenges. This approach has characterized much of the lesbian and gay legal-rights strategy since the *Bowers* decision, and it is particularly evident in the fight for same-sex marriage (Salokar 1997, 396).

Several variables affect the extent to which an interest group will pursue a litigation strategy and whether that strategy will target the state or national-level court system, or whether a movement would be better off using its resources to target state legislatures, local governments, the President, or Congress. These variables include the following: the current political climate, the courts' general ideological balance, the nature of judicial doctrine, and the policies that emerge from the President, Congress, and state legislatures (Pacelle 1996, 197). In one way or another, virtually all of these variables have been present in the recent debates over the military ban or over same-sex marriage. We now turn to a discussion of these two case studies. The goal is to highlight some of the earlier themes of this chapter and to assess the utility of a legal-rights strategy with respect to these two incendiary policy areas.

The Ban on Military Service

At the core of the political-process model of social movements discussed in Chapter 1 is the belief that expanding political opportunities help to determine the movements' overall strength. With the election of President Bill Clinton in November 1992, many perceived that, after twelve long years of Republican Party control of the White House, the opportunity now existed for forceful presidential leadership on behalf of sexual minorities.[12] There was tremendous jubilation in the lesbian and gay community on the night of Clinton's election. Pollsters estimate that Clinton received some 75 percent of the lesbian and gay vote and that the community had contributed some $3 million to his campaign (Kaiser 1997, 333–34). Indeed, there was great hope and excitement because for the first time a presidential candidate had courted the lesbian and gay vote, had been elected with the support of the community, and now would have to govern with that reality in mind (Rimmerman 2000).

What had Clinton done during the campaign to warrant such support? On May 18, 1992, then-candidate Clinton gave a speech to the Los Angeles–based organization ANGLE (Access Now for Gay and Lesbian Equality). Some 650 lesbians and gays spent at least a hundred dollars each to hear Clinton's speak about his vision of a more inclusive America:

> Finally, let me say again, this is not an election, or it should not be, about race or gender or being gay or straight or religion or age or region or income. What kills the country is not the problems it faces. . . . What kills the country is to proceed day in and day out with no vision, with no sense that tomorrow can be better than today, with no sense of shared community. What I came here today to tell you in simple terms is: I have a vision and you are part of it. (Rimmerman 2000, 43)

Video-taped copies of Clinton's speech were distributed throughout the country and played at lesbian and gay fundraisers all fall. Many perceived that Clinton's words signaled a serious commitment to address the concerns of lesbian and gay communities.

During the 1992 presidential campaign, Clinton pledged that he would not forget the interests of his lesbian and gay constituents if he did get elected. At various points during the campaign, Clinton pledged to do much more substantively and symbolically on behalf of lesbians and gays than previous presidents had done. He would provide lesbians and gays greater access to his administration and would appoint openly lesbian and gay officials. He promised to escalate the federal government's response to AIDS, by creating the office of AIDS czar and increasing funding for AIDS research, and he pledged to overturn the ban on lesbians and gays in the U.S. military through executive order. Clinton made additional promises as well: to support a gay civil rights bill and to issue an executive order that would bar discrimination on the basis of sexual orientation in all federal agencies. The promise began to take shape at the 1992 Democratic National Convention when Roberta Achtenberg, a California lesbian, and Bob Hattoy, a gay man who has AIDS, were both given speaking opportunities. Eventually, both Achtenberg and Hattoy received appointments in the Clinton administration.

As governor of Arkansas, Bill Clinton had no record of supporting lesbian and gay rights. But in an October 1992 interview with New York *Times* reporter Jeffrey Schmalz, Clinton admitted that his Los Angeles fund-raising event forced him to realize that "running for President would require me to think about things that I just didn't have to deal with as Governor" (Kaiser 1997, 330). Rahm Emanuel, one of Clinton's political advisors and the finance director for the campaign, put the issue more bluntly: "The gay community is the new Jewish community. It's highly politicized, with fundamental health and civil rights concerns. And it contributes money. All that makes for a potent political force, indeed" (ibid., 330–31).

And who could blame the lesbian and gay movements for supporting candidate and president-elect Clinton? After twelve years of Republican presidencies openly hostile to lesbian and gay concerns, Clinton's election was viewed as an opportunity. The 1980s had been the decade of Reagan, Bush, *Bowers v. Hardwick,* and, above all, the grim reality of the AIDS crisis. Things just had to be better in the 1990s, and Bill Clinton's election allowed people to envision new opportunities for meaningful change.

How much power do presidents have to make unpopular decisions in our political system? And to what extent should political and social movements at the margin look to presidential leadership to promote significant progressive change? At one level, an important legacy of the constitutional framers is that individual presidents have the freedom to make the choices regarding the opportunities and constraints facing them as they exercise presidential power. Yet in their efforts to promote liberty and impede majority tyranny, the architects of the Constitution may have performed their task too well. Nowhere is this more evident than when a president attempts to sustain the momentum of his honeymoon period by building the governing coalition that he needs in Congress and in the electorate to translate his campaign promises into concrete public policy.[13] All presidents soon learn that our fragmented political system makes it difficult for presidents to accomplish their domestic policy goals in a timely manner. This was especially true as Clinton attempted to carry out his campaign promise to overturn the ban on military service ban through an executive order (Rimmerman 2000, 46–47). In addition, divided public opinion regarding the military ban also undermined Clinton's ability to move quickly and decisively by issuing an executive order.

At the start of his presidency, Bill Clinton had virtually no governing coalition since he had won with just 43 percent of the popular vote. He was in a particularly vulnerable position, despite the fact that Democrats controlled both the House and the Senate. As the political scientist David Rayside has suggested, it was easy "to conclude that Clinton's victory had been a negative vote—a rejection of President Bush" (Rayside 1998, 221). In addition, Ross Perot's strong showing as a third-party candidate had denied Clinton the important symbolism of winning more than half of the vote.

While the Democrats had control of both the House and Senate, they were hardly united on how or even whether to address lesbian and gay concerns. Most had other and, to them, more important domestic concerns on their minds—the budget, the economy, health care, social security, trade, welfare reform—that were central elements of Clinton's own successful campaign strategy.

This is the broad context in which the military-service issue appeared on the policy agenda soon after Clinton was elected. If the political-process model is accurate, then "movements depend on their external environments (and especially on political opportunities) to coordinate and sustain collective action" (Tarrow 1994, 10). But to what extent were political opportunities really available to lesbian and gay movements once Clinton was elected? Of course, the political and social landscape looked very different to lesbian and gay movements in November 1992 than that same period looks in hindsight. For example, we now know that Clinton's own honeymoon period was very short indeed. One reason for its brevity was the furor caused by his attempt to overturn the military ban on lesbians and gays through executive order. At a Harvard University forum in the fall of 1991, then-candidate Clinton was asked whether he would issue an executive order to rescind the ban on lesbians and gays in the military. Clinton responded "Yes," and explained further: "I think people who are gay should be expected to work, and should be given the opportunity to serve the country." He continued to articulate this pledge as a presidential candidate and as President-elect (Rimmerman 1996b, xix).

What happened after Clinton took office is important because it suggests how quickly political opportunities for groups at the margin may close, and how they are often subordinate to elites' short-term political interests. First, President Clinton failed in the important leadership role of educating the public about why he believed that the military ban should be overturned. In a previous study of this episode, I outlined several reasons for his failure to do so (Rimmerman 1996, 112). Then Clinton clearly recognized that he did not have the required votes in Congress to sustain an executive order overturning the ban. In addition, compromise came easily to Clinton: building consensus characterized his approach to governance. This is what he later attempted with his "Don't Ask, Don't Tell" compromise proposal.[14] Another explanation is that Clinton embraced policy positions associated with the New Democrats, those who believe that the Democratic Party should move in a more moderate direction.[15] In this context it made good sense for Clinton and his advisors to distance themselves from so-called liberal special-interest groups such as lesbian and gay organizations. Finally, Clinton was worried about squandering valuable political capital in fighting the ban early in his first term, capital that he would surely need in his budget and health-care fights with Congress.

During the campaign, Clinton's promise had provoked little response from President George Bush or Vice President Dan Quayle. Although the August 1992 Republican national convention was characterized by considerable antigay vitriol, which public opinion polls indicated mirrored the attitudes of much of mainstream America, Bush and Quayle generally avoided using antigay rhetoric during their election campaign. In doing so, they perhaps gave Clinton and his lesbian and gay supporters a false sense of optimism regarding the possibility of overturning the military ban. Soon after Clinton confirmed his intention to make good on his campaign promise (at his first news conference following his election), the Christian Right began to mobilize. They had the strong support of Senator Sam Nunn (D-Georgia, then chair of the Senate Armed Services Committee), veterans' groups, and antigay personnel in the military hierarchy. Clinton's own perceived weakness on military issues—he had managed to avoid being drafted during the Vietnam War—gave further ammunition to those opposed to lifting the ban, as did his determination to focus "like a laser beam" on the economy immediately upon taking office. As it became increasingly clear that overturning the ban would entail considerable political peril and erosion of political capital, Clinton and his advisors distanced themselves from the issue.

The result was a compromise proposal, one that shattered the hopes of Clinton's lesbian and gay supporters, who expected he would have the political courage to follow through with his original plan. On April 16, 1993, Clinton had even met with six lesbian and gay representatives—the first publicly announced session of gay representatives with any president in the Oval Office—to discuss the military ban. Tom Stoddard, the head of the Campaign for Military Service, attended the session and reported that the President was "completely sympathetic" and "understood all the points that were raised" (Kaiser 1997, 334). Stoddard and several of his colleagues mistook access to the President for substantive support, a mistake that many in the lesbian and gay movements were to make over the course of his presidency. In addition, the Campaign for Military Service, a largely Washington, D.C.–based organizing effort, was formed only in late January. As late as March 22, Tom Stoddard spoke of a grassroots campaign "revving up" (Rayside 1996, 176). The organization was roundly criticized for failing to communicate with and thus to mobilize lesbian and gay people to act.[16] It did not help, either, that the lesbian and gay movements were divided over whether the military ban should even be on their agenda. As Urvashi Vaid astutely points out, "Rather than uniting behind the effort to overturn this form of government discrimination, gay people argued about whether it was the right goal. Our division undermined our leadership and ultimately helped our enemies" (Vaid 1995, 358).

To no one's surprise, but to considerable disappointment, Clinton ultimately offered a compromise in the form of his July 1993 "Don't Ask, Don't Tell, Don't Pursue" proposal. Senator Nunn toughened Clinton's proposal so that lesbians and gays serving the military were dealt with even more harshly than in the Clinton compromise. Ultimately, Nunn's changes were codified into law by Congress, thus making it much more difficult for opponents of the ban to win significant structural reforms in the future. While the previous ban was based on an executive order, and could be changed through presidential action, any changes to Nunn's statute would require congressional consent.

As one would expect, lesbian and gay activists and their supporters were furious with Clinton's compromise plan. Torie Osborn, executive director of the National Gay and Lesbian Task Force, argued that the plan was "simply a repackaging of discrimination." Tom Stoddard, coordinator of the Campaign for Military Service, said, "The President could have lifted up the conscience of the country. Instead, he acceded without a fight to the stereotypes of prejudices he himself had disparaged." But perhaps a *New Republic* editorial best captured the anger of those who had expected far more from the President: "And the most demeaning assumption about the new provisions is that they single out the deepest moment of emotional intimacy—the private sexual act—as that which is most repugnant. Its assumption about the dignity and humanity of gay people, in and out of the military, in public and in private, is sickening" (quoted in Bawer 1993, 62).

The subsequent implementation of the plan has done nothing to allay the concerns of the President's strongest critics. The Service-members Legal Defense Network has conducted yearly studies of the military's application of the "Don't Ask, Don't Tell" policy and has repeatedly found a pattern of violations that often render the policy little more than "Ask, Pursue, and Harass."[17]

One study revealed that Clinton's leadership did have positive consequences for public opinion on allowing lesbians and gays to serve openly. Political scientists Clyde Wilcox and Robin Wolpert found that Clinton's stand may have mobilized increased support for lifting the ban among those who liked him (Wilcox and Wolpert 1996, 142). But the reality is that the ban is still in place, and it took the July 1999 beating and murder of Army private Barry Winchell, who was suspected of being gay, to provoke public discussion and a Department of Defense review of the policy. Yet that review provides little hope that the ban will be overturned in the foreseeable future. Even Michelle Benecke, co-director of the Service-members Legal Defense Network, a Washington-based organization that provides legal aid for those who have been harassed by the military, believes that the "Don't Ask, Don't Tell" policy is solidly entrenched in the short term. Benecke points out that "the acceptance of blacks and women in the military had a 50-year time line. We thought that if we had a time line half that long, we would be doing pretty well. The resistance to [allowing gays and lesbians to serve openly] cannot be underestimated" (Bull 2000b, 27).

With the failure of the President and Congress to overturn the military ban, lesbian and gay movements have turned to the courts, embracing a case-by-case legal strategy to challenge the discriminatory nature of the ban. Their legal challenge will likely rest on one or more of several principles. The first is the right to privacy, whereby an individual has a right to engage in any private consensual sexual conduct, as upheld in the Supreme Court's earlier decisions allowing abortion, contraception, and miscegenation. A second approach emphasizes that the military's policies against lesbians and gays violate the Fourteenth Amendment's equal-protection clause. The last argument is that even if the federal government could establish homosexual conduct among military personnel, it would have to prove why such conduct made an officer unsuitable for the armed forces (Rimmerman 1998b, 264).

What lesbian and gay advocacy groups found in the short term is that the courts have been somewhat supportive of lesbian and gay efforts despite the Clinton administration's attempts to pursue a more regressive policy. Interestingly, the Clinton administration defended the military's old lesbian and gay policy in court in an effort to establish precedents that would make challenges to the policy more difficult. On June 1, 1994, a Seattle federal judge ordered the military to reinstate Col. Margarethe Cammermeyer, who was forced out of the Washington State National Guard after admitting her lesbianism. Judge Thomas Zilly of the federal district court "ordered Cammermeyer back to the job she held in 1992, ruling that the military's policy on homosexuals at that time was based solely on prejudice and was a clear violation of the Constitution's equal-protection clause."[18] Judge Zilly ruled that "there is no rational basis for the Government's underlying contention that homosexual orientation equals 'desire or propensity to engage' in homosexual conduct" (Schmitt 1995).

The Clinton and congressional compromise has also been successfully challenged in the courts. On March 30, 1995, Judge Eugene Nickerson of the federal district court in Brooklyn ruled in *Able v. the United States* that the "Don't Ask, Don't Tell, Don't Pursue" compromise violated the First and Fifth Amendments and also catered to the prejudices and fears of heterosexual troops. The case came before Nickerson three times in three consecutive years. To Nickerson the fact that the new policy attempted to distinguish between sexual orientation and the possibility of acting on such an orientation was "nothing less than Orwellian." Nickerson ruled, as well, that the new policy denies lesbians and gays the protection of the Fifth Amendment by unfairly discriminating against them. His final decision in the *Able* case, on July 2, 1997, offered his strongest denunciation of the "Don't Ask, Don't Tell" policy. Nickerson wrote, in part:

> A court should ask itself what it might be like to be a homosexual. . . . For the United States government to require those self-identifying as homosexuals to hide their orientation and to pretend to be heterosexuals is to ask them to accept a judgment that their orientation is in itself disgraceful and they are unfit to serve. To impose such a degrading and deplorable condition for remaining in the Armed Services cannot in fairness be justified on the ground that the truth might arouse the prejudice of some of their fellow members. (Keen 1997, 1)

Both the original Zilly and Nickerson decisions were encouraging to lesbians and gays who embraced the legal approach at a time when the President and Congress were unwilling to rescind the ban. But the *Able* case was reversed on appeal by the Second Circuit "on grounds of deference to the military," and lesbian and gay litigators chose not to apply for certiorari (Cain 2000, 201). Patricia Cain explains this decision:

Enough was enough. The Supreme Court had denied certiorari in every single military case, whether litigated under the old 1980s policy or the new 1990s policy. Not a single court of appeals had ruled against the 1990s policy. In consultation with each other, the public interest gay rights lawyers that had been fighting the military for over a decade finally decided it was time to quit. No writ of certiorari would be requested in *Able*. (Cain 2000, 201)

The judicial appeals process in the *Able* case reveals the limitations of a legal strategy. Yet the military-ban debate suggests how legal doctrine can influence political decisions and debates. As we have already seen, the *Bowers v. Hardwick* decision had serious implications for what has come to be known as the status-conduct debate. Homosexual status (sexual orientation alone) and homosexual conduct (engaging in homosexual acts) are the basis of this contentious distinction.[19] The courts have clearly been divided over precisely this issue. Most appeals courts have ruled "that discrimination based on sexual orientation could not be subject to heightened scrutiny under the equal protection clause because it was constitutionally permissible under Hardwick for a state to criminalize sodomy, and participation in sodomy defined the class homosexual" (Hunter 1995b, 139). In the absence of "a privacy-based defense against criminalization of that conduct, advocates and some judges argued that sexual orientation was first and foremost a status, not contingent on conduct." The debate over homosexuality as conduct or status has rested on a single case and is "purely an artifact of the categories of legal doctrine." Yet as legal scholar Nan Hunter has pointed out, it has been used over and over again to justify the military ban (ibid., 139–40).

Except for the *Able* decision, the recent cases considering the military's policy on lesbians and gays have made clear that the military can justify banning homosexual conduct. As legal scholar Peter Jacobson suggests, "the issue, therefore, is whether the military is justified in assuming that homosexual orientation is tantamount to homosexual behavior (that is, being a homosexual predisposes the person toward homosexual conduct)" (Jacobson 1996, 54). This important issue will continue to be addressed by the courts. But the judicial debates and decisions suggest that it will be a long, uphill battle if the goal is ultimately to eliminate the military ban.

Given the unwillingness of the President and Congress to extend basic civil rights to lesbians and gays in the military and in the larger society, some believed that the movements should turn to the judicial system. But as this chapter has pointed out, many pitfalls face activist organizations who rely on the courts to effect political and social change. One important limitation is the inability of the judicial system to construct coherent public policy. In addition, victories in the courts energize opponents, who often work to block those gains through other venues. We may well see this latter development if lower court rulings favor individual plaintiffs challenging the military ban. It is a development that has already arisen in the battle over same-sex marriage.

Same-Sex Marriage

Since the adoption of the United States Constitution, family life issues, including child custody, divorce, and marriage were presumed to be regulated by individual states. Given this history, it is no surprise, then, that the federal government and the federal judiciary have been quite "reluctant to tread into this last bastion of state sovereignty" (Brewer, Kaib and O'Connor 2000, 401). This is certainly true with respect to marriage.

The campaign for same-sex marriage has depended on success in the courts. It was inspired not through consensus among activists but by a relatively small coterie of lawyers. Thus the campaign is rooted in litigation, though it has now garnered the support of most major national lesbian and gay organizations, including the Lambda Legal Defense and Education Fund, the National Gay and Lesbian Task Force, and the Human Rights Campaign.[20] Its status as one of the leading issues of the 1990s for the mainstream lesbian and gay movements is evidenced by Lambda's Evan Wolfson's contention that, in the wake of the Hawaii Supreme Court's 1993 *Baehr v. Lewin* decision, there should be no "intra-community debate over whether to seek marriage. The ship has sailed" (Warner 1999, 83). For strategic reasons, Wolfson believes that the lesbian and gay movements should present a united front in support of same-sex marriage if homophobic Christian Right initiatives are to be defeated.

There are vocal critics of same-sex marriage within the lesbian and gay movements, however. For example, Paula Ettlebrick argues from a feminist perspective that all marriage reinforces patriarchy and for that reason alone should be rejected. Instead, she argues, lesbians and gays should form their own families.[21] William Eskridge points out that most of the responses to Ettlebrick's position embrace a central tenet of liberalism—that lesbians and gays should have the same choices that are available to straights. Indeed, this classical liberal argument dominates the case for same-sex marriage. Nan Hunter, however, offers a slightly different critique of Ettlebrick's position, suggesting that the oppressive aspects of marriage should be undermined. But if this were done, Hunter admits that traditionalists might well be correct to argue that same-sex marriage would ultimately undermine marriage because it is an attack on the most patriarchal elements of marriage, such as that a man's primary role is to be the breadwinner while the woman's is to care for the home and family (Eskridge 1999, 288). But Hunter believes that this is precisely the set of attitudes and values that need to be undermined.[22] Finally, Michael

Warner offers a scathing critique of marriage based on two arguments: first, that it reinforces the worst elements of heteronormativity by "normalizing" the lesbian and gay movement; and second, that by embracing same-sex marriage, lesbian and gay movements endorse the real economic benefits and privileges associated with marriage as an institution in the United States, such as health care coverage, inheritance rights, social security survivors' benefits, and tax breaks.[23] Warner is particularly concerned with those national organizations that have "accepted the mainstreaming project and, in particular, the elevation of the marriage issue as the movement's leading goal" (Warner 1999, 146).

Before reviewing the lesbian and gay movements' interactions with the legal system over the marriage issue, it is important to recognize that besides legal recognition of same-sex relationships, there are several other ways that same-sex couples have achieved legal recognition, including expanding definitions of family and domestic partnership benefits and ordinances.[24] But for some, the right to marry is now a crucial goal. Indeed, the Fourteenth Amendment's due-process clause guarantees that the right to marry is a fundamental liberty.

The issue of whether the due-process clause protects same-sex marriage has been central to the lesbian and gay movements' legal strategy.[25] Prior to the *Baehr* decision, the court ruled against "same sex couples who challenged the refusal of the state to grant them marriage licenses." For example, in three cases that preceded *Baehr*,[26] the court offered three similar constitutional and statutory arguments:

> First, plaintiffs argued that the Supreme Court had declared the right to marry to be a fundamental right and that the refusal to grant them a marriage license violated their fundamental right to marry. The courts uniformly rejected this argument, holding that the term marriage by its definition is the union between one man and one woman. Thus, the fundamental right is defined in terms of a heterosexual couple and does not apply to a same-sex union. Second, plaintiffs argued that they were being discriminated against on the basis of sex, since a man could marry a woman but not a man. This argument was rejected on the grounds that the law applied equally to male and female same-sex couples. Finally, in some states, the marriage license law does not explicitly state that marriage must be between a man and a woman. Plaintiffs argued that the statute itself did not preclude the issuance of a marriage license. The courts rejected this argument by again saying that by its terms, marriage means the union of one man and one woman. (Dolkart 1998, 316)

None of these arguments provided much hope to the legal activists who turned to the judicial system to press their grievances on a case-by-case basis. Indeed, when three lesbian and gay couples challenged Hawaii's marriage laws, most lesbian and gay litigation and political groups were hardly enthusiastic. Why? First, the plaintiffs proposed little in the way of new arguments that had not already been rejected by various state courts some twenty years earlier. Second, lesbian and gay rights organizations hesitated to enter into a legal battle where there was little prospect of tangible success. Third, these same organizations worried about setting bad precedents and feared a political backlash. Besides Lambda, which "joined the case as co-counsel when the possibility of judicial success became clear," not a single other lesbian or gay group had hired a marriage project director full-time (Lewis and Edelson 2000, 199).

The broad legal-rights strategy adopted by the lesbian and gay movements finally received judicial legitimacy with the Supreme Court of Hawaii's *Baehr v. Lewin* decision. The relevant background to the case is as follows: In 1991, three couples who were all residents of Hawaii challenged Hawaii's marriage law by filing a declaratory judgment that the law was unconstitutional because it "denied same-sex couples the same marriage rights as different-sex couples." They based their claims on the privacy and equal-protection clauses of the Hawaii state constitution. The Hawaii Supreme Court's 1993 decision rejected the privacy argument by "holding that Hawaii's guarantee of privacy has been interpreted to be co-extensive with the U.S. Constitution's right to privacy, in which the right to marry has been linked with the rights of procreation, child-birth, and child rearing, clearly contemplating a union between a man and a woman" (Dolkart 1998, 316–17).

The Hawaii court responded more positively to the equal-protection argument. It found nothing in the state constitution that prevented lesbian and gay marriage, and it argued that denying same-sex couples access to the benefits and rights associated with marriage is a form of sex discrimination. The court also ruled that "sex-based classifications are suspect" and, as a result, are subject to strict scrutiny. The Hawaii statute restricted a vital personal right—the freedom to marry—to female/male couples. In order to justify this statute, the state would have to show a compelling reason for restricting marriage to opposite-sex couples, and it would further have to prove that the gender classification was narrowly tailored to accomplish the state's purpose.[27]

The Supreme Court remanded the case to the state trial court, affording Hawaii the opportunity to present evidence at trial to justify the marriage statute. This new trial was held during the summer of 1996, and because it found "that the state had failed to prove a compelling interest in denying same-sex couples the right to marry," the trial court ruled the Hawaii marriage law unconstitutional. The decision itself "was stayed pending appeal" (Dolkart 1998, 316–17). The case returned to the Hawaii Supreme Court, which on December 9, 1999, issued a ruling of fewer than five hundred words stating, in essence, that the state of Hawaii can bar lesbian and gay couples from obtaining marriage licenses. The Hawaii Supreme Court also ruled that a 1998 initiative passed by voters legitimized a previous statute that restricted marriage licenses to one man and one woman. However, the court also opened the door to the possibility that same-sex couples could still be eligible for "the same benefits of marriage—even without the license" (Keen 1999b, 1).

Shortly after the 1993 *Baehr* decision, there was an enormous conservative backlash. For example, the Hawaii legislature passed legislation forbidding same-sex marriage, thus codifying the heterosexual character of marriage. Later, after the trial judge's 1996 decision, the Hawaii state legislature also proposed a constitutional amendment "that would permit the legislature to restrict marriage to opposite-sex couples." This amendment, which appeared on the ballot during the 1998 November elections, was accepted by Hawaii voters, thus dealing same-sex marriage advocates a serious blow. Interestingly, the Hawaii state legislature awarded same-sex couples "the broadest package of domestic partner benefits ever provided by a governmental entity" at the very same time that it proposed the constitutional amendment (Dolkart 1998, 317). This politically brokered compromise enabled supporters of the referendum to win moderate and liberal support. The message is very clear. Domestic partnership under this new law is available to those who cannot marry, thus reinforcing the idea that marriage is only available to couples of the opposite sex. In this way, Hawaii has ultimately supported the beliefs of the Christian Right. Worse yet, the backlash against the 1993 *Baehr* and 1996 court of appeals decisions have led more than half the states to enact some form of a specific ban on same-sex marriages.[28] The President and Congress also acceded to the Christian Right's agenda by passing the virulently anti-lesbian and gay 1996 Defense of Marriage Act (DOMA). Given their history of organizing against lesbian and gay "advances" over time, it is no surprise that the Christian Right led the opposition to same-sex marriage. For example, three days before the 1996 presidential caucuses in Iowa, a coalition of eight conservative religious groups publicly touted what it called a Marriage Protection Resolution. All of the Republican presidential candidates signed the resolution, and three even addressed a rally sponsored by the conservative groups (Lewis and Edelson 2000, 200).

But many were surprised by the Clinton administration's response, once the issue was forced onto the national policy agenda by the Christian Right. Understandably, President Clinton received strong criticism from some members of the lesbian and gay movements when he signed

DOMA on September 21, 1996. The law is designed to accomplish two goals: "(1) prevent states from being forced by the Full Faith and Credit Clause to recognize same-sex marriages validly celebrated in other states, and (2) define marriages for federal purposes as the union of one man and one woman" (Strasser 1997, 127). Unlike the military ban issue, however, Clinton was at least consistent on lesbian and gay marriage: he had announced his opposition in the 1992 campaign. But those most critical of the president argued that DOMA was both unnecessary and highly discriminatory, and that Clinton could have vetoed DOMA while still opposing the principle of lesbian and gay marriage.[29] Others understood, however, that Clinton was forced to sign DOMA in order to avoid attacks by the Christian Right during the 1996 presidential campaign. Indeed, the Dole campaign had run a radio ad that criticized Clinton for supporting an end to the military ban. The Clinton forces responded by releasing their own ad celebrating the President's signing of DOMA. This ad was run on Christian radio stations across the country, despite the fact that the President criticized the authors of DOMA for attempting to inject such a difficult issue into presidential politics during an election year. In fact, Clinton actually signed the bill after midnight so that there would be as little attention drawn to his decision as possible. Nevertheless, lesbian and gay movement members protested loudly when the Clinton campaign advertisement was broadcast on Christian radio. In response, the Clinton campaign pulled the ad in two days (Chibbaro 1996a, 24).

Could the movements have done more to force the Clinton administration to support same-sex marriage? In answering this question, it is important to remember that same-sex marriage is not a crucial issue for many movement members. Those who think it should be a key goal—individuals such as Andrew Sullivan[30] and Bruce Bawer—generally represent the movements' more moderate to conservative element. But as we have already learned from the military ban debate, the movements cannot control when specific issues will come to the fore. And in many ways, the issue of same-sex marriage could not have come up at a worse time. The Republicans now controlled both houses of Congress, it was a presidential election year, and the movements simply did not have the time, organizational skills, or resources to mount an effective organizing and educational campaign on an issue that appeared to be unpopular with the American public—certainly not a campaign equal to challenging the Christian Right's vast organizational resources. Indeed, the Republicans were searching for a popular election-year wedge issue when they introduced the Defense of Marriage Act on May 8, 1996. Rich Tafel, executive director of the Log Cabin Republicans, supported several of these points when he said, "Marriage is so visceral, such a negative in the polls.

My experience in debating this issue is that if I have an hour or two hours, I can win, but if I have five minutes, I can't. This is all being done in five minutes" (Gallagher 1996, 21). As a campaign issue, opposition to same-sex marriage served several purposes. It was an opportunity for some politicians to reach out to both the center and the right, given the larger public's apparent lack of support for the issue. And it forced President Clinton to tackle a difficult issue at a time when he did not want to relive the military fiasco of several years before. Clinton had no choice, then, but to alienate some members of his voting base.

How might Clinton have handled the situation differently? He certainly could have forbidden his campaign team from broadcasting a radio ad supporting DOMA on Christian radio. That the campaign ran such an ad suggests how badly Clinton and his campaign advisors wanted to straddle all sides of the issue, especially given his public statements that Republicans were putting him in a difficult situation by introducing DOMA in the middle of an election campaign. He might also have vetoed DOMA while still expressing his own opposition to same-sex marriage, but arguing that such legislation was inappropriate at the time and was being used as a political weapon, without the kind of lengthy public education and discussion that the issue deserved. We should not be surprised that Clinton did not follow this latter strategy, given his previous record on the military ban. For him to take a bold and creative position, one rooted in educational leadership, would have been out of keeping with his political character.

But fortunately for advocates of same-sex marriage, the issue moved out of the national arena and back to the states with Vermont's Chief Justice Jeffrey Amestoy's historic December 1999 decision that Vermont's state legislature must grant lesbian and gay couples the "common benefits and protections" that heterosexual couples receive (Freiberg 2000b, 1). As in Hawaii, however, the unanimous decision by the Vermont Supreme Court in *Baker v. Vermont* stopped short of stating that its legislature must afford lesbians and gays the legal right to marry. Instead, the Vermont state legislature was given the authority to decide just how such "such common benefits and protections" would be extended to lesbians and gays. Chief Justice Amestoy put it this way:

> We hold that the State is constitutionally required to extend to same-sex couples the common benefits and protections that flow from marriage under Vermont law. Whether this ultimately takes the form of inclusion within the marriage laws themselves or a parallel "domestic partnership" system or some equivalent statutory alternative rests with the Legislature. Whatever system is chosen, however, must conform with the constitutional imperative to afford all Vermonters the common benefit, protection, and security of the law. (Keen 1999b, A1)

The reaction to the court's decision by advocates of same-sex marriage was euphoric. In a typical response, Mary Bonauto, an attorney for Gay and Lesbian Advocates and Defenders, a Boston-based legal organization that assisted in representing the couples, said, "It's a legal and cultural milestone. For the first time a state supreme court has recognized that gay couples exist and have the same needs for legal protections as other couples" (Gallagher 2000, 28). This euphoria may have been premature, especially if the long view is taken into account. Most analysts predicted that, as had happened in Hawaii, the Vermont state legislature would adopt some form of domestic partnership law, one that extended certain key benefits but stopped short of endorsing lesbian and gay marriage. Their predictions were essentially turned into reality when Vermont Governor Howard Dean signed into law the first-in-the-nation "civil unions" bill, which extended to lesbian and gay couples "all the rights and benefits of marriage granted by state law" (Freiberg 2000, 1) but failed to endorse "marriage." While many lesbian and gay activists celebrated this development, others, such as Andrew Sullivan, lamented Vermont's withholding of one of the most basic civil rights.

Not surprisingly, a conservative backlash soon emerged against the original Vermont Supreme Court decision. Vermont state legislators who supported the civil unions legislation were targeted for defeat by Christian Right organizers, and some lost their re-election bids in the 2000 elections. Conservative forces throughout the United States immediately moved to pre-empt attempts to recognize same-sex marriages in their own states. In late December 1999 and January 2000, activists and legislators in seven states displayed interest in prohibiting same-sex marriages. These states are Colorado, Massachusetts, Missouri, Nevada, New Hampshire, New York, and Ohio. For example, only two days after the December 20, 1999, Vermont Supreme Court decision, New Hampshire State Rep. Gary Torressen (R–Center Harbor) introduced a bill that would prohibit same-sex marriages from being recognized in New Hampshire. Voters in Nevada and Nebraska gave overwhelming support in the November 7, 2000, elections to referenda that would outlaw same-sex marriages and civil unions. Such actions raise important questions about the implications of the same-sex-marriage debate for the broader lesbian and gay movements' strategy. The publicity surrounding the original Hawaii case appears to have done much more for opponents of lesbian and gay marriage than for its proponents. Further, the marriage issue vaulted to the forefront of the movements' agenda without a full and frank discussion of what this rights-based strategy would mean for lesbian and gay movements' organizing and education efforts, and for the direction of both short-term and long-term political and cultural change.

CONCLUSION AND IMPLICATIONS

Lesbian and gay movements have understandably looked to the legal system for rights-based change when elected officials have been unwilling to extend individual rights to those people who do not meet "acceptable" standards of heteronormativity. In the decades of the 1950s and 1960s, the movements' legal efforts were generally uncoordinated and much more fragmented than those of other social movements of the period, and the legal "victories" were often narrowly circumscribed and failed to provide the legal precedents needed for future advances. They also established the important principle that guides lesbian and gay litigation even today— the conduct/status distinction. By the time of Stonewall, however, the legal-rights strategy had begun to be more coherently developed, as reflected in the challenging of various state-level sodomy laws in the early 1970s and 1980s. These challenges mirrored the ascendancy of the lesbian and gay liberation movements in the 1970s, which attacked stereotypes and celebrated sexual freedom.

By the more conservative 1980s, however, and with the Supreme Court's reactionary *Bowers v. Hardwick* decision in 1986, the lesbian and gay movements began to publicly de-emphasize efforts to overturn sodomy laws, although such efforts continued behind the scenes. This is not surprising given how the *Bowers* decision provided a legal framework for responding to lesbian and gay rights claims, and given the much more repressive political and social environment that accompanied the rise of AIDS. The way that the *Bowers* decision has been interpreted and used by other courts over the years also suggests how little protection the law provides for those who are most hated and despised by society.

In recent years, the legal-rights strategy has been generally unquestioned by lesbian and gay movement "leaders," most of whom work in hierarchical organizations that focus on achieving access to the mainstream political and legal system, largely at the national level. This legal-rights strategy achieved at best mixed results in the 1990s, if eliminating the ban on military service and embracing same-sex marriage are accepted as central movement goals. Of course, any strategy that relies on the legal system can only produce incremental change. This is because, first and foremost, the courts react to the decisions and actions of other actors in the political system. Second, the courts lack the ability to inspire fundamental changes in people's attitudes and behavior. Third, they are constrained to the extent that they can only rule on cases that appear before them. Fourth, there are many structural barriers at the state and local levels that undermine the timely implementation of judicial decisions. The judicial process cannot possibly construct coherent public policy, and lesbian and gay movements who turn to the courts may focus on narrow legal issues at the expense of larger movement goals. This has certainly happened, especially in the movements' response to same-sex marriage in light of the Hawaii Supreme Court's 1993 *Baehr* decision.

Worse yet, the Christian Right has galvanized in response to lesbian and gay legal-rights advances, most notably in the area of same-sex marriage. This has been true both at the state and national levels. The 1996 Defense of Marriage Act, proposed by conservative members of Congress but signed into law by a so-called "friend" in the White House, is a testimony to how the Christian Right has established the legal framework within which same-sex marriage can be discussed. Much of the political, organizing, and legal activity around same-sex marriage will remain at the state level, which suggests the relevance of a new judicial federalism and the importance of examining state-level politics. But any activity that addresses same-sex marriage at the state level is now constrained by the provisions of the Defense of Marriage Act. If one of the criteria for the effectiveness of a legal-rights strategy is that individuals are increasingly able to live their lives free from harassment and discrimination, then our discussion of the military ban and same-sex marriage suggests failure in these two crucial policy areas, at least in the short term.

But perhaps this approach to political, social, and legal change is far too narrow insofar as it legitimates an incremental and reactive policy process rooted in hierarchical notions of liberal democracy and pluralism. Indeed, a successful legal strategy would be part of a broader movement for progressive political and social change, one that would challenge the classical liberal paradigm that focuses on the individual and identity-based group rights and assumes an interest-group, pluralistic approach to political and social change. This new progressive strategy, which is discussed more fully in Chapter 6, would attempt to incorporate and go well beyond this narrow legal-rights approach. It would arise from the grass roots in a participatory, democratic manner, thereby challenging the top-down, hierarchical model of political and social change. But at this time, we do not even have the resources to discuss such a strategy, much less plan for both the short and long term. The assumptions of the current strategy, then, go unquestioned and unchallenged. This is largely due to the dominance of the assimilationist model of political change, one that is generally supported by our national organizations, who have the financial resources to articulate their vision for the broader movements.

If there are fundamental flaws with electoral-politics and legal-rights strategies, then perhaps we should devote more of our attention and resources to a grassroots, unconventional political strategy for meaning-ful political and social change. To what extent would such a strategy allow the larger movements to move beyond a mainstream, assimila-tionist strategy and embrace progressive change that is transformative in nature? We explore that question in historical and contemporary context in Chapter 4.

4   Unconventional Politics
as a Strategy for Change

Contrary to predictions that AIDS would be the death knell of gay liberation, the AIDS crisis instead created new solidarities across generations, genders and sexualities, political commitments, and cultures and helped galvanize the formation of queer theory and sustain, despite the constant presence of illness and death, the AIDS movement.

—Paula Treichler

AIDS IS A GAY DISEASE! There. I said it. And I believe it. If I hear one more time that AIDS is not a gay disease, I shall vomit. AIDS is a gay disease because a lot of gay men get AIDS. Nationally, gay and bisexual men still account for more than half of all AIDS cases. More important, most of what has been noble about America's response to AIDS has been the direct result of the lesbian and gay community. All this AIDS-is-not-a-gay-disease hysteria is an insulting attempt to downplay the contributions of lesbians and gay men.

—Michael Callen

WHY HAVE THE lesbian and gay movements turned to unconventional politics over the years? Are unconventional politics a viable political and social strategy? What is the connection between unconventional outsider politics and the insider-based electoral and legal strategies? If we accept that there are fundamental flaws with the electoral-politics and legal-rights strategies, should the lesbian and gay movements reject a mainstream assimilationist strategy and embrace progressive change that is transformative in nature? These are the questions at the core of this chapter, and they will be explored in both historical and contemporary context.

Unconventional politics require participants to go outside the formal channels of the American political system (voting and interest-group politics) to embrace the politics of protest, direct action, and mass involvement. This form of politics was employed with great success by the African-American civil rights movement and has been used in contemporary American politics by groups across the ideological spectrum, including Earth First!, ACT UP, Operation Rescue, and the militias.[1]

This chapter explores the use of unconventional politics within the contemporary lesbian and gay movements. It devotes considerable attention to AIDS policy and to the way AIDS altered the landscape of lesbian and gay politics in the 1980s and 1990s, as large numbers of newly politicized activists mobilized in the midst of a hideous epidemic. ACT UP, Queer Nation, and the Lesbian Avengers all developed at the height of the AIDS crisis. As we will see, the movements associated with AIDS "pioneered new and sophisticated forms of cultural politics" (Escoffier 1998, 179). The "sex-panic" debates and the debates over the de-gaying and re-gaying of AIDS in the 1990s provide a window for assessing the contemporary landscape of lesbian and gay politics in light of the epidemic. The chapter also considers marches and demonstrations and the debate over whether valuable movement resources should be used to promote such unconventional politics, with specific attention to the 1993 March on Washington and the 2000 Millennium March. Finally, several activists and scholars identified a decline in political activism and unconventional politics in the 1990s. If such a decline is real, what accounts for it? The most provocative and interesting explanation is that lesbian and gay consumerism has heightened in response to the intersection among capitalist market economies, advertising, and the growth of lesbian and gay communities that are organized around this market-driven imperative. The chapter ends with a discussion of this phenomenon and begins to assess the implications of this development for the politics of contemporary movements.

The core argument of this chapter is one that underlies this entire book. It is difficult to foster and maintain a relationship between the mainstream, assimilationist lesbian and gay movements and outsider, lesbian and gay activists organizing at the grass roots, as we have seen in the discussion of conflicts over various organizing strategies. Yet this relationship is an important one and it needs to be developed and encouraged, as the case study of AIDS policy in this chapter suggests. AIDS first appeared on the scene in the summer of 1981, when the New York *Times* reported on July 3 that forty-one gay men were dying from a rare cancer as well as infectious complications that stemmed "from an unexplainable depression of the immune system" (Kayal 1993, 1). By 1982 and 1983, the seriousness of the AIDS epidemic "was widely experienced by gay men, not only as a threat to new-found sexual freedoms, but to the broad social and political gains of the community as a whole" (Odets 1996, 121). How the lesbian and gay movements responded to these challenges is a central focus of our inquiry.

UNCONVENTIONAL POLITICS IN HISTORICAL CONTEXT

The importance of the civil rights movement of the 1950s and 1960s for other political and social movements, including the emerging lesbian and gay movements, should not be underestimated. One scholar has called it "the second reconstruction" (C. Vann Woodward, quoted in Eagles 1986, ix). Another credits it with having "a profound impact on American society" (Morris 1984, 286) for two central reasons. First, it dismantled those features of the American political system that severely restricted the right of African Americans to vote. Second, "the movement altered and expanded American politics by providing other oppressed groups with organizational and tactical models, allowing them to enter directly into the political arena through the politics of protest" (ibid., 286–87; Rimmerman 1997, 52). Third, it also afforded African Americans equal access to public accommodations—schools, universities, buses, and lunch counters.

The goals of the civil rights movement were largely achieved through the use of unconventional politics, by which participants operated outside the formal channels of the American political system through mass involvement and protest. Civil rights organizers used the boycott, marches and demonstrations, and nonviolent civil disobedience to attract media coverage and to highlight racial injustices, thereby helping to dramatize their grievances. These techniques helped mobilize African Americans throughout the nation and created a base for further successful political and social struggle. In addition, these strategies disrupted "normal patterns of life," specifically the ability of business and government to conduct their daily activities (Rimmerman 1997, 52–53).

Over the years, all of these protest techniques have been used with some success by the lesbian and gay movements. For example, Franklin Kameny led protests in the 1960s at a number of federal government buildings, including the Pentagon and State Department. In his view, such action was justified because government anti-homosexual policies established a negative example for private employers and contributed to societal prejudice. But more conservative movement members denounced Kameny and the protests, fearing that they would alienate potential allies. Despite this criticism, Kameny and his supporters persevered with their very public actions, recognizing that media attention was important if the movements were to achieve tangible progress. Protests, demonstrations, and picketing clearly garnered more media attention than any other form of politics (Alwood 1996, 55). In his fine study of the media's coverage of the lesbian and gay movements, Edward Alwood assesses the impact of a confrontational style: "The confrontational style was affecting media coverage and beginning to change the mind-set among gays accustomed to hiding. Through their activism, gays and lesbians willing to confront prejudice publicly became symbols of the growing resistance to invisibility and silence as a way of life" (ibid.).

A confrontational style has been used at various points in the movements' history. For example, we have already seen how the Stonewall riot helped to spark a nationwide movement for lesbian and gay liberation, one that was inspired by the New Left politics of the time.[2] Young people associated with the New Left were already galvanized by their fervent opposition to the Vietnam war and a shared distrust of hierarchical institutions that wielded power in undemocratic ways. John D'Emilio points out that "gay liberation used the demonstrations of the New Left as recruiting grounds and appropriated the tactics of confrontational politics for its own ends." Some of the same ideas that undergirded the youth protests of the 1960s were adopted by lesbian and gay liberation, modified to fit their own oppression. During this time, young radicals staged political events daily throughout the United States, and these events enabled lesbian and gay liberationists to dramatize their existence and share their ideas. The network of activists associated with the New Left helped to publicize the ideas of lesbian and gay liberation (D'Emilio 1983, 233).

The lesbian and gay liberation movements used "zaps" and demonstrations in the early 1970s to dramatize their grievances and to disrupt the activities of those perceived to be openly hostile to their interests. Zaps are carefully orchestrated disruptions of meetings or proceedings by protestors, who often use satirical humor as a way to capture attention (Cruikshank 1992, 77). For example, when hostile articles appeared in *Harper's* and the *Village Voice,* members of the gay liberation movement occupied the publishers' offices. A bloody confrontation with police ensued in San Francisco after a demonstration against the *Examiner.* The 1970 convention of the American Medical Association was disrupted by the Chicago Gay Liberation chapter, and the San Francisco Gay Liberation organization zapped the American Psychiatric Association's annual meeting. During the reading of a paper on aversion therapy at the American Psychiatric Association in San Francisco, D'Emilio recalls that "a young bearded gay man danced around the auditorium in a red dress, while other homosexuals and lesbians scattered in the audience shouted 'Genocide' and 'Torture!' " Politicians campaigning for office were consistently and visibly challenged by lesbian and gay movement supporters. While these unconventional forms of protest alienated some observers, they did garner liberationists the attention that they sought. More importantly, such actions inspired others to come out of the closet and to join the larger lesbian and gay liberation movements (D'Emilio 1983, 235).

Perhaps the greatest policy success of the early 1970s was the American Psychiatric Association's 1973–74 decision to remove homosexuality from its "official Diagnostic and Statistical Manual list of mental disorders." This decision did not come about because a group of doctors suddenly changed their views; it followed an aggressive and sustained campaign by lesbian and gay activists (Loughery 1998, 345). In order to bring about this important policy change, the movements used a combination of insider and outsider strategies with considerable skill and effectiveness. These involved a "louder watchdog presence at psychiatric conferences, behind-the-scenes lobbying, alliances with friendly and influential members of the APA, contact with regional psychiatric societies, the presentation of alternative papers, and a parade of 'healthy homosexuals.'" Most importantly, activists recognized, in the words of Ronald Gold, "when to scream and when not to. It's an art. It's the art of politics" (Loughery 1998, 346). Some ten years later, in the midst of the AIDS crisis, the ability to understand when insider and outsider politics might be most effective proved crucial to the maturing lesbian and gay movements. The "grassroots politics of knowledge" that the movements developed in their struggle with the American Psychiatric Association had consequences for later challenges to the federal government's policies on AIDS research (Escoffier 1998, 139).

UNCONVENTIONAL POLITICS IN THE AGE OF AIDS

This section assesses the development and effectiveness of unconventional politics in the face of AIDS. The discussion is placed within a broad historical and policy context, with specific attention to the responses of Congress and of Presidents Reagan, Bush, and Clinton. How did the lesbian and gay movements react to the lack of a systematic and sustained federal governmental response to AIDS? In answering this important question, we assess the de-gaying and re-gaying of AIDS strategies, and evaluate the approach to political and social change embraced by ACT UP and the development of the Treatment Action Group (TAG). We begin by providing an overview of the federal government's response to AIDS over time.

The Federal Government's Response: The Executive Branch

AIDS first appeared on the American political scene in 1981, a time when Christian Right fundamentalists were achieving greater power in American politics. The growth of the Christian Right is epitomized by the rise of the Moral Majority, an organization rooted in religious fundamentalism and committed to grassroots mobilization of its constituency to elect conservative politicians at all levels of government. Galvanized by the 1980 election of Ronald Reagan as president and the defeat of a number of liberal Democratic senators, the Moral Majority and other Christian Right groups called for the ouster of members of Congress who opposed their conservative moral agenda. The Christian Right and other antigay conservatives consistently identified homosexuality as evidence of moral degeneracy in society as a whole and AIDS as a punishment for homosexual behavior.[3] The new conservatism engendered hostility toward those with AIDS, who were scapegoated and stigmatized (Koop 1991, 198). It was widely reported, as well, that Christian Right groups, such as the Moral Majority, successfully blocked funding for AIDS education programs and counseling and other services for people with AIDS (PWAs). At various points in the epidemic, conservatives called for the quarantining and tattooing of PWAs. Jerry Falwell, the leader of the Moral Majority, was quoted as saying that AIDS " 'was the judgment of God. . . . You can't fly into the laws of God and God's nature without paying the price' " (in Clendinen and Nagourney 1999, 488).

The rise of the Christian Right and a general climate of conservatism was coupled with the presidential campaign and election of Reagan in 1980. When AIDS was first reported in 1981, Reagan had just assumed office and was pursuing his conservative agenda by slashing social programs and cutting taxes, while at the same time embracing traditional moral values. Reagan did not even mention the word "AIDS" publicly until 1987, when he spoke at the Third International AIDS Conference held in Washington, D.C. His administration did little to support medical research, expedite the testing and release of AIDS-related drugs, or to promote AIDS education. Reagan's only concrete proposal as of 1987 was to call for widespread, routine AIDS testing. The death of his close friend Rock Hudson from AIDS in 1985 had no significant impact on Reagan's policies, although he is said to have been deeply affected (Cannon 1991, 814). For Reagan and his advisers, AIDS was not a national problem; instead, it was a series of local problems to be dealt with by states and localities and not the federal government. This stance helped to fragment the limited governmental response early in the AIDS epidemic.

Presidents frequently maintain a low profile with respect to newly identified public health hazards, perceiving them to offer little political gain and many risks.[4] The response of Presidents Ronald Reagan and George Bush to AIDS fits this pattern. In this case, Reagan and Bush were clearly uncomfortable with a major health problem that targeted those at the margins of American society—gay men and intravenous drug users residing largely in inner cities. Their views of the world simply did not allow for those most despised by society at large to receive their support. Indeed, many of those who assumed power in both administrations embraced political and personal beliefs hostile to gay men and lesbians. The prevailing conservative climate enabled the Reagan and Bush administrations' indifference toward AIDS.

For Reagan, AIDS presented serious political risks. As a presidential candidate, Reagan had promised to eliminate the role of the federal government in the already limited U.S. welfare state, as well as to inject "family values" into social policy. In the critical years of 1984 and 1985, according to his White House physician, Reagan thought of AIDS as though "it was measles and it would go away." Reagan's biographer Lou Cannon characterizes the president's response as "halting and ineffective" (Cannon 1991, 814). It should be no surprise, then, given his own ideological proclivities and the strong conservative ethos of almost all of his appointees, that the administration barely responded to the emerging health crisis at all. For example, in the early 1980s, senior officials from the Department of Health and Human Services (DHHS) maintained publicly, for political reasons, that they had enough resources to address the AIDS crisis while behind the scenes they pleaded for additional funding. The administration undercut federal efforts to confront AIDS in a meaningful way by refusing to spend the money Congress allocated for AIDS research.

Reagan and his close political advisers also successfully prevented his surgeon general, Dr. C. Everett Koop, from discussing AIDS publicly until Reagan's second term. Congress mandates that the surgeon general's chief responsibility is to promote the health of the American people and to inform the public about the prevention of disease. In the Reagan administration, however, the surgeon general's role was to promote the administration's conservative social agenda, especially pro-life and family issues. Thus, at a time when the surgeon general could have played an invaluable role in public health education, Koop was prevented from addressing AIDS publicly. Then, in February 1986, Reagan asked Koop to write a report on the AIDS epidemic. Koop had come to the attention of conservatives in the Reagan administration because of his leading role in the anti-abortion movement. Reagan administration officials fully expected Koop to embrace conservative principles in his report on AIDS.

When the "Surgeon General's Report on Acquired Immune Deficiency Syndrome" was released to the public on October 22, 1986, it was a call for federal action in response to AIDS, and it underscored the importance of a comprehensive AIDS education strategy, beginning in grade school. Koop advocated the widespread distribution of condoms and concluded that mandatory identification of people with HIV or any form of quarantine would be useless in addressing AIDS. As part of Koop's broad federal education strategy, the Public Health Service (PHS) mailed AIDS information to 107 million American households. Koop's actions brought him into direct conflict with William Bennett, Reagan's Secretary of Education. Bennett opposed Koop's recommendations and called for compulsory HIV testing of foreigners applying for immigration visas, for marriage license applicants, for all hospital patients, and for prison inmates.[5]

Not surprisingly, the Reagan administration did little to prohibit discrimination against people with HIV/AIDS. The administration placed responsibility for addressing AIDS discrimination issues with the states rather than with the federal government. In the face of federal inaction, some states and localities passed laws that prohibited HIV/AIDS discrimination, but many remained passive in the face of federal governmental indifference. It took the Supreme Court, in its 1987 *School Board of Nassau County, Fla. v. Arline* decision, to issue a broad ruling that was widely interpreted as protecting those with HIV/AIDS from discrimination in federal executive agencies, in federally assisted programs or activities, or by businesses with federal contracts (Rimmerman 1998, 400).

Reagan did appoint the Presidential Commission on the Human Immunodeficiency Virus Epidemic in the summer of 1987; it was later renamed the Watkins Commission, after its chair, Admiral James D. Watkins. With the appointment of this commission, Reagan was able to appease those who demanded a more sustained federal response to AIDS. He also answered the concerns of the New Right by appointing to the commission few scientists who had participated in AIDS research and few physicians who had actually treated PWAs. In addition, the commission included outspoken opponents of AIDS education.

In retrospect, it is clear that the commission was created to deflect attention from the administration's own inept policy response to AIDS. The Watkins Commission's final report did recommend a more sustained federal commitment to address AIDS, but this recommendation was largely ignored by both the Reagan and Bush administrations. In fact, none of the commissions studying AIDS over the years has recommended a massive federal effort to confront AIDS at all levels of society. How might history view the Reagan approach to AIDS policy? Don Francis, a Center for Disease Control official, gave one answer in his testimony before a congressional committee on March 16, 1987:

> Much of the HIV/AIDS epidemic was and continues to be preventable. But because of active obstruction of logical policy, active resistance to essential funding, and active interference with scientifically designed programs, the executive branch of this country has caused untold hardship, misery, and expense to the American public. Its effort with AIDS will stand as a huge scar in American history, a shame to our nation and an international disgrace. (Andriote 1999, 143–44)

As Reagan's vice president in 1987, George Bush nominally headed the AIDS Executive Committee of the National Institutes of Health (NIH).

Bush also had to balance his role as Reagan's adviser with his role as a presidential candidate in the 1988 election. As a candidate, Bush appealed to the Christian Right by endorsing policies that would publicly identify people who were HIV-positive and that would require mandatory HIV tests when people applied for marriage licenses. On the campaign trail, Bush argued that HIV testing is more cost effective than spending money on treatment. After Bush's election in 1988, he continued most of the policies of the Reagan era. Bush did appear, however, to be more sensitive to the magnitude of the AIDS crisis.

The Bush administration continued Reagan's fiscal austerity with respect to AIDS. In addition, Bush embraced mandatory testing to prevent the spread of AIDS. Finally, his administration argued that local officials should design and implement AIDS educational strategies, although federal resources could be used to gather more AIDS information. His surgeon general, Dr. Antonia Novello, generally maintained a low profile on AIDS issues.

It was not until March 30, 1990, almost nine years after AIDS was first identified and over a year into his presidency, that George Bush gave his first speech on AIDS. He praised his administration's efforts in dealing with the AIDS crisis and asked the country to end discrimination against those infected with HIV. At the same time, Bush refused to eliminate a federal policy that placed restrictions on HIV-positive foreigners who wished to enter the United States. The speech was heralded as the strongest public commitment ever articulated by a president, even though most AIDS activists argued that it was the kind of speech that should have been given in the early 1980s. Bush was also criticized for not endorsing a comprehensive federal policy for addressing AIDS and for perpetuating discrimination against HIV-positive individuals who wished to enter the United States. However, Bush did sign the Ryan White Comprehensive AIDS Resources Emergency (CARE) Act into law in 1990, although he consistently opposed funding this legislation to the level its congressional supporters requested. The legislation was originally designed to provide federal assistance for urban areas that were hardest hit by AIDS. The role of Congress in the formulation of this law will be assessed shortly.

The election of Bill Clinton to the White House in 1992 created hope that a new administration would offer a sustained and comprehensive federal effort to address AIDS. Clinton had campaigned actively for lesbian and gay support and had insured that Bob Hattoy, an openly gay man who had been diagnosed with AIDS, would address the Democratic National Convention in New York in the summer of 1992. Clinton promised that if elected, he would appoint a national AIDS policy director, or "AIDS czar," to coordinate AIDS policy from the White House, and that he would commit more funding to AIDS research and education than had his Republican predecessors. In addition, he ridiculed the Bush administration's retrograde policy banning the immigration of HIV-positive foreigners to the United States (Rimmerman 1998, 401).

AIDS activists and PWAs were soon disappointed. Although Clinton discussed AIDS more often than had his predecessors, he failed to propose the kind of comprehensive plan that activists had expected. The Clinton administration argued that only so much could be done, given the budget deficit they had inherited from the Reagan and Bush administrations. Soon after taking office, Clinton decided not to challenge Congress when it voted to reinforce the Bush policy of preventing HIV-positive foreigners from entering the United States.

It also took the Clinton administration considerable time to settle on an AIDS czar. After much delay, the choice was Kristine Gebbie, a nurse and Washington state health official without extensive policy-making experience.[6] Gebbie departed about a year later in the wake of criticism by AIDS groups. She was replaced by Patricia Fleming, who had served on the staff of former U.S. Representative Ted Weiss of New York, advising him on AIDS issues. Fleming was succeeded in 1997 by Sandy Thurman, the former executive director of an AIDS service organization in Atlanta, Georgia (Moss 1995, 22–28).

Another high-profile Clinton appointee was Dr. Jocelyn Elders, an Arkansas physician and professor of pediatrics, as surgeon general. Elders's outspoken endorsement of sex education and AIDS-prevention outreach earned her many critics among conservatives, who derisively dubbed her the "condom queen." Following Republican victories in the 1994 congressional elections, Clinton forced Elders's resignation when she angered conservatives by appearing to call for the teaching of masturbation to schoolchildren; in fact, Elders had simply endorsed comprehensive sex education programs (Rimmerman 1998, 401–2). Her original comments had obviously been distorted by conservatives.

Clinton again disappointed his supporters in the AIDS activist community when he failed to endorse a promised needle-exchange program to target injecting drug users. Adopting a cautious middle ground, the administration called for a federally funded study on needle exchange and concluded that more research was needed before any needle-exchange policy could be proposed. In addition, in the face of conservative criticism, the Clinton administration eliminated mandatory AIDS education programs for federal workers, to the dismay of AIDS activists.

In February 1996, President Clinton agreed to sign a defense authorization bill that included a proposal to discharge all HIV-positive personnel from the military. As signed into law, this provision would have caused over one thousand healthy, asymptomatic people with HIV to be discharged from the military. Clinton issued a public statement acknowledging that this provision was both abhorrent and unconstitutional, but he explained that he had to support the full defense-authorization measure. He promised that his attorney general, Janet Reno, would not defend the new policy in court when its constitutionality was challenged. That provision of the law was ultimately rescinded by Congress.

From the vantage point of the lesbian and gay movements, however, Clinton's approach represented a significant improvement over the policies of Reagan and Bush. Clinton embraced full funding of the Ryan White CARE Act. He created the National Task Force on AIDS Drug Development, whose goal was to examine how new drugs could be released to the market more quickly. Clinton's Department of Justice took action to address discrimination against people who were either HIV-positive or diagnosed with AIDS. In June 1993, the Clinton administration announced that rules governing the eligibility of people infected with HIV for disability benefits would be relaxed considerably. Finally, Clinton's 1992 election meant that more federal money was allocated for AIDS research. For example, in fiscal year 1994, funding for AIDS research increased by 18 percent (Foreman 1994, 123).

AIDS remained a low-profile issue in the 1996 presidential elections, although some saw a political motive in the Clinton administration's decision to extend Medicaid coverage to include a class of AIDS drugs called protease inhibitors. Shortly after Clinton's reelection, he outlined a six-point AIDS agenda for his second term. The list included the search for a cure and a vaccine, a reduction in new HIV infections, guaranteed services for those with HIV, opposition to AIDS-related discrimination, support for international efforts in fighting HIV/AIDS, and the effective practical application of advances in scientific knowledge concerning HIV/AIDS.

Although Clinton was far more attentive to AIDS than his predecessors, many AIDS activists believe that he and his administration could have done more, especially given Clinton's 1992 campaign promises. Underlying this critique is an assumption that has pervaded the discussion of AIDS since its emergence in 1981—that, of all the political figures in the United States, the president is best situated to educate the public and to provide moral and political leadership in a public health crisis. But Congress plays an integral role in formulating national health care policy as well, and the next section discusses how it has responded to AIDS.

The Federal Government's Response: Congress

Members of Congress calling for a sustained federal response to AIDS in the early to mid 1980s had to operate within the conservative moral and fiscal climate as well. The most active Senators and Representatives in the early years of the AIDS crisis represented districts or states with large gay constituencies. For example, in the House of Representatives, four Democrats, Barbara Boxer and Phil Burton of San Francisco, Henry Waxman of Los Angeles, and Ted Weiss of New York, were active in calling for a committed federal governmental response to AIDS. But they and their supporters faced an uphill battle given the Reagan administration's cuts in spending for social programs and its refusal to acknowledge the gravity of AIDS.

From June 1981 to June 1982, the period generally considered the first twelve months of the epidemic, the Centers for Disease Control and Prevention (CDC) spent $1 million on AIDS, compared with the $9 million it devoted to the much smaller problem of Legionnaires' disease. In late 1982, Congress allocated $2.6 million for AIDS research by the CDC, but the Reagan administration claimed that the CDC did not need the money and opposed any congressional supplemental appropriations designed to fund federal governmental AIDS policy efforts (Rimmerman 1998, 149).

In the absence of presidential leadership, Congress was forced to ascertain on its own how much money doctors working inside government needed to address the AIDS epidemic. The Reagan administration resisted these efforts but refused to exercise an on-the-record veto of supplementary AIDS funding efforts (Shilts 1987, 214). In the crucial early years of the epidemic, when federal resources could have been profitably spent on basic research and prevention education, federal AIDS researchers relied on supplemental funding in the form of continuing resolutions initiated by Congress. Year after year, Congress significantly increased AIDS funding relative to the Reagan budgetary proposals.

Under the leadership of Rep. Ted Weiss, who was chair of the Subcommittee on Human Resources and Intergovernmental Relations, and Rep. Henry Waxman, who chaired the Subcommittee on Science and Technology, Congress in 1983 investigated the U.S. Public Health Service (PHS) response to AIDS. Both subcommittees held hearings and jointly requested a study of the AIDS-related activities of the CDC and the National Institutes of Health (NIH). The Weiss report highlighted AIDS funding problems in the Reagan administration and lengthy delays in research into AIDS-related drugs, as well as management problems in funding, coordination, and communication within the PHS (Panem 1988, 31–35). The highly public, adversarial relationship between Congress and the Reagan administration regarding governmental responses to AIDS continued throughout Reagan's two-term presidency.

One way that congressional Democrats attempted to force the administration to increase funding and other forms of support for people with

HIV/AIDS was to publicly highlight the large numbers of people affected by the epidemic. This strategy helped the public appreciate the scope of the AIDS problem. By 1987 congressional concern was so pervasive that the Senate, which had been much less active than the House in addressing AIDS, called for the Reagan administration to establish an AIDS commission. In response to the request of both Republican and Democratic Senators, Reagan appointed what came to be known as the Watkins Commission.[7]

There was, of course, considerable conservative resistance in Congress to spending federal tax dollars on AIDS-related measures. For example, Senator Jesse Helms (R–North Carolina) was highly critical of federal spending on AIDS education. On October 14, 1987, Helms appeared on the floor of the Senate during a debate over a federal AIDS appropriation bill to denounce a safer-sex comic book published by Gay Men's Health Crisis of New York. Although Helms thought the comic book had been federally funded, a subsequent investigation revealed that no federal funds were used to support its production. Nonetheless, the Senate voted overwhelmingly to pass the Helms amendment to the AIDS appropriation bill. This amendment prohibited the use of federal tax dollars for AIDS education materials that "promote or encourage, directly or indirectly, homosexual activities." Since 1987, Helms continued to offer his amendment to each appropriation bill. With these amendments, Helms and his conservative supporters in Congress, notably former California Republican Representatives Robert Dornan and William Dannemeyer, helped limit federal funding for safer-sex education targeting lesbians and gays (Vaid 1995, 139–40).

During the last year of the Reagan presidency, Congress considered the AIDS Federal Policy Act of 1987. This was the first legislation considered by Congress that took into account the larger societal implications of the epidemic, and that went beyond mere funding of AIDS prevention, research, and treatment efforts. The legislation, passed by Congress and ultimately signed into law by President Reagan, prohibited discrimination against individuals with disabilities, including those who were infected by HIV or AIDS, in certain forms of housing and employment. This legislation set the foundation for the passage of the more comprehensive Americans with Disabilities Act (ADA) in 1990, a law that protects all Americans with disabilities, including those who are infected by HIV or AIDS, from discrimination in public accommodations and the workplace. AIDS is not specifically mentioned in the law, but people with HIV/AIDS are included owing to a variety of subsequent judicial and regulatory decisions.

During the 1992 presidential campaign, candidate Bill Clinton was critical of the administration of President George Bush for supporting an immigration policy that prevented HIV-positive individuals from entering the United States. Congress had originally imposed this ban in 1987 but voted to rescind it in 1990. In May 1993, Congress reinstated the ban without a challenge from President Clinton, much to the dismay of AIDS activists and others who expected Clinton to keep his campaign promise to make immigration policy less restrictive.

In 1990 Congress passed and President Bush signed the Ryan White Comprehensive AIDS Resources Emergency (CARE) Act, named after the Indiana teenager who died of AIDS just four months before its passage. It was originally designed to provide federal assistance for urban areas that were hardest hit by AIDS, and money was distributed under the act according to formulas based on local caseloads. The CARE Act had an immediate impact; in the first two years of its implementation, it provided more than $847 million to fund nationwide AIDS services (Andriote 1999, 232). Unfortunately, despite having signed the legislation, Bush consistently opposed funding the Ryan White CARE Act to the extent that its congressional supporters asked.

With the election of Clinton and a Democrat-controlled Congress in 1992, there was considerably less conflict between Congress and the president on AIDS policy concerns. Indeed, Clinton quickly followed through on his campaign promise to increase federal funding for the Ryan White CARE Act. The reauthorization of the original legislation was introduced in 1995, and supporters claimed that because AIDS had spread to smaller cities and rural areas, the funding formula needed to be adjusted to provide these areas with much-needed federal support. The reauthorization discussion, however, took place within a more conservative Congress. Republicans had swept the 1994 midterm elections and took control of both houses of Congress for the first time in four decades (Rimmerman 1998, 150).

The new Republican majority in Congress meant that virtually all federal efforts with respect to AIDS would undergo considerable scrutiny. This was especially true of the Clinton administration's policy initiatives, such as they were. But this did not stop proponents of a more active federal role from supporting the AIDS Cure Act, which was first introduced in May 1994 and reintroduced in March 1995. If funded, the act would have cost $1.84 billion over five years. Its goal was to promote the search for an effective treatment for AIDS without duplicating the research that was already being done by the major pharmaceutical companies. Underlying the legislation was a belief that the major drug companies could not be trusted to come up with timely drug treatments on their own; under the AIDS Cure Act, the research efforts of smaller drug companies would have received more federal support than ever before.

By 1996 conflict between the President and Congress over AIDS-related policy initiatives had become the norm. Over the years, Congress has attempted to balance competing pressures, appease an array of interest groups across the ideological spectrum, and placate the general public. In doing so, Congress joins the presidency in earning well deserved blame for the halting and largely ineffective federal response to AIDS.

THE RESPONSE OF THE LESBIAN AND GAY MOVEMENTS

AIDS policy and AIDS activism in the 1980s and 1990s altered the landscape of lesbian and gay politics as newly mobilized activists became involved in politics and their communities for the first time. The formation of ACT UP in 1987 represented the rebirth of one form of unconventional politics—one rooted in participatory democratic principles and dedicated to nonviolent civil disobedience.

In the early days of the epidemic, a few gay people insisted that the President, Congress, and the media should pay attention, and they called on the federal government, at a bare minimum, to increase AIDS-related research funding (Andriote 1999, 221). As more and more gay men became sick and died, and in the face of continuing government indifference, lesbians and gays began to organize throughout the United States. By the mid 1980s, the failures of government policy makers were clear. Veteran movement activist Virginia Apuzzo lists these: (1) lack of support at all levels of government, (2) failure to expedite AIDS-related research, (3) failure to educate a public in hysteria about AIDS, (4) an unwillingness to address specific questions about the safety of the blood supply, (5) failure to include affected groups in the public-policy decision making, and (6) failure to respect people's right to confidentiality and privacy (ibid., 223).

These failures of leadership at all levels of government forced lesbian and gay activists to confront two key dilemmas, summarized by Urvashi Vaid: "How were we going to get a response from an administration that did not care about us? And how were we going to motivate and mobilize a community that was largely in the closet and invisible?" (Vaid 1995, 72–73). As the following discussion elaborates, lesbian and gay movements pursued four overlapping strategies in their response to AIDS: (1) the de-gaying of AIDS, (2) organizing for heightened visibility of the lesbian and gay movements, (3) separating AIDS-specific reform from structural reform of the overall health care system, and (4) direct action in the form of unconventional politics (ibid., 74).

The De-gaying of AIDS

In the mid 1980s, AIDS leaders made a crucial decision to publicize the message that "AIDS is not a gay disease." The goal was to gain greater funding and public support, and to convey the importance of AIDS prevention to all sectors of the population. The assumption was that the public and politicians would be more receptive if gay men were not the targeted beneficiaries of increased AIDS-related funding. That this strategy had to be used suggests how much gay men remain despised by the larger society and how little progress has been made in combating prejudice and hatred seemingly woven into the fabric of the larger culture. Thus, for roughly the next eight years, many AIDS groups de-emphasized lesbian and gay participation, denied that they were "gay organizations" per se, "and attempted to appeal to the 'general public' by expunging gay references and sanitizing gay culture" (Rofes 1990, 11). A central goal was to capture the attention of straight society by stressing that heterosexuals—and particularly women and children—were at risk of contracting HIV.

We can see why the de-gaying of AIDS might have made strategic sense at the time. The early years of the epidemic posed formidable strategic problems for lesbian and gay rights activists. The public culture of the time was overwhelmingly conservative, as we have seen. Given this reality, how might lesbian, gay, and bisexual advocates attract positive attention from legislatures throughout the United States? And more importantly, how might this positive attention be translated into much-needed AIDS education, prevention, and funding, when the targeted groups were at the margins of American society? By de-gaying AIDS, organizers allowed non-gay public-health officials to lobby on behalf of AIDS-specific issues, while avoiding lesbian-and gay-rights concerns. In essence, we allowed public officials to speak for lesbian and gay interests because we assumed that they had greater moral and strategic standing in the larger society. We assumed that organizations such as the Washington, D.C.–based AIDS Action Council, founded in 1988, should play this vital role.[8] De-gaying advocates argued that we had no choice given the increasing numbers of deaths that were wiping out entire friendship networks. Years later, Vic Basile, director of the Human Rights Campaign Fund (HRCF) from June 1983 until 1989, expressed this pragmatism well: "The moral imperative [of AIDS politics] is to find a cure for AIDS . . . [and] not to see any more of my friends die" (Andriote 1999, 229). Urvashi Vaid describes the negative consequences of the de-gaying of AIDS especially well:

> With our frequent pleas to the government to spend funds for AIDS because straights can get ill too, we promoted the homophobic subtext that AIDS would not be as important if only gay or bisexual people were susceptible. . . . By emphasizing the risks to heterosexuals and playing down the staggering destitution of the gay community, AIDS organizations and many AIDS activists established the fledgling AIDS movement as something separate from the gay and lesbian civil rights movement. In a sense it is—more

straight people are involved with AIDS organizations than are in gay groups, and the AIDS-specific movement has focused narrowly on services and securing a response to the epidemic. But in our attempt to get a governmental response to AIDS, we employed a strategy that left the gay movement at the mercy of the homophobic, sex-phobic, and racist government. (Vaid 1995, 75)

Perhaps even more importantly, in our efforts to force a positive governmental response, we failed to address the crucial issue of antigay prejudice. An unintended consequence of the de-gaying of AIDS has been to deny the tremendous activist response of the broader lesbian and gay community as it promoted "safe sex" and attempted to respond to a crisis with limited resources. Ultimately, the pragmatic response has overwhelmed any conscious political strategy that makes the crucial connection between AIDS politics and lesbian and gay liberation. And what did this de-gaying strategy signal to gay men? Writing in 1993, British AIDS activist and educator Edward King provides a plausible answer: "The over-riding impression is that the epidemic has somehow lifted up and moved on, taking away any significant risk to gay men, when in reality it has merely expanded, with gay men still in the epicenter, still most at risk. Worse, there are some indications that this mistaken message has also been picked up by many gay men themselves" (King 1993, 189). King admits "that heterosexuals can and do become infected with HIV." But he wonders if it is "too much to ask that some sense of perspective is maintained between the hysterical extremes of those who believe that 'everyone is equally at risk' and those who believe that 'straight sex is safe'?" (Watney 1997, 86).

Given this reality, King and other lesbian and gay activists argue that we must now re-gay AIDS, a movement that began in 1992.[9] At its core, the re-gaying of AIDS requires that gay men and lesbians play a much larger role in rethinking and restructuring community-based organizations' responses to AIDS. The "heterosexual agenda" associated with the de-gaying of AIDS needs to be reversed. Gay organizations "that had become progressively more straight acting" need to rethink their priorities and how their messages are communicated to gay men so that they receive an appropriate share of HIV-prevention resources (Scott 1997, 322). Most important of all, the re-gaying of AIDS pivots on this fundamental premise, in the words of King: "Gay and bisexual men are far more at risk of HIV than anyone else, now and for the foreseeable future" (Watney 1997, 86–87). In both Britain and the United States, this premise must inform the allocation of scarce education and prevention resources. This process of re-gaying AIDS has begun to occur in both Britain and the United States in recent years.[10]

Heightened Cultural Visibility

A second consequence of the AIDS epidemic was to heighten the visibility of the lesbian and gay movements. Media activism, which had characterized the movements since the 1950s, played an increasingly important role in the AIDS movements of the 1980s and 1990s (Vaid 1995, 79). Well before AIDS, lesbian and gay media were the principal outlet for information pertaining to lesbian, gay, bisexual, and transgendered issues. They helped build community, and they were crucial arenas for political debate. The lesbian and gay media remain a vital information source even after the advent of AIDS. For example, in the early years of the epidemic, the New York *Native* provided some of the most forthright, accurate, and courageous reporting on AIDS. Dr. Lawrence Mass, then the paper's medical writer, authored the first news report and first feature article about AIDS, both of which appeared in the *Native* soon after the disease began striking gay men in early 1981.[11] These were the first articles about AIDS to appear in the nonscientific press. Sadly, Mass was threatened with the loss of his job at the New York City Health Department for speaking out publicly about AIDS (Blasius and Phelan 1997, 574). The role of the New York *Native* and other lesbian and gay media sources cannot be ignored, especially given that the mainstream press largely shunned coverage of AIDS in the early years of the epidemic.

In his book *Straight News*, Edward Alwood reports that by the end of 1982, the major networks had dedicated a combined total of only thirteen minutes' airtime to the coverage of AIDS. And when they and other mainstream media sources did report AIDS-related news, they devoted little attention to the epidemic; their treatment of the issue often suggested that homophobia lurked just below the surface.[12] For example, in the early years, medical experts often referred to the symptoms associated with what came to be known as AIDS as "gay-related immune deficiency" (GRID). Following the medical establishment's lead, the mainstream press used this term and created the erroneous impression that only gay men were at risk. In addition, the New York *Times* banned the use of the term "gay" in its pages until the summer of 1987, soon after Max Frankel replaced Abe Rosenthal as executive editor. And as recently as 1991, major newspapers refused to mention the surviving lover of a gay person in their obituaries.

In the early years of the crisis, the mainstream press also ignored the grassroots organizations that were committed to education and prevention. For example, in 1982 the Gay Men's Health Crisis (GMHC) was founded by Larry Kramer, Lawrence Mass, and others, including Alvin Friedman-Kien, who had diagnosed the first AIDS cases in New York and who served as a faculty member at the New York University Medical Center. GMHC became the first grassroots AIDS service-related organization in the United States. Upon its creation, Kramer targeted the mainstream media, hoping they would highlight the organization's AIDS prevention and education efforts. But few showed any interest in the story at all. Claiming that this yet-unnamed disease posed too many unanswered questions, they did not wish to contribute to a public panic over something that was still poorly understood (Alwood 1996, 214–15). In ignoring Kramer's request and the request of other concerned activists in major cities throughout the United States, the media abdicated their important reporting and education responsibility.

By the late 1980s, however, mainstream newspaper coverage of AIDS gradually began to improve, perhaps because, as Cathy Cohen suggests, newspapers such as the New York *Native* "provided outside pressure and information for reporters at the *Times* eager to write about the emerging medical crisis." Later, unconventional protest politics, often sponsored by ACT UP, also pushed the *Times* and other mainstream newspapers to improve their coverage of AIDS (Cohen 1999, 156–57). Such aggressive political activism clearly helped to heighten the political and cultural visibility of the lesbian and gay movements and AIDS.

The AIDS memorial quilt project played a major role as well in raising public awareness of AIDS, yet it caused controversy within the lesbian and gay movements. The October 11, 1987, March on Washington for Lesbian and Gay Rights was the occasion for the Names Project's first display of the AIDS memorial quilt. March participants as well as the general public were reminded by the 1,920 panels, which covered the equivalent of two football fields, that AIDS had already claimed many lives. The timing of the quilt's appearance was deliberate: the 1988 presidential campaign was underway, and the quilt "provided a powerful symbol of the gay community's political struggle for equal rights and of the casualties of the simultaneous struggle for sexual liberation" (Andriote 1999, 365). But much to the consternation of some activists, the opportunities for enhanced public education and greater movement visibility brought by the AIDS quilt did not begin to make up for the de-gaying of AIDS that characterized the Names Project's way of representing the disease. One letter writer reported his frustration on visiting the Names Project's AIDS quilt in Washington, D.C.:

> That evening the candlelight march was led by invited parents of people with AIDS as thousands of mostly gay people marched behind them in the silent arc of candles. While this gesture towards parents was certainly admirable and appropriate, it was unforgivable for the project not to show the same level of respect for the partners of people who had died of AIDS. Surely it is not too much to expect an overwhelmingly gay-run organization to strive to recognize gay relationships in a more sensitive manner than society has shown. (Rofes 1990, 12)

Other activists were frustrated with the Names Project's seeming neglect of politics. For example, Urvashi Vaid argued that it "didn't do enough to politicize people" (Andriote 1999, 367). And worse yet, the project did little to build the lesbian and gay rights movements. Vaid commented, "that George Bush, who did so little, could be quoted on the back of the Names Project book reveals the irony of the depoliticization of the AIDS movement" (Vaid 1995, 78).

In the end, the lesbian and gay movements met with mixed success in their attempts to achieve heightened cultural visibility around the AIDS issue. As at other points in their history, this strategy encountered resistance by mainstream institutions, such as the media and the medical establishment. In addition, however, the strategy was undermined by considerable disagreement within the movements over just what this strategy should entail, what the messages to the larger public and lesbian and gay communities should be, and ultimately how they should be communicated.[13]

AIDS-Specific Reforms

Besides mobilizing lesbians and gay men in communities throughout the United States, AIDS has fostered the creation of new organizations at the national and local levels. The grassroots response to AIDS was particularly noteworthy in the decade of the 1980s. In the absence of appropriate action by federal and state governments, lesbian and gay communities recognized the crucial importance of creating organizations, many of them community based, to respond to a staggering health crisis.[14] Barry Adam points out that with the creation of these new organizations, we witnessed "the institutionalization of gay and lesbian politics in the form of AIDS service organizations" (Adam 1995, 161).

These developments raised additional tensions over strategy and goals within the lesbian and gay movements. What should be the relationship between the newly created AIDS service organizations and the broader lesbian and gay movements? Should such organizations critique the prevailing health care system, or should they simply focus on providing basic services in a time of crisis? It is certainly understandable why many, faced with scarce resources and a serious public health crisis, embraced a more narrow response. But this more "pragmatic" option has been the target of considerable criticism from those who believe in a liberationist approach to political and social change. For example, Urvashi Vaid has said that "the AIDS-service organizations . . . positioned themselves within the health care system and sought to accommodate us to it," rather than offering any meaningful structural critique of the inequalities associated with medical care in the United States. In adopting this strategy, Vaid points out that "the AIDS service movement reproduced the dominant class, race, and gender biases within the organizations, legislation, and delivery system it created" (Vaid 1995, 87).

The founding and original goals of Gay Men's Health Crisis and the AIDS Action Council support Vaid's critique. When Larry Kramer and others met in his Greenwich Village apartment in the summer of 1981 to discuss the onset of what eventually came to be known as AIDS, they decided that New York City needed an organization that was "founded by the gay community for the gay community" (Rom 2000, 222). Philip Kayal indicates that GMHC's many volunteers subsequently helped to organize "the country's first major support programs for People with AIDS and AIDS-related complex (ARC) and their lovers, families, friends, and carepartners." Over the years, the GMHC has provided counseling, education, and social services in support of the sick in ways "that a family, community, or group of friends would" (Kayal 1993, 2). In addition, it has lobbied for entitlements and drug reviews and instigated hospital treatment protocols. Until ACT UP was founded in fall 1987, GMHC delivered a wide range of social services to more than three thousand persons with AIDS a year and was also the most outspoken advocate on behalf of PWA entitlements (ibid., 3). The organization's social service efforts are premised on the notion of "bearing witness," which suggests that "volunteering personalizes AIDS by drawing carepartners out of themselves and placing them in the situation of another person as hated for his gayness as they are" (ibid., xviii). GMHC's organizational structure and approach have served as a model for similar organizations that have been created in other cities, including AIDS Atlanta, the AIDS project in Los Angeles, NO AIDS in New Orleans, the AIDS Arms Network in Dallas, and San Francisco's Kaposi Sarcoma Education and Research Foundation (Rom 2000, 230).

Since its creation in 1981, GMHC has become thoroughly institutionalized. By the late 1990s, the organization had served more than seventy-five thousand clients annually with a support staff of over two hundred and nearly seven thousand volunteers. Its yearly budget was $22 million; two-thirds of its funding came from private donors. Over time, representatives of GMHC have participated in AIDS-related meetings at all levels of government. While founded as a local organization, GMHC has had an important national presence, and it has embraced a quintessential conventional, insider approach to political change (Rom 2000, 222). Specifically, GMHC has largely avoided addressing larger, structural inequalities in the health-care system. Ruth Finkelstein, a former public policy director for GMHC, recognized the limitations of the organization's approach:

> I really feel there aren't any more AIDS-specific fixes. The reason that everything is going so badly is that what remains to be done in AIDS is [to] deal with the [systemic] issues we haven't dealt with. There's no more confi-

dentiality to fix. There are no more categorical programs to design and write and pass. We've done things I'm proud of: the ADA [Americans with Disabilities Act], the [Ryan White AIDS] Care Act, a model of community planning, participation, and empowerment [and a source of] money and services. But we've also done things I'm not proud of. In the face of systemic problems, we've sought exceptions for our people. (Vaid 1995, 88)

Finkelstein offered those observations in 1993, but they are still relevant today as we consider the relationship of the AIDS movements to the larger lesbian and gay movements. Her observations are also appropriate as we evaluate the role played by the AIDS Action Council in both movements.

Founded in 1984, the AIDS Action Council has been a leading national voice on AIDS, representing thirty-two hundred of America's AIDS organizations and the millions of Americans whom they serve. The organization's mission statement asserts that "AIDS Action is the only organization solely dedicated to responsible federal policy for improved HIV/AIDS care and services, effective HIV prevention and vigorous medical research." In 1998 the AIDS Action Council's income came from four different sources: (1) community-based AIDS service organization members (38 percent); (2) program grants (33 percent); (3) national and community events (17 percent); and (4) individual support (12 percent). A former director of the organization told me that "we realized that there had to be a non-gay voice associated with the policy aspects of AIDS and that is why the AIDS Council was created" (personal interview, February 19, 1997). In this way, the organization has played an integral role in the de-gaying of AIDS discussed earlier.

Like GMHC, the AIDS Action Council has pursued conventional insider approaches to change. Urvashi Vaid reports that the organization has had considerable access to people in power, of a kind that has been denied to lesbian and gay organizations. While working at the National Gay and Lesbian Task Force in the period 1986–92, she personally saw how various AIDS lobbyists had access to important Bush administration officials. She writes: "NGLTF and I failed for two years to secure a meeting with [Health and Human Services] Secretary Louis Sullivan on gay and lesbian teen suicide, only to witness representatives of the AIDS Action Council (of which NGLTF was a member) meet with the secretary at least twice and work closely with his staff on several AIDS policy matters" (Vaid 1995, 78). Vaid's frustration is clearly understandable, especially given that the AIDS Action Council has played such an important national role in AIDS funding battles, while generally neglecting to connect its political organizing to a critique of the U.S. health care system and widespread economic inequalities. And worse yet, there does not seem to be much evidence that such a strategy was even considered. However, a former executive director of the organization has acknowledged that "in the context of AIDS, there was conflict over short-term responses to AIDS and long-term political and policy planning" (personal interview, February 19, 1997).

It is easy to see why the AIDS Action Council embraced a de-gaying or mainstreaming strategy and why this strategy ultimately succeeded in winning tangible accomplishments. For example, this approach led to increased funding for AIDS and major legislation in the form of the Ryan White CARE Act. Another former executive director of the organization, Jean McGuire, recognizes now that politicians were most receptive to the message that they could "do something for AIDS by helping women and kids—as small a segment of the AIDS population as they may have been" (Andriote 1999, 234).

Over the years, a chasm has grown up between the AIDS-centered organizations and progressive lesbian and gay groups. Tensions have erupted over funding, strategy, and purpose. But they also reflect the inability of the AIDS service groups to organize people on behalf of any kind of meaningful political action, a failure that is reflected in the depoliticization that has occurred within the broader movements. Perhaps most importantly, discord has arisen from what Eric Rofes identifies as "the conflicting forces of government funding, community participation, and the politics of the time ... whipped into a frenzy by fear, grief, and exhaustion" (Rofes 1990, 8). These conflicts were surely exacerbated by the stinting governmental response, especially in the early years of the AIDS crisis, which largely ignored the serious structural deficiencies of the American health care system. In the end, what was missing was unconventional, outsider politics as a political strategy for capturing the attention of public policy decision makers. Such a strategy emerged with the birth of ACT UP in 1987.

Direct Action and the Rise of Unconventional Politics

ACT UP, the commonly used acronym for the AIDS Coalition to Unleash Power, is a grassroots organization associated with nonviolent civil disobedience. In the late 1980s and early 1990s, ACT UP became the standard-bearer for protest against governmental and societal indifference to the AIDS epidemic. As we have seen, the group is part of a long tradition of grassroots initiatives in American politics, especially in the African American civil rights movement, which used unconventional politics to promote political and social change. ACT UP has been influenced by the civil rights movement to the extent that it, too, has used boycotts, marches, demonstrations, and nonviolent civil disobedience to attract media coverage of its direct action. With the birth of ACT UP, we witnessed a return to a style of political organizing that had connections to the lesbian and gay liberation movements of the early 1970s, although ACT UP was more successful in garnering national and international attention.

The organization was founded in March 1987 by playwright and AIDS activist Larry Kramer. Kramer had become increasingly unhappy with the GMHC's focus on providing social services and its "bearing witness" approach to those services.[15] Finally, he publicly disengaged himself from what he labeled "GMHC's Red Cross role" (Kayal 1993, 223).[16] In a speech at the Lesbian and Gay Community Services Center of New York, Kramer challenged the lesbian and gay movements to organize, mobilize, and demand an effective AIDS policy response. He informed the audience of gay men that two-thirds of them might be dead within five years. In Kramer's view, the mass media ought to be the central vehicle for conveying the message that the government had hardly begun to address the AIDS crisis. In his speech, he asked, "Do we want to start a new organization devoted solely to political action?"

Kramer's speech inspired another meeting at the Community Services Center several days later, which more than three hundred people attended. This event essentially signaled the birth of ACT UP. Thereafter, ACT UP/New York routinely drew more than eight hundred people to its weekly meetings. As the organization grew, it remained the largest and most influential of all the chapters. By early 1988, active chapters had appeared throughout the country, including in Los Angeles, Boston, Chicago, and San Francisco. At the beginning of 1990, ACT UP had spread around the globe, with more than a hundred chapters worldwide (Vaid 1995, 94–95).

ACT UP's original goal was to demand the release of experimental AIDS drugs. It identified itself as a diverse, nonpartisan group, united in anger and committed to direct action to end the AIDS crisis. This central goal is stated at the start of every ACT UP meeting. ACT UP's commitment to direct action emerged as a response to the more conservative elements of the mainstream lesbian and gay movements. Underlying ACT UP's political strategy is a commitment to radical democracy and principles of participatory democratic theory.[17] For example, no one member or group of members had the right to speak for ACT UP; this was a right reserved for all members. There were no elected leaders, no appointed spokespeople, and no formal structure to the organization.

Throughout its existence, ACT UP has made an effort to recruit women and minorities into the organization. This made considerable sense given that AIDS has clearly broadened the lesbian and gay rights movements' agenda. Women in ACT UP organized a series of national actions aimed at forcing the U.S. Centers for Disease Control and Prevention to change its definition of AIDS to include those illnesses contracted by HIV-positive women.[18] But despite its efforts at inclusion, many ACT UP chapters were riddled with gender conflicts.[19] Arlene Stein attributes these to "real, persistent structural differences in style, ideology, and access to resources among men and women" (Stein 1995, 148). Lesbians and gay men often experienced the same kinds of divisions that arose between heterosexual men and women (ibid.).

ACT UP/New York attempted, without great success, to recruit African Americans and Latinos into the organization. The experiences of those who did participate suggest that many ACT UP chapters were not really open to racial diversity. It is understandable, then, that with the arrival of AIDS in 1981, a number of racial minority AIDS service and political organizations were created over the years, many of which are located in cities throughout the United States. Some examples are the Minority AIDS Project in Los Angeles, New York's Minority Task Force on AIDS, and IMPACT DC, an organization based in Washington, D.C.

Efforts to build diversity into ACT UP have provoked considerable criticism from those who believe that the interests of minority gay men were de-emphasized in ACT UP's quest to transcend its largely white, male, middle-class membership. The organization, some critics say, has embraced the de-gaying of AIDS. For example, Robin Hardy believes that ACT UP's failure to ground itself in the politics of identity is a serious problem:

> ACT UP's failure to ground its politics in the identity of 98 per cent of its members has diverted it from goals which are critical to gay men. As ACT UP embraces the politics of inclusion, it cuts itself off from the community which has provided the core of its tactics, theory, membership and funding. . . . Implicit in ACT UP's brand of coalition politics is an assumption that homosexuals must subordinate their gay/lesbian identity to attract other communities to the ranks of AIDS activism. No one has stopped to ask what attention to the political agendas of other minorities might be costing the gay community. Or if it's even working. (King 1993, 192)

Once again, we see that lesbian and gay movements have experienced conflicts over the fragmentation of identity—this time within the context of AIDS. Other social movements have certainly experienced serious divisions over strategy and membership. But it is this deep conflict over the politics of and organizing around identity that makes the lesbian and gay movements a new social movement.

Over the years, ACT UP has broadened its original purpose to embrace a number of specific practical goals. It has demanded that the U.S. Food and Drug Administration (FDA) release AIDS drugs in a timely manner by shortening the drug testing and approval process, and it has insisted that private health insurance as well as Medicaid be forced to pay for experimental drug therapies. Ten years into the AIDS crisis, ACT UP questioned why only one drug, the highly toxic azidothymidine (AZT), had been approved for treatment. ACT UP also demanded federally controlled and funded needle-exchange and condom-distribution programs and a serious sex-education program in primary and secondary schools, to be created and monitored by the U.S. Department of Education (personal interview, April 13, 1993).

Since its creation in 1987, ACT UP has also challenged the prices charged and profits garnered by pharmaceutical companies for AIDS treatment drugs. The goal was to pressure them to reduce the cost of the drugs and make them more affordable to people with HIV/AIDS from all class backgrounds. Class and political-economy concerns are not central to ACT UP's ideology, however, but are raised only to publicize the group's belief that pharmaceutical companies pursue profits at the expense of lives.

Thousands of people joined ACT UP chapters in response to what they perceived to be an outrageous governmental inattention to AIDS. Many were motivated by anger but also shared Larry Kramer's belief that direct political action on behalf of their lives should be a key element of any organizing strategy. The media were a central target of the group, led by ACT UP members with experience in dealing with the media through their professional backgrounds in public relations and reporting.

ACT UP embraced slogans such as "Silence = Death" and used political art to convey its message to the public.[20] The organization succeeded in securing media attention from the start and, as a result, was able to communicate greater awareness of AIDS issues both to the lesbian and gay communities and to the larger society. The media covered ACT UP's first demonstration, held on Wall Street in New York on March 24, 1987. The goal of this demonstration was to heighten awareness of how the FDA's bureaucratic procedures prevented it from releasing experimental drugs in a timely fashion. This demonstration became a model for future ACT UP activities. It was carefully staged to attract media attention and to convey a practical political message (Vaid 1995, 100–101).

Over the years, other ACT UP demonstrations received considerable media coverage, although much of it was quite negative.[21] A 1987 protest at New York's Memorial Sloan-Kettering Hospital called for an increase in the number of anti-HIV drugs. Another demonstration, also in 1987, targeted Northwest Airlines for refusing to seat a man with AIDS, and the editorial offices of *Cosmopolitan* magazine were invaded in 1988 as protesters challenged an article claiming that women were unlikely to contract HIV or develop AIDS. In 1988 more than a thousand ACT UP protesters surrounded the FDA's Rockville, Maryland, headquarters building. In 1989, ACT UP activists demonstrated at AIDS hearings held by the U.S. Civil Rights Commission to protest its inept response to AIDS. Also in 1989, ACT UP/New York's "Stop the Church" demonstration disrupted Roman Catholic cardinal John O'Connor's mass in Saint Patrick's Cathedral to protest his opposition to condom distribution. In one especially memorable action, ACT UP members invaded the studio of the *MacNeil/Lehrer NewsHour* on January 22, 1991, chained themselves to Robert MacNeil's desk during a live broadcast, and flashed signs declaring "The AIDS Crisis Is Not Over."

Following some of these actions, particularly the "Stop the Church" demonstration, ACT UP found itself responding to critics arguing that it had gone too far. The confrontational and, many believed, offensive "Stop the Church" demonstration strategy engendered considerable criticism of ACT UP from both within and outside the lesbian and gay movements. David Brudnoy, a now openly gay conservative Boston radio-talk show host, captured this sentiment well:

> Now and again a group of AIDS activists will make news by jeering at newly ordained seminarians or tossing condoms at priests in their churches. I find myself infuriated, not at their passionate concern for what matters to them and certainly matters as well to me but at their cruelty in offending the most deeply held sentiments of the people whom they taunt and the faith they mock. (Brudnoy 1997, 100–101)

"Stop the Church" and other actions exacerbated an already existing tension within the movements, between those who favored more traditional, insider lobbying activities and those who embraced the radical direct action associated with ACT UP. Many ACT UP activists became increasingly intolerant of those who worried that direct action alienated important policy elites. In addition, ACT UP came under renewed criticism from within for the chaotic, unwieldy, and often unfocused nature of its weekly meetings.

By 1992 there were also divisions within ACT UP over what should be appropriate political strategy. Since ACT UP's creation in 1987, AIDS activists had directed their anger toward perceived enemies, including the U.S. Congress and president, federal agencies, drug companies, the media, religious organizations, and homophobic politicians. The divisions within ACT UP undermined organizational and movement solidarity (Vaid 1995, 104) and helped spawn other organizations, many of whose members had previous connections to ACT UP.

Queer Nation, a short-lived, radical lesbian and gay organization, appeared in June 1991 with a goal of radicalizing the broader AIDS movement by reclaiming the word "queer" and embracing confrontational politics. "Queer" politics rejected the politics of assimilation and the labels "lesbian" and "gay." Edward Stein points out that "the lesbians, gay men, bisexuals, transgendered people, and others who embraced the label 'queer' did not want to assimilate, and they proudly announced their difference from heterosexuals by their slogan 'We're here; we're queer; get used to it'" (Stein 1999, 10). Perhaps the most controversial tactic promoted by Queer Nation members and supporters was "outing," a strategy designed to embarrass and challenge various closeted lesbians and gays who occupied positions of power in American society. Understandably, outing has been a source of great controversy within the lesbian and gay movements, as some question whether such a tactic will ultimately prove to be counterproductive. Those targeted for outing have often taken public stances that are inimical to broader goals associated with the lesbian and gay movements. The media then become a crucial vehicle for publicizing an individual's sexual orientation. Understandably, outing has been a source of great controversy within the lesbian and gay movements, as some question whether such a tactic will ultimately prove to be counterproductive.

The Lesbian Avengers also embraced unconventional politics. Founded in the fall of 1992, the organization was the idea of six lesbian friends— Ana Maria Simo, Anne-Christie D'Adesky, Maxine Wolfe, Marie Honan, Ann Maguire, and Sara Schulman—most of whom had been active in AIDS, feminist, and other forms of progressive politics. They came together to create this new organization because they believed that more lesbians needed to engage in direct street action on their own terms, and they were frustrated with the unwillingness of gay men to address sexism in meaningful ways.[22] The organization has used tactics similar to those used by ACT UP in its efforts to secure media attention. One example occurred when Denver's mayor, Wellington Webb, visited New York to promote Colorado tourism shortly after the antigay Amendment 2 initiative was ratified by Colorado voters. In the fall of 1992, the Lesbian Avengers distributed three hundred lavender balloons to children entering a Queens public school, which was located in a district that refused to implement New York City's lesbian and gay–positive Rainbow Curriculum. The balloons said, "Ask about Lesbian Lives." The organization has become known for its Dyke Marches, which have almost always taken place without a permit. The 1993 Gay and Lesbian March on Washington was the occasion of the first Dyke March (Trice 1998, 40–41). Finally, the organization has done some important grassroots organizing on behalf of lesbian and gay communities located in states that are fighting hostile referenda (Keen and Goldberg 1998, 232–33). Their cross-state grassroots efforts may well be a model for other groups that wish to shift the battleground for lesbian and gay rights from the national level to the state and local levels.

But the fissures within ACT UP did not only produce radical alternatives. In 1992 activists committed to a political strategy emphasizing the treatment of individuals with HIV/AIDS left ACT UP/New York and formed the Treatment Action Group (TAG).[23] Unlike ACT UP, which had a democratic organizational structure, TAG accepted members by invitation only, and membership could be revoked by the board. In addition, TAG members received salaries, and the group accepted a $1 million check from the pharmaceutical company Burroughs Wellcome, the manufacturer of AZT, in the summer of 1992. TAG used this money to finance members' travels to AIDS conferences throughout the world, to pay salaries, to hire professional lobbyists, and to lobby government officials (Rimmerman 1998, 40).

TAG's central goal has been to force the government to release promising AIDS drugs more quickly and to identify possible treatments for opportunistic infections (Burkett 1995, 339–40). It has done so by lobbying for improved clinical trials of protease inhibitors and other anti-HIV drugs. In addition, it has called for a more coordinated AIDS research effort at the National Institutes of Health by strengthening the Office of AIDS Research. TAG has been quite effective in lobbying government officials to address its organizational goals in a timely manner. However, considerable criticism has been directed toward TAG by some ACT UP members and other activists. Because the organization is perceived by some as small, elitist, and undemocratic, it has been attacked for not fully representing the interests of the entire AIDS activist movement. These criticisms are unfortunate to the extent that they fail to recognize TAG's important contributions in forcing government officials to support more aggressive AIDS research. The sociologist Steven Epstein has identified the meaning of these and other conflicts for the larger AIDS movements:

> Gender and racial divisions, as well as debates over internal participatory mechanisms, insider/outsider strategies, and overall priorities and goals, are the kinds of issues that can tear apart any social movement. What particularly complicated the internal battles of the AIDS movement was the additional overlay of the politics of expertise. It was not simply that some people were working on the inside while others were outside—just as important, those who were on the inside were increasingly mastering specialized forms of knowledge with which their fellow activists on the outside did not come into contact. (Epstein 1996, 292–93)

These conflicts were compounded by differences of class, gender, race, and education, all of which can divide any social movement, as Epstein suggests.

Despite these challenges, from its inception ACT UP has had a considerable impact on AIDS-related public policy. The organization successfully used its nonviolent, direct-action approach to force the FDA to accelerate drug trials for AIDS and to consider ACT UP's "parallel track" proposal. Under this proposal, people with AIDS are given drugs before they complete the time-consuming and bureaucracy-ridden FDA approval process. ACT UP's protests also led Burroughs Wellcome to dramatically reduce the price of AZT. Other pharmaceutical companies have been shamed into cutting the prices of drugs that have demonstrated effectiveness in helping people with AIDS. In addition, ACT UP forced the redefinition of AIDS to include women and to insure that women with AIDS received disability benefits and were included in drug trials. ACT UP members have established needle-exchange programs, which are now widely credited with helping to reduce the rate of HIV infection among both injecting drug users and their sexual partners (Rimmerman 1998, 40–41).

By 1996, plagued with internal divisions over tactics and its relationship to the larger AIDS and lesbian and gay movements, and depleted by the deaths of many members, ACT UP still existed but was widely considered moribund. ACT UP suffered as well with the election of Bill Clinton. Without a clear enemy in the White House, ACT UP's efforts were undermined. Nonetheless, the organization's use of direct-action politics demonstrated the effectiveness of unconventional politics in challenging unresponsive policy elites. ACT UP's radicalism has also allowed other lesbian and gay organizations to seem much more moderate in their work on AIDS-related issues. A former executive director of the AIDS Action Council perceives that ACT UP has been quite successful in keeping "mainstream organizations from enjoying their seats at the table too much" and that "multiple political strategies have a tremendous effect" (personal interview, February 19, 1997).

In recent years, the few remaining chapters that exist in major cities, including New York City, San Francisco, and Washington, D.C., have flourished by building creative new alliances. These range from work with the Rainforest Action Network to support for the 2000 Green Party presidential candidate, Ralph Nader. In early 2001, ACT UP members in San Francisco protested the thirty-nine pharmaceutical companies that sued the South African government for choosing to produce its own AIDS drugs.[24] As it has broadened its political strategy, ACT UP has embraced a more progressive, social justice agenda, one that transcends identity politics (Bull 1999, 18–19). In this and in other ways, ACT UP has made an invaluable contribution to saving people's lives in the face of governmental and societal indifference.

MARCHES AND DEMONSTRATIONS

Like other social movements in the United States, the lesbian and gay movements have used marches and demonstrations as vehicles for voicing anger, communicating ideas for political and social change, and attracting media attention. The largest of these marches have logically taken place in Washington, D.C. The first March on Washington occurred on October 14, 1979; march organizers estimated that around a hundred thousand people participated.[25] Lucia Valeska, co-director of the National Gay Task Force, claimed that it symbolized "the birth of a national gay movement" (Anderson in Thompson 1994, p. 187). Reflecting on the major differences between it and the first march against the Vietnam war, held ten years earlier (on October 15, 1969), another march participant, James M. Saslow, said, "Then the order of the day was Quaker solemnity, panicky outrage, and some rather naive notions about the ingredients of social change. The men made speeches, and the women made coffee. I am a decade older now, and so is Stonewall; today the women lead off the march, and there is a mood of celebration, a sense that this time we're all marching not merely against something, but *for* something" (Saslow in ibid., p. 190).

By the second March on Washington in October 1987, the political and social landscape had radically changed. Ronald Reagan had been President for six years, and the lesbian and gay movements were experiencing the holocaust called AIDS. The news media dutifully reported the police estimate that some two hundred thousand marched, but others on the scene believed that number was too low. Regardless of the actual figure, many more marchers participated in 1987 than in 1979. This is no surprise, given the changed historical circumstances of the time, most notably the urgency of the AIDS crisis, made visible by the Names Project's AIDS Memorial Quilt. More than six hundred people were arrested during a protest on the steps of the U.S. Supreme Court, the largest number of people who participated in any act of civil disobedience since the antiwar demonstrations. The mainstream news media offered considerably more coverage of this march than it had in 1979, although inexplicably the three national newsmagazines, *Newsweek, Time,* and *U.S. News and World Report,* provided no coverage at all. Urvashi Vaid, then media director of the National Gay and Lesbian Task Force, devised a smart strategy for attracting the attention of those journalists who did cover the march. She advised protesters that they should carry signs identifying the city and state they represented. Vaid recognized that reporters needed a local angle in order to satisfy their hometown editors, and if the organizers provided that, they would receive important coverage in their local press. She explained, "I told the press they would see protesters from every corner of the nation, and when they held up their signs, the media swarmed all over them. It was the best. We gave the media what they wanted, and the people who got the coverage went on to be major spokespersons in their media at home" (Alwood 1996, 251–52).

This march may well have been a turning point for many participants, who found themselves galvanized politically in new ways. There is some evidence, for example, that the march inspired increased lesbian and gay activism at the grassroots (Vaid 1995, 117). But it apparently had little effect on Congress. Soon thereafter the Senate overwhelmingly passed Senator Jesse Helms's amendment to an AIDS appropriations bill. This amendment prevented federal funds from being spent in support of AIDS education material that "promotes or encourages homosexuality." Three days after the march, Helms arrived on the Senate floor brandishing a copy of GMHC's "Safe Sex Comix." He threatened to "throw up" after examining the booklets and video, which were meant to instruct gay men on techniques for safe sex. Helms claimed that the materials were funded by taxpayers and called them "pornographic" (Andriote 1999, 144). Although it was demonstrated subsequently that no taxpayer dollars had supported the materials in question, his arguments obviously proved effective with members of Congress and served as a reminder of just how little support the mainstream national policy process offered lesbians, gays, bisexuals, and transgendered people.[26] Congress's action also raised questions about the effectiveness of marches and demonstrations, at least in their ability to influence policy, and these questions resurfaced around the 1993 March on Washington.

This 1993 march attempted to define itself by its name: the March on Washington for Lesbian, Gay and Bi Equal Rights and Liberation. The march liberally invoked the memory of Dr. Martin Luther King and championed a strategy modeled on the African American civil rights movement and its 1963 March on Washington.[27] As the march platform suggests,[28] this civil rights strategy now completely dominated the broader movements' approach to political and social change. Indeed, despite the reference to "liberation" in its title, very little in the platform suggested a broadly political, cultural, and liberationist strategy. The amount of media coverage for this march was "unprecedented." Gregory Adams, the communications director for the march, said that "the media really seemed to get it this time. Consistent and distinct messages of justice, fair treatment, and equality ran through nearly every article or broadcast we saw." Ohio University professors Joseph Bernt and Marilyn Greenwald supported Adams's assessment with their empirical analysis of march coverage in thirty newspapers. Bernt said, "It extended over a long period of time, including the week after the march. This [march] generated much more sophisticated stories; it got into local gay and lesbian communities" (Alwood 1996, 311). Despite the fact that more people participated in this march than in either 1979 or 1987, there was controversy within the larger lesbian and gay movements over whether such marches have any meaningful, tangible impact.

Rep. Barney Frank (D-Mass.) was among the strongest critics. Over the years, Frank had maintained a fairly close and favorable relationship to the direct-action wing of the lesbian and gay movements, "despite publicly voicing criticism of some tactics, and a distaste for the all-or-nothing purism he sees as widespread in them" (Rayside 1998, 272). One ACT UP member offered this endorsement of Frank in 1992: "He maintains a certain distance from direct-action groups, but there aren't many people in the halls of Congress who call ACT UP and Queer Nation on a regular basis and ask what they're up to" (ibid.). But Frank broke with many direct-action group members when he publicly voiced his disapproval of the 1993 March on Washington:

> It's not that the people in the gay and lesbian community are not energetic. They are very energetic; they just wasted all their energy. When they came to Washington they surrounded the Capitol and turned their backs and held hands. That had zero impact on public policy—zero. But it took a lot of energy, and they thought it would have an impact. The debate about whether or not we are 300,000 people or a million people [at the March on Washington] is irrelevant. The point is that nobody in Congress cares. Literally, nobody cares. What they care about is how many of those people they heard from. And if there were a million people but nobody heard from them, that is not as good as 10,000 people everybody heard from. . . . The March was an important cultural event; it was an important self-actualizing event; but it had no short-term political impact for us. . . . So by May I was very discouraged about our inability to make the transition from a marginal to a mainstream political group. And that is the problem when people have the preference for the tactics of the margins—sit-ins, demonstrations. When is the last time the NRA had a sit-in, or a demonstration, or a shoot-in? They don't do that. Who is more influential? (Rayside 1998, 274)

Frank's frustration erupted during the debate on the military ban. He joined other "insider" politicians in lamenting the failure of the lesbian and gay movements to do the tough day-to-day organizing and lobbying of Congress that were clearly needed if the ban had any chance at all of being overturned.[29]

Frank's critique is also relevant as we consider the planning for the 2000 Millennium March, which took place on April 30, 2000. In February 1998, two organizations—the Human Rights Campaign (HRC) and the Universal Fellowship of Metropolitan Community Churches (UFMCC)—publicly announced that they were starting to organize another march on Washington. With the encouragement of organizer Robin Tyler, the two organizations made preliminary decisions about the march itself and agreed to provide funding for the planning efforts. A number of critics quickly pointed out that no other organizations had been consulted in advance, nor had the broader lesbian and gay communities. And decisions had already been made: The march would be held in the year 2000, it would be called the "Millennium March," and the central organizing theme would be issues of "faith and family" (Boykin 2000, 89–90).

This was hardly the kind of open and democratic process that organizational and community members had a right to expect. Should such a march even be held? Might the resources of the movements better be used in other ways? If the march did occur, what should its message be? And who should be involved in planning the march? These questions were never satisfactorily addressed early in the planning process, a failure that caused considerable consternation within the broader lesbian and gay movements.[30] Elizabeth Birch, executive director of HRC, eventually came to believe that the original call for the march was "a colossal error in judgment," but the damage had already been done (Gamson 2000, 18). To some critics, "the Millennium March [came] to symbolize . . . a movement increasingly run by what is essentially a national, corporate, business-as-usual political lobby [HRC], which collects funds while local and state groups struggle against attack" (ibid., 16). The so-called planning for this march also reflected the top-down, hierarchical proclivities of the mainstream lesbian and gay movements. Worse yet, the march organizers did not seem to have seriously engaged the thoughtful criticisms that Barney Frank offered regarding the 1993 March on Washington. The controversy over the march is an important reminder that many movement members resist this model of political organizing, and believe it is crucial to have open, participatory, and democratic conversations about strategy, message, and use of resources.

THE DECLINE OF POLITICAL ACTIVISM AND UNCONVENTIONAL POLITICS?

Some observers believe that, in recent years, activist, outsider, unconventional, grassroots politics has declined within the lesbian and gay movements, a decline that some attribute to the creation of lesbian and gay markets and the concomitant rise of lesbian and gay consumerism. To what extent is this perception accurate? And if it is accurate, what does it say about the current state of lesbian and gay social movements? Before we can address these questions, we need to highlight a few of the arenas where such activism still occurs, within the context of the broader policy areas already addressed in this chapter. Chapters 5 and 6 will also explore various forms of grassroots organizing that are still prevalent.

ACT UP remains active in a few cities, as Democratic presidential candidate Al Gore can attest. On June 17, 2000, the group heckled him during a campaign stop for his position on generic drugs. Bill Dobbs, cofounder of Queer Watch, an ACT UP–affiliated organization, believes that ACT UP's obituary is far too premature: "As the epidemic continues to evolve, there is as much need for street activism as ever. The difference now is because it's smaller and less confrontational, it's much harder for the media to see what the group is doing" (Bull 1999, 18). But the remaining chapters, located in major cities such as New York, Philadelphia, San Francisco, and Washington, D.C., have thrived by creating new alliances. These range from working with Ralph Nader to connecting with the Rainforest Action Network, a radical environmental group. To the extent that ACT UP chapters embrace these sorts of activities, they are clearly adopting a more progressive political agenda. Other chapters have reached out to people of color with AIDS (Philadelphia), organized a local ballot measure that would legalize the medical use of marijuana (Washington, D.C.), and promoted a ballot initiative that would repeal San Francisco's ban on bathhouses (San Francisco). This latter effort represents the kind of grassroots, outsider politics that we have already witnessed in New York City.

Some of the most interesting grassroots debates and actions have come in response to the closing of bathhouses in cities such as San Francisco and New York. Debates over the regulation of public sex venues under the umbrella of HIV prevention erupted in the 1980s, when, at the height of the AIDS epidemic, a number of cities closed gay male sex clubs, back rooms, theaters, and bars. The lesbian and gay communities were sharply divided over these decisions. Opponents identified them as politically motivated, and predicted that they would have dire consequences for the future of AIDS activism.[31] In 1997 a number of activists and academics, including Douglas Crimp, Ann Pellegrini, Eva Pendleton, and Michael Warner, founded Sex Panic! in New York City, an organization created to challenge the puritanical notions underlying the crusade against public sex and to celebrate sexual freedom. While their target was the administration of New York mayor Rudolph Giuliani, they also aimed their criticisms at prominent figures in the gay community, including Bruce Bawer, Larry Kramer, and Andrew Sullivan, whom they perceive as having marginalized "queer sex and sexuality." The organization identifies itself as a pro-queer, pro-feminist, anti-racist, direct-action group whose goal is "to defend public sexual culture and safer-sex in New York City from police crackdowns, public stigma, and morality crusades" (Trice 1998, 43). It attempts to voice concerns that other, more mainstream organizations do not articulate. Specifically, the organization has embraced: "1) the right to sexual and reproductive self-determination; 2) the right to publicly accessible sexual culture; 3) the right to a sexual life free from shame and stigma; and 4) freedom from government intervention" (ibid.). Sex Panic! founders explain the name of their organization by placing it in historical context:

> This is not the first time that officials have launched repressive measures against sex in the name of the public good. Since the nineteenth century, it has been a recurrent pattern: public morals and health have been invoked; scapegoats have been found in homosexuals, sex workers, and others who are unlikely to fight back, and a fantasy of purity is held as the norm. Historians have come to call this pattern a "sex panic." We have taken this name, with a sense of irony, to publicize our belief that we are in the middle of one. (Trice 1998, 43)

Like ACT UP, Sex Panic! embraces unconventional, direct-action politics as a vehicle for attracting media attention and challenging repressive government policies. For example, it joined ACT UP New York in a demonstration protesting GMHC's position on HIV names reporting. It offers supporters a venue to reject the mainstream organizations' emphasis on marriage and family, as well as the scapegoating of HIV-positive, sexually active people (Trice 1998, 43). In this way, the organization has already made an invaluable contribution to grassroots politics and the public discourse. As Michael Warner puts it, Sex Panic! enables supporters to transcend the "normalizing" tendencies of the mainstream movement organizations.[32] Vocal critics of Sex Panic! have included Gabriel Rotello, Michelangelo Signorile, Larry Kramer, and John-Manuel Andriote. Andriote has offered a succinct critique of the organization: "Nothing was surer than the devastation of the AIDS epidemic. Not only did SexPanic! flout the epidemiologic facts of AIDS, but it ignored the fact that gay men because of the epidemic now shared so much more than a priapic brotherhood of sexual rebellion insisting on a dubious 'right' to promiscuity" (Andriote 1999, 413). Despite these criticisms, Sex Panic! has provided a thoughtful alternative to the mainstream movements' assumptions about the meaning of sex, freedom, and privatism. In addition, the organization's efforts suggest that perhaps the outsider, unconventional politics associated with grassroots political organizing is not nearly as moribund as some observers fear.

What accounts for the belief that grassroots activism has been in decline among the lesbian and gay movements since the early 1990s? A major reason is that increasing numbers of lesbians and gay men "embrace a politics of privatization that offers them both property value and an affirmation of identity in a language of respectability and mainstream acceptance" (Warner 1999, 164). This issue has been the subject of recent articles and books. The arguments are worth considering here and will be considered again in Chapter 6, as they are relevant to our analysis of the current state of lesbian and gay movements in the United States.

Like Michael Warner, Joshua Oppenheimer perceives that "since the early 1990's, there has been a spectacular decline in American grassroots AIDS and queer activism." Oppenheimer also blames the opening up of the lesbian and gay market in the 1990s for undermining grassroots activism. He cites the claim by Jeff Yarbrough, former editor of *The Advocate,* that American direct-action organizations of the late 1980s and early 1990s scared away advertisers who might have targeted their messages to lesbians and gay men. In support of these claims, Oppenheimer offers this thoughtful analysis:

> Advertisers were fearful that following some particularly brash demonstration, the Christian right would organize a boycott of firms marketing to "militant homosexuals." The demise of ACT UP made marketing to gays and lesbians more attractive to big business. In turn, the arrival of big business to gay shopping streets and lifestyle magazines promised far greater income to landlords leasing property on the gay commercial strips, and far greater advertising revenues to gay magazines. To accommodate mainstream advertisers, the lifestyle magazines went glossy and professional, and the community papers, unable to compete, have all but disappeared. This mainstreaming of lesbian and gay markets marks a profoundly significant moment in gay economic life. (Oppenheimer 1997, 292)

"Mainstreaming" refers to a trend whereby non-lesbian and non-gay firms replace lesbian and gay-identified and -owned companies and firms. Economic mainstreaming is linked to political and social mainstreaming to the extent that it encourages "assimilationism and anti-activist sentiment" (Oppenheimer 1997, 292). If people who can afford to do so spend much of their discretionary time shopping, this leaves little time for the commitment that grassroots organizing requires.

But what about the argument that direct-action, grassroots organizing is no longer needed because the lesbian and gay movements have won access to mainstream policy makers? This argument presumes that direct action has outlived its usefulness because mainstream "professional organizations are best poised to follow up the campaigns which the grassroots organizations successfully initiated" (Oppenheimer 1997, 288). As we have already seen in Chapters 2 and 3, access does not necessarily mean influence in terms of affecting the outcomes of public policy. In addition, access to mainstream policy makers and medical institutions has not been won permanently and uniformly. We also cannot assume that the mainstream national organizations will represent the perceived interests of grassroots communities, interests which, in and of themselves, are often fragmented (ibid.). A key argument of this book is that we surely need both insider and outsider political organizing. The lesbian and gay movements have benefited enormously from the courageous efforts of those who have rejected mainstream, pluralist, interest-group politics and who have agitated at all levels of government for meaningful political, social, and cultural change.

Finally, the advertising and marketing strategies that some identify as a sign of progress focus on those lesbians and gay men who can afford to consume. But these are a minority within the broader lesbian and gay community. The economist Lee Badgett points out that, "lesbians and gay men earn no more than heterosexual people; indeed, in some cases gay men appear to earn less than comparable heterosexual men" (Badgett 1998, 2). Badgett's empirical work has exploded the myth that lesbians and gays are more affluent as a group than heterosexuals.[33] This leaves an important question: what about those lesbians, gays, bisexuals, and transgendered people who cannot afford a consumerist lifestyle? Where do they fit in this identity-based, market-niche strategy embraced by advertisers and affluent members of mainstream organizations?[34] And perhaps most importantly of all, to what extent does the economic agenda of marketers coincide with the political, social, and economic agenda of lesbian and gay movements? These important questions are explored in much more detail in the last chapter of this book.

CONCLUSION AND IMPLICATIONS

The evidence presented in this chapter suggests that unconventional politics, often working in tandem with more conventional, insider politics, is a viable strategy. We have seen how, over time, the lesbian and gay movements successfully combined conventional and unconventional politics to force the American Psychiatric Association to remove homosexuality from its list of mental disorders in 1973–74. The activists working through ACT UP and TAG have also had a considerable impact on AIDS-related public policy. Of course, these successes have come despite searing conflicts that have divided the broader lesbian and gay social movements.

But unconventional, outsider politics do not necessarily guarantee that the larger lesbian and gay communities will move beyond a mainstream, assimilationist approach and embrace progressive change that is transformative in nature. The groups and organizations discussed in this chapter have generally failed to link their critiques to structural and class-based concerns over access to quality medical care and other basic resources that are generally considered privileges in most liberal democracies. In addition, they have largely failed to transcend identity politics. Interestingly, none of the groups discussed here have embraced the critique of the market-driven advertising strategy that has encouraged an identity-based lesbian and gay consumerism in recent years.

As we think about the implications of the analysis presented in this chapter for the lesbian and gay movements, we need to recall Urvashi Vaid's 1989 statement, which is still relevant today: "We can't go on just living through AIDS. We have to think in terms of living beyond it if this movement's going to survive" (Rist 1989, 199). In many ways, the lesbian and gay movements have embraced Vaid's exhortation over the past decade. AIDS has been de-gayed and we are now told by movement "leaders" that marriage, the military ban, and the Millennium March for equal rights are the central issues on our movements' agenda. The mainstream, assimilationist, civil rights strategy has largely prevailed, at least in the short term. But what we have not done is reconcile that more narrow strategy with a progressive liberationist approach to political, cultural, and social change. In other words, there are still divisions within the movements over both the substance of the message and how that message is articulated politically and culturally, and the Christian Right has been able to take advantage of these. Chapter 5 examines the strategies it has employed to exploit these divisions as well as conflicts in the larger society over the politics of sexual orientation.

5 The Christian Right's Challenge

The ability of the Christian Right to register voters, to penetrate the grass roots, and to shape the narrower congressional and broader public agendas all show that it has been an important force in American politics, worth studying both generally and in terms of its transformation over time.
—Matthew C. Moen

Indeed, it is not an exaggeration to say, and no doubt many conservative Christians themselves would agree, that by the mid-1990s the battle between the CR and the lesbian and gay movement was one of the most significant arenas of social struggle in the United States.
—Didi Herman

HOW HAVE THE Christian Right and lesbian and gay movements intersected over time? What are the sources of antagonism that fuel the conflicts between the movements? What factors and motivations underlie the Christian Right's antigay politics? Why and how have Christian Right antigay strategies shifted over time?[1] Finally, what do the Christian Right's mobilizing efforts imply for the political strategies embraced by the lesbian and gay movements? This chapter addresses all of these questions by examining the Christian Right in both historical and contemporary contexts. While the chapter is organized by decade, beginning with the 1970s and ending with the 1990s, it is not meant to be a comprehensive overview of all of the ways that the Christian Right and the lesbian and gay movements have intersected over time. Any attempt to do so would require a book in and of itself.

Much of the conflict between the two movements has occurred within state and local arenas. As a result, while this book has largely emphasized national policy making, this chapter will devote considerable attention to the politics surrounding state and local initiatives. In attempting to understand the intersection between the movements, and the resistance to the extension of lesbian and gay rights, I will integrate elements of resource-mobilization theory and political-process approaches to studying social movements. Underlying this chapter are three key arguments. First, the Christian Right has proven itself to be remarkably adaptable to changes in the political and social landscape over time. It has been able to modify its own strategic choices in response to perceived gains on the part of lesbian and gay movements and changing political opportunities. Of course, the Christian Right has access to institutional and financial resources that dwarf those available to the lesbian and gay movements, as this chapter discusses. Second, the lesbian and gay movements have been thrown on the defensive over the years and forced to respond to the claims of the Christian Right and its changing organizing strategies as a result. Third, and finally, the response to the lesbian and gay movements' advances in recent years suggests even more strongly the importance of reconsidering and rethinking the movements' messages and political organizing strategies at all levels. As we have seen, serious conflicts persist over both the substance of the message and how that message is articulated politically and socially, as the debates over lesbian and gay marriage, the ban on military service, and the Millennium March suggest. The Christian Right has been able to exploit these divisions as well as the conflicts in the larger society over sexual orientation. Ultimately, how the lesbian and gay movements have been shaped by and responded to these developments is integral to the core analysis of this book.

UNDERSTANDING THE CHRISTIAN RIGHT'S ORGANIZING EFFORTS

Didi Herman observes that "the opposition to gay rights is led, invigorated, and inspired by Christians, and the Christian faith" (Herman 1997, 1). It is important to recognize, however, that the Christian Right does not speak with a single voice; indeed, a wide range of organizations with differing concerns and approaches make up this social movement. But although it does not have a single, monolithic approach to lesbian and gay rights, some broad commonalities can be identified. The groups that compose the Christian Right are generally rooted in a conservative, evangelical Protestantism. Their primary social agenda focuses on issues that are among the most contentious in American politics, including banning a woman's right to a legal abortion, eliminating laws that would protect lesbians and gays from housing and job discrimination, and altering public school curriculums "to prevent favorable depictions of lifestyles that they regard as sinful" (Wilcox 1996, 8). Herman lists several organizations in the forefront of antigay activity in the United States: Focus on the Family, which is headed by James Dobson; the Family Research Council, which was led by Gary Bauer, a 2000 presidential candidate; and the Christian Coalition, which has supposedly moderated its position on lesbian and gay rights in recent years, in the interest of "pragmatic politics aimed at achieving the widest possible consensus" (Herman 1997, 16).

The Christian Coalition does not stress lesbian and gay rights in the legislative arena, but it does emphasize these concerns in fundraising appeals (Wald 2000, 6). Herman, however, rejects the notion that the Christian Right has moderated its views. On the contrary, she believes that the anti-gay movement is part of the radical goal of forming a Christian state, one that would have sweeping powers to repress what it perceives to be immoral behavior.

The political scientist John Green has extended Herman's analysis by identifying three ideal types of opposition to lesbian and gay rights: instrumental, reactive, and proactive. According to Green, each represents "a different mix of motives, means, and methods." Instrumental opposition uses antigay rhetoric to secure political power; the goal "is to implement a broad agenda of traditional morality, of which opposition to gay rights is one part" (Green 2000, 126). The implementation strategy used to further this ideology is the mobilization of resources, which are then used to support general-purpose organizations of the kind that we will discuss in this chapter.

Reactive opposition focuses on blocking changes in laws that are perceived as dangerous to the community. The central avenue for such opposition is what Green identifies as the "'mobilization of outrage' in a narrow context, and then reaching out to other kinds of traditionalists. Thus, gay rights is the only focus of the activity, the methods employed arise directly from the occasion, and the effort dissipates once the controversy has passed." These efforts focus on preserving the status quo regarding lesbian and gay rights. Many of the battles are fought in the legislative arena as opponents of lesbian and gay rights bring pressure to bear on legislators who might support public policies perceived to favor the lesbian and gay movements (Green 2000, 126).

Finally, Green discusses proactive opposition, which refers to "the preemption of attempts to promote gay rights." The central goal is to hinder lesbian and gay rights advocates from pursuing their objectives. Green explains that the chief means for expressing such opposition "is the mobilization of bias against the 'special interests' of the gay community; organization and resources arise from the prospect of stalling a subversive enemy." Various methods are employed, depending on the context. However, the goal is to prevent the advancement of lesbian and gay rights by constricting the politics surrounding the issue (Green 2000, 127).

Many of the Christian Right's organizing efforts have occurred at the state and local level. For example, opponents of lesbian and gay rights have used the citizen's initiative and voter referendum effectively. Elements of the Christian Right have perceived that the citizen's initiative, which enables groups to force legislation onto the ballot after obtaining the required number of voter signatures, is a viable mechanism for impeding lesbian and gay advances at the state and local levels.

In order to better understand the Christian Right's organizing efforts, we first need an analytical framework with which to contextualize the discussion that follows. Chapter 1 provided an overview of the resource-mobilization and political-process approaches to movement organizing. Elements of both are relevant to the discussion here. Resource-mobilization theory informs us that the resources internal to the group are of crucial importance. These include leadership, organizational capacity, and wealth, qualities that are integral to both the short- and long-term success of social movements.

Chapter 1 also pointed out that those who embrace the resource-mobilization model tend to advocate a "work within the system" approach to political and social change. Theirs is an insider, elite-centered, pluralist politics. I argued that the model, with its narrow focus, has limited utility for helping us to understand lesbian and gay movements because it cannot take into account the full range of organizing activities—both inside and outside the system—that have characterized them over time. But while the Christian Right has been enormously successful in mobilizing supporters at the grass roots, it also generally embraces the insider, elite-centered, pluralist politics associated with the resource-mobilization approach. For this reason, the approach is a good one for understanding how the Christian Right has organized over the past twenty-five years.

The political-process model is also helpful in understanding the Christian Right because the model describes insurgency as a response to factors both internal or external to the movement. With this in mind, considerable attention is devoted to those factors that shape insurgency, including "the confluence of expanding political opportunities, indigenous organizational strength, and the presence of certain shared cognitions within the minority community that is held to facilitate movement emergence" (McAdam 1982, 58–59). These three factors are used to evaluate insurgency as seen in the Christian Right.

We will see how perceived political opportunities have helped structure the Christian Right's response to the lesbian and gay movements' advances over the years. Such political opportunities include changes in who occupies the White House, who controls Congress, and the political, cultural, and social milieu. At the same time, we will devote some attention to the various organizations and informal networks that have mobilized opposition to the lesbian and gay movements over the years. Finally, we will evaluate how the Christian Right has modified its political and social strategies in response to changing conditions.[2] Their ability to do so has been a major factor in their successes in challenging the lesbian and gay movements. The

Christian Right's anti-lesbian and gay agenda has also clearly benefited from the centrality of religion, and fundamentalism more specifically, in the United States. As a result, lesbians and gay men have faced difficulties that their counterparts in other countries have been able to escape.[3]

THE 1970s

In the aftermath of the 1969 Stonewall rebellion, newly formed political groups sought laws that would protect lesbians and gays from harassment and discrimination. Within several years, these new groups succeeded in prompting the enactment of ordinances banning discrimination on the basis of sexual orientation in a number of localities throughout the United States: Boulder, Colorado; Columbus, Ohio; Dade County, Florida; Detroit, Michigan; Seattle, Washington; San Francisco, California; and Washington, D.C. (Keen and Goldberg 1998, 6). In addition, twenty states had legalized sodomy by the late 1970s.

The Christian Right reacted to these developments with hostility and a commitment to grassroots organizing. During the 1970s, the Christian Right organized effective opposition to homosexuality, as lesbian and gay rights suffered major setbacks both locally and nationally. Six antigay referenda appeared in 1977 and 1978 alone. Additionally, as Didi Herman explains, "Local lesbian and gay rights ordinances were repealed and in some cases banned permanently; statewide initiatives prohibiting future, similar legislation were launched; state gay rights legislation and proposed legislation was challenged or killed" (Herman 2000, 140). Specific antigay statutes were proposed and/or enacted in some cases.

The 1970s also witnessed an increase in anti-lesbian and gay violence as "fag bashings" became more commonplace. The first publicized killings occurred in San Francisco, and they soon spread throughout the country. Oklahoma teenagers created a Ku Klux Klan chapter with the expressed purpose of assaulting gays, and University of Oklahoma students wore T-shirts that said "Bury a Fairy" and "Do the World a Favor—Shoot a Faggot." Gay men in New York City were particularly vulnerable. A former policeman opened fire with a machine gun inside a gay bar, killing two men and wounding six others. Crime statistics from this period indicated that "one New Yorker a day was physically attacked because of his sexual orientation." And mysterious fires—most attributed to arson—broke out in bathhouses and theaters in New York, New Orleans, San Francisco, and Washington. These tragic fires killed dozens of gay men and injured hundreds of others (Streitmatter 1995, 211–12).

Antigay violence attracted considerable public attention in 1978 when Dan White, a member of the San Francisco Board of Supervisors, climbed into an open City Hall window, and then shot and killed openly gay board member Harvey Milk and Mayor George Moscone, who had supported Milk and lesbian and gay rights more generally. White had been the only member of the San Francisco board who voted against the city's gay rights law. At his trial, White invoked what became known as the "Twinkie defense," arguing that a diet of junk food had caused him to act irrationally on the day of the killings. When a jury accepted this defense, finding White guilty of voluntary manslaughter and not the more serious charge of murder, gay San Francisco exploded in riots and protests that hearkened back to Stonewall some ten years earlier (Streitmatter 1995, 212).

Numerous reasons have been proposed to account for the virulent opposition to extending the rights of gays and lesbians. Some saw homosexuality as a disease that needed a cure rather than governmental sanction and support. Herman (1997) suggests that economic concerns were another factor, specifically that "the cost of concession would be paid in the unacceptable growth of state bureaucracy, and the diminution of private-sector freedoms" (p. 3). Some protested that the rights of those who opposed homosexuality would be threatened by prohibitions on discriminatory practices. But what is most important for the analysis in this chapter is that opposition to lesbian and gay rights was most often grounded in religious arguments based in holy scriptures. Those who supported this line of thinking claimed that "lesbian and gay rights were akin to 'adulterer's rights' or 'murderer's rights' " (ibid.). They argued that homosexuality was unnatural. Religious fundamentalists worried that without a public taboo against it, homosexuality might engulf all of humanity. As a part of their campaign, they aroused fears that young people would be the targets of sexual abuse (Nichols 1996, 86–87). Jerry Falwell, the head of the Moral Majority, said publicly that "so-called gay folks would just as soon kill you as look at you" (Streitmatter 1995, 211). By the late 1970s, his bile and venom appeared to be rewarded, as the Moral Majority grew to four million members and embraced an aggressive anti-lesbian and gay media campaign, one that fought "to have the death penalty instituted as the standard punishment for being homosexual" (ibid.).

Indeed, the emerging lesbian and gay movements were perfect targets for the right's fund-raising efforts by the late 1970s. For example, conservative activist Richard Viguerie astutely recognized that the knee-jerk antigay views of many rank-and-file conservatives could be targeted in political campaigns. Viguerie compiled the first of his legendary computerized lists of individuals who could be counted upon for money and political support. His success in building a base of support for the conservative agenda secured his standing as a prominent Republican campaign consultant and his leadership of a generation of young, angry conservatives who came to be known as the "New Right."[4] By the early 1980s, Viguerie had articulated the "special rights" argument that the Christian Right would embrace to fight efforts to overturn bans on policies that discriminated against lesbians and gay men (Bull and Gallagher 1996, 13–14).

Anita Bryant and the Save Our Children Campaign

It was a former Miss America, Anita Bryant, who helped to galvanize conservative opposition to lesbian and gay rights in 1977. On June 7 of that year, with her successful efforts to persuade voters to rescind a six-month-old Dade County, Florida, civil rights ordinance, the fight over lesbian and gay rights finally received considerable national attention in the mainstream press (Alwood 1996, 167). Bryant's celebrity status certainly helped her cause. As an evangelist singer, national promoter for Florida orange juice, and the mother of two children, Bryant was a perfect spokesperson. In challenging the Dade County ordinance, Bryant made two arguments that helped her cause. First, she insisted that the new law "discriminates against my children's rights to grow up in a healthy, decent atmosphere" (Loughery 1998, 373). Second, she claimed that God had called her to fight against "preferential legislation" that endorsed a degraded "lifestyle" (ibid., 374). Both of these arguments have been invoked by opponents of lesbian and gay rights over the years, but the latter was particularly important. One activist concluded that "Gay rights was in trouble, the day 'special rights' was born."

The reactionary climate of the late 1970s was ripe for Bryant's campaign. The Save Our Children organization, which led the Dade County fight, represented a profile of anti-lesbian and gay forces. It galvanized conservative religious leaders and politicians; the campaign itself was founded on fundamentalist church networks, and Bryant obtained active support from the National Association of Evangelicals, which represented "more than three million people from 60 denominations" (Adam 1995, 110). The association's television programs, the PTL Club, 700 Club, and The Old-Time Gospel Hour, afforded Bryant a national platform and raised funds on her behalf. Moral Majority founder Jerry Falwell campaigned against the Dade County ordinance in person, and the direct-mail political lobby, Christian Cause, extended its organizing efforts into Jewish and Roman Catholic hierarchies. Opposition to the Dade County ordinance arose at the local level as well. For example, Miami's archbishop distributed a pastoral letter to local Roman Catholic churches, exhorting their congregations to vote against lesbian and gay civil rights. The president of the Miami Beach B'nai B'rith and twenty-eight rabbis publicly lent their support to Bryant's cause (Adam 1995, 110).

In order to overturn the Dade County ordinance, Bryant needed ten thousand names on petitions submitted to the Dade County Elections Department. The Save Our Children campaign gathered so many signatures that county officials simply stopped counting when they reached 13,457. In a 6–3 vote, the Metro Commission put the referendum on the ballot in a special election scheduled for June 7, 1977 (Clendinen and Nagourney 1999, 299).

Twenty-one years later, John Loughery summarized the Dade County campaign as "a contest between two diametrically opposed viewpoints, the fundamentalist and the homosexual, that managed to bring middle-class America (which was neither one nor the other) into the debate. The result was an overwhelming defeat for the advocates of gay rights" (Loughery 1998, 376). The pro-lesbian and gay forces were represented by the Dade County Coalition for Human Rights (DCCHR) and the Miami Victory Campaign. But only the Miami Victory Campaign engaged in the kind of popular mobilization that we associate today with mature organizing efforts. And these efforts occurred in the latter stages of the campaign. The DCCHR embraced "a professionally directed media campaign" that failed to canvass door-to-door and largely ignored Miami's large African-American and Cuban communities. This strategy was embraced by gay businessmen and by gay club leaders belonging to the Democratic Party. With this kind of inept organizing by the local lesbian and gay community, and the carefully orchestrated campaign by Anita Bryant and her fundamentalist supporters, it is no surprise that equal rights were repealed on June 7, 1997, by a huge margin: 202,319 to 83,319 votes (Adam 1995, 111).[5]

In the final weeks of the campaign, Bryant's speeches became increasingly hateful. She argued that God was the cause of California's drought because that state was too tolerant of lesbians and gays. She publicly referred to lesbians and gays as "human garbage," and warned that if the Dade County ordinance was allowed to stand, it would "protect the right to have 'intercourse with beasts'" (Clendinen and Nagourney 1999, 306). This kind of hate-filled rhetoric manifested itself with increasing regularity as the more conservative 1980s began. The Christian fundamentalist right had won an overwhelming victory in Dade County, Florida. Clendinen and Nagourney review the true meaning of this victory for the lesbian and gay movements:

> Indeed, it seemed that Anita Bryant could not have hoped for anything more. There was a new movement afoot, of fundamentalist conservatives, and it had found a rallying point, a cause that seemed likely to stir more passions than the fight against abortion rights or for prayer in schools. The vote seemed to be a repudiation of homosexuals by the American public.

And the Dade County results revealed that the movement remained painfully unsophisticated, divided and dominated by extreme personalities, and apparently unprepared for the fights that lay ahead. (Clendinen and Nagourney 1999, 309)

The civil rights ordinance resurfaced in 1998, when the Miami–Dade County commissioners voted 7–6 to ban discrimination based on sexual orientation. Even the narrow margin of the vote could not alter the importance of this victory for the lesbian and gay movements. But Duberman (1999) cautions that since it was passed by elected officials and not by voters, this measure, "like the earlier one, could be rescinded through a referendum" (p. 329). Given how the Christian Right has consistently responded to progress by the lesbian and gay movements over the years, their mobilizing against this new ordinance appears to be a foregone conclusion.

The 1977 repeal had attracted considerable press attention and Anita Bryant was now a national figure. She capitalized on her victory by launching an anti-gay-rights campaign throughout the United States. By June 1978 voters in Eugene, Oregon; Saint Paul, Minnesota; and Wichita, Kansas, had also rescinded local ordinances that had protected the basic rights of lesbians and gays. Fundamentalist churches, with the financial support of the business community, constituted the foundation of the antigay movement. By 1978, then, the conservative opposition against lesbian and gay rights had solidified and gained momentum. But this did not mean that the opposition was invincible. The lesbian and gay movements proved that they could organize an effective response (Button, Rienzo, and Wald 1997, 69). One of their most successful organizing campaigns came in California.

The Briggs Initiative

The day after the 1977 Miami vote, California state senator John Briggs, from conservative Orange County, announced his plans to introduce legislation that would prevent lesbians and gays from teaching in California's public schools. When it became obvious that the legislation had little chance of passing, Briggs altered his tactics and organized a campaign to have his proposal placed on the ballot in the form of a statewide initiative (D'Emilio 1992, 89). Within eleven months of Bryant's victory, Briggs filed the half million signatures that he needed to introduce a voter referendum that would force the removal of lesbian and gay teachers from California's public schools. In May 1978 Briggs had hoped that his teachers' initiative, his support for a second initiative that would expand the use of the death penalty in California, and his public association with Anita Bryant would help make him a strong candidate for governor (Clendinen and Nagourney 1999, 376). Briggs attempted to build on some of the organizing strategies used by Bryant. Although he lacked her connections to the Christian Right, he tried to appeal to the same forces in California, and nationally, with the help of Bryant's contributor list. But Briggs miscalculated severely. In the end, the voters in California, which is an unpredictable state politically (it has elected both Ronald Reagan and Jerry Brown as its governors), overwhelmingly defeated his Proposition 6.

California lesbian and gay activists initially expected to lose the fight against the Briggs initiative. They did not expect California to defy a national trend, which by 1978 revealed considerable public hostility toward laws that protected lesbians and gays from discrimination.[6] Even Harvey Milk shared this pessimism, although this did not stop him from organizing against the Briggs amendment. Milk often spoke publicly against the initiative and debated Briggs on several occasions. Milk's efforts were supported by the Concerned Voters of California, a new coalition of anti-Briggs activists from Los Angeles and San Francisco. The anti-Briggs effort also received considerable funding support from David Goodstein, then editor of *The Advocate*.

The deputy managers of the campaign were David Mixner and Peter Scott, veteran gay political activists. Mixner and Scott made perhaps one of the most important strategic decisions of the entire campaign when they visited Governor Ronald Reagan and asked him to oppose the Briggs amendment. They offered two arguments for Reagan's consideration. First, they claimed that the Briggs initiative would destroy school discipline by enabling students to blackmail teachers. Second, they argued that if passed, the initiative would lead to pointless litigation that would waste taxpayers' money. When Reagan subsequently announced his opposition to the Briggs initiative, the campaign turned around almost overnight. California pollster Mervin Field found that at the beginning of September 1978, voters supported the initiative by 61 percent to 31 percent. By the end of the month, voters favored it by a statistically insignificant 45 to 43 percent, with 12 percent undecided. Field was convinced that the changes in public opinion were due to the "increasing number of influential voices now being raised against the measure." His statement is a clear reference to the impact of Reagan's public opposition to the initiative.

Reagan's opposition was not the only reason that the amendment failed. The lesbian and gay movements won endorsements from an array of unions, including the auto workers, culinary workers, postal workers, steelworkers, and Teamsters, and the support of various African American and Chicano leaders including Angela Davis and United Farm Workers leader Cesar Chavez (Adam 1995, 113). The work of lesbian and gay organizers and Reagan's high-profile public opposition led to Proposition 6's overwhelming defeat on November 7, 1978, by a margin of 58 percent to 42 percent. On the same night, Seattle voters defeated an initiative that would have repealed its gay rights law, by a margin of 63 percent to 37 percent (Clendinen and Nagourney 1999, 389). As the decade of the 1970s approached its final year, these were two important and highly visible victories for the lesbian and gay movements.

Nevertheless, the Christian Right had made considerable progress over the past five years in fighting lesbian and gay rights. After the Miami–Dade County referendum, gay activist Ethan Geto observed bitterly, "In 1965, if the federal civil rights act was voted on in Selma, Alabama, what would have happened? Of course they would have taken away blacks' civil rights. A referendum is a lousy vehicle to extend or expand the rights of a minority" (Clendinen and Nagourney 1999, 311). Geto's observations proved prescient as major fights over lesbian and gay rights erupted at the state and local levels in the 1990s. And while Governor Reagan had helped to secure victory in the Briggs initiative fight, the ushering in of his conservative presidency in January 1981 provided new political opportunities for the Christian Right. For the lesbian and gay movements, with Reagan's election and the emergence of AIDS in June 1981, the worst was yet to come.

THE 1980s

A Gallup poll had predicted that the 1980 presidential election between Ronald Reagan and the incumbent Democrat Jimmy Carter would be close, but Reagan won with surprising ease—and with considerable help from the New Right and the fundamentalist Christian Right. The political landscape had been fundamentally altered, and not only with respect to the presidency. Republican challengers also upset nine incumbent Democratic Senators, including such liberals as Birch Bayh, Frank Church, John Culver, and George McGovern, thus giving the Republican Party control of the Senate for the first time in nearly thirty years. Republicans gained seats in the House as well. These surprising results left political observers searching for explanations. Jerry Falwell, the head of the recently created Moral Majority, credited conservative Christians for electing Reagan and for defeating so many liberal Senate Democrats (Wilcox 1992, xiii). Falwell's explanation was generally accepted by the mainstream press, and the Moral Majority and other Christian Right organizations attracted tremendous public attention for their impressive grassroots organizing abilities and national voter-turnout campaigns. Other New Right leaders also claimed responsibility for the dramatic changes in the national political landscape. The successes of Richard Viguerie,

Terry Dolan (of the National Conservative Political Action Committee), Howard Phillips (of the Conservative Caucus), Phyllis Schlafly (of the Eagle Forum), and Paul Weyrich (of the Committee for the Survival of a Free Congress) galvanized the modern conservative movement in support of "profamily, single-issue, and religious-right organizations for the capitalist class" (Adam 1995, 121).

For lesbians and gay men, there was little to cheer in the 1980 elections. Despite Reagan's opposition to the Briggs initiative two years earlier, he had courted the most conservative elements of the Republican Party in his bid for the presidency. As a result, he embraced a conservative social agenda, one that celebrated the traditional family and waged an all-out war against those who did not conform to his view of morality. Galvanized to seek the political opportunities that Reagan's election and a more conservative Congress had provided, fundamentalist Christians renewed their assault on lesbians and gays. They were undoubtedly delighted when Senator Roger Jepsen (R-Iowa) introduced the "Family Protection Act" in 1981, an act that would prevent lesbians and gays from receiving Social Security, veterans, or welfare benefits. President Reagan endorsed this legislation. That same year the House of Representatives passed legislation that "prohibited the Legal Services Corporation from accepting discrimination cases filed by [lesbians and] gays" (Streitmatter 1995, 211). Reagan's appointment of Gary Bauer, a close associate of James Dobson, who was president of Focus on the Family, as domestic policy advisor also obviously cheered the Christian Right, despite the fact that Bauer had little actual influence over public policy (Bull and Gallagher 1996, 21).

How did the Christian Right contribute to the dominance of conservatism in national politics during the 1980s? First, it registered hundreds of thousands new voters who could generally be counted upon to support its pro-family views. Second, it successfully infiltrated the Republican Party by recruiting new people at the grass roots to participate in party politics. Third, the Christian Right helped to reshape the political and cultural agenda by taking abortion, school prayer, and pro-family issues more generally, and placing them on the "narrower congressional and broader public agendas" (Moen 1992, 8–9).

AIDS and the Christian Right

It was against this political and cultural backdrop that AIDS emerged in the summer of 1981. In response, some Christian Right organizations, such as the Moral Majority, exploited AIDS hysteria as central elements of their political organizing and fundraising strategies. Jerry Falwell was particularly effective in doing so. For Falwell and other religious conservatives, AIDS represented divine and just retribution for immoral homosexual behavior (Bull and Gallagher 1996, 25–26). As Diamond (1989) put it, "homosexuals [could] now be blamed for the modern-day Plague, fulfilling the time-honored role of scapegoat" (p. 101).

Chapter 4 of this book has already detailed how the President and Congress largely ignored AIDS for the first seven years of the crisis. It is worth recounting how the Christian Right's agenda on AIDS influenced public policy at all levels of government. First and foremost, conservatives vigorously objected to any public school efforts that would introduce safe-sex and AIDS-education programs into the curriculum. Their successes at the height of the epidemic helped to spawn new HIV infections that might well have been prevented by more serious AIDS-education efforts. And as we saw in Chapter 4, conservatives had a vigorous ally in Senator Jesse Helms. The House and Senate both passed the 1987 Helms amendment, which prohibited the use of federal tax dollars for AIDS education materials perceived to "promote or encourage, directly or indirectly, homosexual activities." Helms was not alone in his efforts to insure that the Christian Right's "family values" agenda was codified into law. Representatives Robert Dornan and William Dannemeyer, both California Republicans, aggressively helped to limit federal funding for safer-sex education targeting lesbians and gays. This is no surprise, given that Dannemeyer once claimed that AIDS spread through "spores." His 1989 book, *Shadow in the Land,* identified lesbians and gays as "the ultimate enemy," and as a horde, much like "Genghis Khan's army" (Herman 1997, 64).

From 1986 until 1989, the antigay right organized on behalf of several California pieces of legislation that would have required "draconian measures" in response to people with AIDS. Proposition 64, which was on the California ballot in 1986, "would have allowed the state to restrict the freedom of people with HIV and AIDS" (Vaid 1995, 83). The initiative was defeated by a margin of two to one after a massive lesbian and gay organizing effort; it reappeared in 1988 as Proposition 69 and was defeated again. Representative Dannemeyer initiated Proposition 102 in 1988. This proposition "would have done away with anonymous antibody testing, required mandatory contact tracing, repealed nondiscrimination laws that protected people with HIV, and allowed insurance companies to carry out testing." California's lesbian and gay communities mobilized yet again and defeated Dannemeyer's measure by a margin of 66 percent to 34 percent. Another 1988 ballot initiative, Proposition 96, actually passed. This initiative permitted the nonconsensual HIV testing of any arrested person when requested by an emergency medical worker, firefighter, or law-enforcement officer (ibid.).

The Christian Right suffered a major national defeat when President Reagan appointed C. Everett Koop as surgeon general in 1981. Initially, conservatives were delighted by Koop's appointment in light of his previous anti-abortion crusades. Koop had also consistently stated that homosexuality was a sin, which reassured the Christian Right. But as we saw in Chapter 4, Koop was a staunch defender of federal funding for sexually explicit AIDS education in the schools. In addition, he believed that schools should provide lesbian- and gay-positive educational material. Koop defended his efforts in this way: "You cannot be an efficient health officer with integrity if you let other things get in the way of health messages" (Bull and Gallagher 1996, 21–22). Koop's courageous stance enraged the Christian Right, and he became a special target of William Dannemeyer, Jesse Helms, and Jerry Falwell.

Paul Cameron also took strong exception to Koop's message. As director of the Institute for the Scientific Investigation of Sexuality in Lincoln, Nebraska, Cameron presided over an entire industry devoted to antigay research. His work attracted greater attention in light of AIDS. Cameron's group would later move to Colorado Springs, Colorado, and change its name to the Family Research Institute, which he described as "scientists defending traditional family values." The institute issued a number of lurid pamphlets that linked various social problems to homosexuality. One flyer identified gay sex as a "crime against humanity." Another showed "a grainy photo of a young girl being threatened by an ax-wielding man, presumably gay." Cameron was discredited after he said in a 1981 debate that a four-year-old boy had suffered sexual mutilation in a Lincoln, Nebraska, shopping mall restroom as the result of a "homosexual act." The Lincoln police failed to provide any evidence to support Cameron's claims; the boy was never even located, and the police ultimately concluded the charges were baseless (Bull and Gallagher 1996, 26).

At the height of the AIDS epidemic, Cameron received considerable publicity for several studies that attempted to "demonstrate that gay men brought AIDS on themselves and the rest of the world." He argued that the AIDS epidemic began when promiscuous American gay men engaged in "unsanitary" sexual practices as they enjoyed "worldwide sex tours." He believed that AIDS warranted universal HIV testing as well as the quarantining of anyone who tested positive for the virus antibodies (Bull and Gallagher 1996, 26). That Cameron's shoddy research and bizarre theories received widespread public attention and entered into mainstream conservative thought says something about the reactionary tenor of the times.[7] Bull and Gallagher believe that Cameron's ideas were important to the Christian Right for strategic reasons: "For all its flaws, the religious right was dependent on Cameron's research to supplement its biblical arguments about the supposed deleterious social consequences of homosexuality" (Bull and Gallagher 1996, 27–28). Over time, the work of the Family Research Institute has been largely discredited by mainstream scholars.

The conservative response to the increased visibility and modest progress of the movements gained considerable momentum during the decade of the 1980s. The movements had to deal not only with the realities of the conservative Reagan era but also with an energized Christian Right. This was the political, cultural, and social milieu in which the devastation of AIDS unfolded. As we have seen in Chapter 3, the Supreme Court's 1986 *Bowers v. Hardwick* decision provided judicial legitimacy to the Christian Right's agenda, especially since the Supreme Court had previously avoided ruling definitely on the issue of sodomy laws. The *Bowers* decision's repercussions continue today as it is cited by courts throughout the judicial system to deny basic lesbian and gay rights.

The 1988 Presidential Election

The 1988 elections offered lesbians and gays hope for the future, most importantly because Ronald Reagan could not serve another term. But those hopes were soon dashed when the Democratic Party nominee, Massachusetts governor Michael Dukakis, distanced himself from the lesbian and gay movements. As governor Dukakis spoke on behalf of equal opportunity and protections for lesbian and gay rights, but his record contained little to back up his rhetoric. On the contrary, he had endorsed a policy that prevented lesbian and gay couples from becoming foster parents, which the Supreme Judicial Court of Massachusetts declared unconstitutional in 1990. Tim McFeeley, former director of the Human Rights Campaign Fund, reports that Dukakis's unwillingness to support lesbian and gay rights stemmed from personal discomfort. McFeeley recalls a meeting with Dukakis in 1985 about the foster parent issue, where Dukakis emphatically pounded his fist on the table and proclaimed that he would not publicly support lesbian and gay rights "because it is wrong!" (Vaid 1995, 119).

But if the lesbian and gay Democratic Party establishment was dismayed by Dukakis's refusal to offer public support, it could not have been too surprised when Pat Robertson announced his candidacy for the Republican presidential nomination in 1987. An ordained Baptist minister whose father had served as a Democratic Senator from Virginia, Robertson had never held elective office, although he had been actively involved in Virginia politics for ten years. What was particularly noteworthy about Robertson's background was his ability to build a business empire, which gave him the necessary capital to support his foray into electoral politics. His business success can be connected to his *700 Club* television show, which proved to be quite different from Jerry Falwell's fundamentalist televangelism. Robertson regularly provided a conservative analysis of daily political events. But the program was essentially run as a religious talk show, where conservative guests shared their views with Robertson and Ben Kenslow, his African American co-host (Wilcox 1996, 38).

The three million people who signed petitions asking Robertson to run for President also provided the financial base for his campaign. Christian Right expert Clyde Wilcox points out that many of these contributors regularly viewed his *700 Club* program; most made gifts of $19.88 to join his "1988 Club." Robertson's first campaign finance report to the Federal Election Commission had to be delivered on a sixteen-foot truck; it contained the names of seventy thousand donors (Wilcox 1996, 39). This is a testimony to Robertson's extensive grassroots support in communities throughout the United States.

Robertson's campaign has been seen as a populist crusade that focused largely on domestic issues and emphasized returning America to its moral roots. For example, Robertson lamented the absence of prayer in the public schools, assailed the same schools for failing to teach "the basics" effectively, condemned abortion, and expressed strong opposition to lesbian and gay rights. In the end, Robertson lost badly to George Bush, and while he spent more money on his campaign than any presidential candidate prior to that point, he was able to secure just thirty-five delegates pledged to vote for him at the Republican national convention. He did not carry a single primary and even lost to Bush in his home state of Virginia (Wilcox 1996, 40).

But the meaning of Robertson's candidacy goes well beyond his smashing defeat in the Republican Party primaries. Wilcox argues that "the Robertson campaign was a vital part of the birth of a new, more sophisticated Christian Right." Robertson campaign activists assembled a cadre of skilled political workers who could turn their energies, commitment, and experience to the next Christian Right mobilizing effort. Some argued that, with Robertson's defeat and the disbanding of the Moral Majority, the Christian Right was all but moribund. As lesbian and gay activists can attest, this was hardly the case. Indeed, Robertson launched the Christian Coalition in 1989 out of his failed presidential bid. Armed with funding, grassroots support, a successful television program, and a large national database of supporters and volunteers, Robertson jump-started an organization that was to dominate Christian Right politics in the 1990s. In support of this claim, Urvashi Vaid offered this assessment of the Christian Coalition in 1995: "Under the leadership of the shrewd Ralph Reed, the Christian Coalition has become the most powerful national political organization in the country. Today it boasts fifty state offices, a network built from the precinct level up, more than 1.5 million members, and a budget of more than $20 million annually. Neither of the parties can match this extraordinary grassroots system nor the discipline and focus of its members" (Vaid 1995, 121). Nor can the lesbian and gay movements begin to approximate the vast network that underlies the Christian Coalition today.

The Robertson candidacy had further consequences for the lesbian and gay movements in the 1988 presidential election. Compared to Robertson, George Bush was perceived as a much more moderate candidate; as a result, he appeared to receive considerable support from lesbian and gay voters.[8] Bush's chief campaign strategist, Lee Atwater, fashioned a winning electoral strategy, which included a smart conservative position on lesbian and gay concerns. It was designed to respond to both pro- and anti-gay supporters. Thus, when Bush was questioned about lesbian and gay rights, he responded by affirming those rights and by arguing that all Americans enjoy the same constitutional rights. But as Vaid has pointed out, Bush's response took rhetorical liberties: "Because gay people do not enjoy the same constitutional status as nongay people, the answer was quite devious: it challenged the most basic premise of our movement while seeming to affirm our equality." Bush also adopted various positions on AIDS that exploited both pro- and anti-gay sentiments. For example, he pledged to increase funding for AIDS-related programs while advocating nondiscrimination. But at the same time, he responded to the Christian Right's worst fears about AIDS when he spoke of "protecting the rights of the uninfected" and expressed enthusiastic support for mandatory HIV testing. Bush's espoused goal was to continue Reagan's conservative approach to governance, but to give it a "kinder, gentler" face (Vaid 1995, 121). At the time, he recognized that he needed the support of Pat Robertson's Christian Coalition members, not an easy task given that Bush was perceived as a moderate from a liberal northeastern state (Connecticut). It is proof of the power of the Christian Coalition, Pat Robertson, and the Christian Right more generally that the Bush campaign and the Republican Party recognized the need to accommodate the party's religious conservative wing.

The 1990s

The Christian Right and its conservative supporters shifted strategic gears in the decade of the 1990s.[9] The 1992 Republican national convention in Houston demonstrated that the Republican Party could ill afford to ignore their demands for a more conservative social agenda, which included opposition to lesbian and gay rights. In his convention speech, Pat Buchanan, who had mounted a spirited but ultimately unsuccessful challenge to George Bush in the Republican presidential primary, claimed that "there is a culture war going on in our country for the soul of America. It is a cultural war, as critical to the kind of nation we will one day be as was the Cold War itself" (Bull and Gallagher 1996, 88). The 1992 Republican convention provided Buchanan and the Christian Right an opportunity to demonstrate their political clout. And while they could not celebrate a presidential victory in 1992, they were ready to challenge Bill Clinton and his lesbian and gay supporters once he took office. In 1993 they helped block President Clinton's plan to overturn the military ban by executive order. By the mid 1990s, the Christian Right had sponsored a series of high-profile, anti-gay-rights ballot measures in a number of states, including Colorado. But the Supreme Court's 1996 *Evans v. Romer* decision ruled such measures unconstitutional. As we saw in Chapter 3, the Christian Right has been active in opposing legal recognition of same-sex marriages. It has also challenged school curriculums that it believes undermines the morals of American society. Finally, a coalition of conservative groups, which has included the Christian Coalition and the Family Research Council, organized a highly visible summer 1998 campaign that was designed to portray "gay people as sick patients who could be 'healed' through prayer and counselling" (Andriote 1999, 410). This section considers all of these organizing strategies. As the discussion proceeds, we will see how the Christian Right has effectively altered its political strategies in response to changing political, social, and cultural conditions. In doing so, it has continually thrown the lesbian and gay movements on the defensive.

When Bill Clinton was elected to the White House in 1992, the Christian Right faced a Democratic President for the first time in twelve years. This was not just any Democratic President, for Clinton was the first presidential candidate to promise lesbians and gays that they would be a part of his electoral and governing coalition. And he immediately acted on this promise by attempting to carry out his plan to overturn the ban on lesbians and gays in the United States military. This issue was discussed at length in Chapter 3, but what is particularly important here is how the Christian Right organized to defeat the measure on Capitol Hill and to provide the newly elected President and the lesbian and gay movements with a stunning defeat. Of course, this could not be accomplished alone. Indeed, the Christian Right had plenty of conservative support among the Joint Chiefs of Staff and members of Congress, including such prominent Democrats as Senator Sam Nunn (D-Georgia), who headed the Senate Armed Services Committee at the time.

As we have seen, the Christian Right had gained strength and clout "by its success in bridging religious and political differences during the Reagan and Bush years, spurred in part by the opportunities opened up within the Republican Party for the exercise of conservative political influence" (Rayside 1996, 173). David Rayside reports that the emergence of the military ban issue in the weeks following the 1992 election created a superb political opportunity for an expanding conservative coalition, and proved to be a "bonanza for building organizations and raising money" (ibid.). The military ban debate helped to galvanize the Christian Right in ways that threw both the Clinton administration and lesbian and gay movements on the defensive. Much of this organizing activity converged in the last week of January 1993, as the Christian Right generated a firestorm of protest against Clinton's proposal. It used its national media resources, a virulently antigay film, *The Gay Agenda*,[10] and its church-centered facilities to rally opposition against the plan. Rayside reports that "for most of that week, the Congressional switchboard was handling more than five times its typical daily total of 80,000 calls, in some offices producing tallies that ran 100 to 1 against Clinton's plan." Veteran Hill staffers claimed that few previous issues had generated such an intense response in so short a period of time. To be sure, most of this activity was carefully orchestrated by the Christian Right, although it reminded politicians of the organizing power of religious conservatives, especially around issues pertaining to lesbians and gays (ibid.). The lesbian and gay movements could not begin to match this kind of public response.[11] But even if they had been able to do so, it probably would not have made much of a difference, given that Clinton had begun to compromise on his original promise, that a congressional majority disagreed with his proposal to overturn the ban, and that the U.S. military hierarchy wished to maintain the status quo.[12] Tanya Domi of the National Gay and Lesbian Task Force, and Bob Hattoy, an openly gay appointee in the Clinton administration, support this line of analysis:

> Even if we had done things differently, we would not have won, because the White House walked, the Pentagon did nothing to help us, and we were left really holding the bag, at the same time dealing with a very vigorous right wing that is—in every single appeal that they do, in every single piece on radio and television, every think tank that's working on right wing issues—focusing on the ban and on the gay and lesbian people of America.
>
> All of a sudden the White House, in one corner here, and the gay and lesbian community . . . all had to go into high gear to do probably the most difficult task that the community has faced—to lift the ban in the military. . . . It was the most difficult because we were up against the military might of the United States of America—we're up against the Pentagon—

we're up against the most institutionalized homophobia that you could find in America today. (Rayside 1996, 178)

These proved to be overwhelming obstacles as the lesbian and gay movements attempted to garner broad support for Clinton's original plan. The entire episode not only points to flaws in the lesbian and gay movements' strategy (for example, trusting Clinton far too much, and failing to recognize the importance of building a grassroots strategy that could be tapped for support) but also highlights the strength of the Christian Right, which had been developing over the preceding twenty-five years.

Much of the battle over lesbian and gay rights has been fought in American cities, counties, and states, principally because the United States has no federal anti-discrimination law. We have discussed the battles that occurred in Dade County, Florida and in California over the Briggs initiative during the 1970s. In the 1980s, as increasing numbers of lesbians and gays came out of the closet and became more visible to the larger society, lesbian and gay-rights legislation was adopted in some forty U.S. cities and counties. Among the major cities to adopt gay-rights legislation were Atlanta, Chicago, Philadelphia, and New York. State-level initiatives to protect lesbians and gays developed much more slowly; Wisconsin became the first state to pass legislation protecting lesbians and gays in 1982, after seven years of debate (Button, Rienzo, and Wald 2000, 273).

During the decade of the 1990s there was a large increase in local laws protecting sexual orientation. Button, Rienzo, and Wald (2000) conclude that "by mid-1993 approximately 12 cities and counties had adopted legislation, and by 1996 the figure had increased to an estimated 160 communities. Thus the first seven years of the 1990s produced the adoptions of as many local gay antibias laws as the two previous decades" (pp. 273–74). There are two explanations for this development. First, "following a political process known as 'diffusion of innovation,' suburban governments and counties began to accept the new legislation from larger and more dominant cities" (ibid., p. 273). Second, as more lesbians and gays kicked down the closet doors, they began to demand more protection against discrimination from their local governments.

Button, Rienzo, and Wald show that the communities implementing lesbian and gay rights measures were varied in both size and geographic region; they cite communities like Brighton, New York; Oak Park, Illinois; Rockville, Maryland; LaGrange, Illinois; Troy, Idaho; Lafayette, Indiana; and Henderson, Kentucky, to show the geographic diversity of the areas. There was also a significant increase in the number of lesbian and gay civil rights laws at the state level during the decade of the 1990s. By 1997, eleven states and the District of Columbia had adopted measures banning antigay discrimination. Nine states had enacted their legislation during the 1990s: California, Hawaii, Minnesota, New Jersey, Rhode Island, Vermont, Connecticut, New Hampshire, and Maine. Governors of eight additional states "had issued executive orders to prohibit discrimination on the basis of sexual orientation in state employment" by the mid 1990s (Button, Rienzo, and Wald 2000, 274–75).

The antigay right responded to these new protections with a vigorous organizing campaign, making the ordinances central targets. Those who oppose lesbian and gay rights have been successful in using the citizens' initiative as a political tool in the battle over sexual orientation. The lesbian and gay movements and the antigay right intersected in campaigns over voter referendums aimed at repealing existing laws protecting lesbians and gays. Major state-level battles occurred in Colorado, Idaho, Maine, and Oregon, and at the local level in cities such as Cincinnati, Portland, Maine, and Tampa.

The most widely publicized referendum of the 1990s occurred in Colorado. The conflict over Amendment 2 to the Colorado state constitution is particularly interesting because it involved intense organizing on each side and received considerable national attention. It is also significant because Colorado voters had overwhelmingly passed a ban on all lesbian and gay anti-discrimination laws in 1992. The attempt to overturn this ban ultimately went to the U.S. Supreme Court; the matter was not finally resolved until 1996, when the Court issued its important *Evans v. Romer* decision.

The Colorado Battle

The 1992 elections gave the lesbian and gay movements two major reasons for celebration. First, Bill Clinton captured the White House and wrested control of the presidency from the Republican Party for the first time in twelve years. And in Oregon an antigay initiative was defeated that would have prevented the state from "promoting" homosexuality and would have nullified existing local lesbian and gay rights ordinances (Bull and Gallagher 1996, 39). But the success of Colorado's antigay initiative dampened the enthusiasm of lesbian and gay activists. It showed, as well, how persuasive the Christian Right's antigay message could be among voters and how much work lesbian and gay movements still had to do in terms of educating and organizing at the state and local levels.

Didi Herman argues that "Amendment 2 was a logical progression in a national, concerted CR antigay effort of over two decades' duration" (Herman 1997, 138). In retrospect, Colorado was a logical site for such an important fight. Opponents of lesbian and gay rights had established themselves in the state long before the 1992 elections; chapters of important national organizations, such as Lou Sheldon's Traditional Values

Coalition,[13] were located there. Various national Christian Right groups were also headquartered there, most notably Focus on the Family, which located in Colorado Springs in 1991 (Bull and Gallagher 1996, 97). The Family Research Council (FRC) is the political organization associated with Focus on the Family, which is headed by James Dobson. Dobson also runs a radio ministry that broadcasts its message daily to listeners on more than fifteen hundred stations.[14] While Dobson and his organization are integral components of the Christian Right, he strongly rejects this label and insists "instead that his organization is pro-family." Scholars of the Christian Right have pointed out, however, that "his background, rhetoric, and agenda clearly fit within the Christian Right mainstream" (Wilcox 1996, 63–64).

Conservative activists had organized in Colorado previously. In fact, the state had been the site for fights over sexual-orientation discrimination laws since the early 1970s. The first battle took place in 1974, when the Boulder city council enacted a measure forbidding discriminatory employment practices that targeted sexual minorities. This law triggered such strong public controversy that the city council decided that the voters should judge its merits. Boulder voters overwhelmingly defeated the ordinance, but in 1987, when asked again whether they wished to prohibit discrimination based on sexual orientation, they said "yes." Keen and Goldberg believe that at least in Boulder, "the gay civil rights movement had made some gains in the 13 years since that first referendum" (Keen and Goldberg 1998, 6).

The lesbian and gay movements had mixed success in Colorado. For example, in November 1998 voters in Fort Collins, Colorado, rejected an amendment to the town's human-rights ordinance that would have protected lesbians and gays. But in 1990 the Denver city council had approved the same ordinance. And when conservatives organized a referendum aimed at repealing the new law, Denver voters turned it down. Another victory occurred when Democratic governor Roy Romer issued an executive order in 1989 that prohibited discrimination against those with AIDS. And the Colorado Civil Rights Commission entered into the fray when it "recommended that the state adopt a law prohibiting discrimination based on sexual orientation" in July 1991 (Keen and Goldberg 1998, 6–8).

But what happened in Colorado Springs in 1991 can now be seen as a harbinger of the Christian Right's success in organizing at the grassroots. In Colorado Springs, politically a much more conservative community than either Boulder or Denver, conservative organizations, including Focus on the Family, organized effectively against the law proposed by the Colorado Civil Rights Commission, and the idea was subsequently dropped. Three leaders of the Christian Right's organizing efforts in Colorado Springs—

David Noebel, Tony Marco, and Kevin Tebedo—were not content with their victory; they wished to repeal other prohibitions on discrimination against lesbians and gays. They formed a new organization—Colorado for Family Values (CFV)—and recruited Will Perkins, a local car dealer, as chairperson. The Denver *Post* summarized their worldview: "America has deteriorated because it has turned away from literal interpretations of the Bible, and fundamentalist church teachings must play a bigger role in government" (quoted in Keen and Goldberg 1998, p. 7). This group launched a statewide campaign that not only defeated the Colorado Springs anti-discrimination ordinance but also succeeded in repealing the governor's executive order and anti-discrimination laws in Aspen, Boulder, and Denver. Their broader agenda was to insure that no further sexual-orientation anti-discrimination measures could be passed in the state. This was the context for the statewide battle that erupted over Amendment 2, one that soon became a national conflict, traveling all the way to the U.S. Supreme Court.

On November 3, 1992, Colorado voters voted 53 percent to 46 percent to approve Amendment 2, which appeared on the statewide ballot through the efforts of the Colorado for Family Values organization. The goal of the initiative was "to amend the state constitution to: (1) repeal any existing law or policy that protected a person with a 'homosexual, lesbian, or bisexual orientation' from discrimination in Colorado and any of its cities, towns, counties, and school boards and (2) prohibit future adoption or enforcement of 'any [such] law or policy'" (Keen and Goldberg 1998, 3). The ballot question stated:

NO PROTECTED STATUS BASED ON HOMOSEXUAL, LESBIAN OR BISEXUAL ORIENTATION. Neither the State of Colorado, through any of its branches or departments, nor any of its agencies, political subdivisions, municipalities or school districts, shall enact, adopt or enforce any statute, regulation, ordinance or policy whereby homosexual, lesbian, or bisexual orientation, conduct, practices, or relationships shall constitute or otherwise be the basis of or entitle any person or class of persons to have or claim any minority status, quota preferences, protected status or claim of discrimination. (Keen and Goldberg 1998, 3)

The question at the core of the debate over Amendment 2 was, "Are gays and lesbians so politically powerless and discriminated against that they merit special legal protection from discrimination?" Colorado voters and the courts were wrestling with the fundamental issue of whether lesbians and gays "are 'genuine minorities' who deserve or need 'special rights'" (Gertsmann 1999, 91).

Antigay activists had already filed initiative petitions from 1992 to 1995 in a number of states—Arizona, Colorado, Florida, Idaho, Maine,

Mississippi, Missouri, Nevada, Oregon, and Washington—in an effort to repeal existing laws that protected lesbians and gays from discrimination (Donovan, Wenzel, and Bowler 2000, 174).[15] Opponents made effective use of political language in challenging these measures. One example is the slogan "equal rights, not special rights." Several arguments were communicated by this adroit use of language, as Donovan, Wenzel, and Bowler (2000, 174) make clear:

> [It implied that] the extension of antidiscrimination protections to certain classes of citizens constituted an extraordinary legal status to which most people were not entitled. The overt argument was that although race, religion, and gender might constitute necessary categories of citizens requiring protections against discrimination, sexual orientation did not. Sponsors of antigay initiatives argued that if ugly people and short people suffered from discrimination yet were protected only by existing laws, why should homosexuals require "special protections?"

Colorado for Family Values' ability to frame the Amendment 2 debate in terms of "special rights" for lesbians and gays clearly helped provide the slim margin of victory.[16] Public opinion polls had indicated that most Colorado voters did not favor measures that would discriminate against lesbians and gays.[17] Proponents of Amendment 2 realized that, in order to secure victory, they would need "to frame the debate not in terms of discrimination, but as a debate over whether gays and lesbians should enjoy a special legal status" (Gertsmann 1999, 91). The discussion was framed so well from the vantage point of CFV and its Christian Right supporters that "many of the voters believed they were debating whether gays and lesbians should benefit from the whole panoply of civil rights that racial minorities receive—especially qualification for affirmative action programs" (ibid.). Proponents invoked constitutional doctrine in an effort to provide legitimacy to their argument "that the debate over Amendment 2 was a debate over whether gays and lesbians should be treated as a 'protected' or 'special' class" (ibid., pp. 91–92).[18]

Many groups that exist to protect civil rights for minorities strongly objected to Amendment 2, including the Anti-Defamation League of B'nai B'rith, Colorado Black Women for Political Action, the Colorado Hispanic League, and the National Organization for Women. These organizations were especially concerned about the portion of Amendment 2 that sought to block lesbians and gays from seeking any further legislative protections. Keen and Goldberg explain their concern: "If CFV and others could convince the public that laws prohibiting discrimination against lesbians and gay men amounted to 'special rights,' it would be easier, then, to characterize existing antidiscrimination laws protecting other minorities the same way." One organization, the Colorado Hispanic League, issued a public statement that spoke to these concerns: "If the civil rights, privacy, privileges and protections of citizens can be restricted because of sexual orientation, what protects Hispanics from similar initiatives based on equally arbitrary reasons?" (quoted in Keen and Goldberg 1998, 12). In response to such concerns, CFV's Will Perkins argued that "special rights" awarded to people based on race or gender were acceptable; the problem was if they were given to people "because of what [they were] doing in their bedroom" (ibid.). CFV also had to be careful not to appear too eager "to convert its religious beliefs about homosexuality into law," thus violating "the Constitution's separation of church and state" (ibid., pp. 12–13). Nevertheless, critics viewed the campaign for Amendment 2 as an attempt by the Christian Right to impose its religious view of homosexuality on Colorado citizens, thus violating both religious freedom and the separation of church and state. When the constitutionality of Amendment 2 was challenged through the legal process, the plaintiffs' lawsuit claimed that "this 'special rights' and 'religious freedom' approach to the law" consigned "gay men, lesbians, and bisexuals to a second-class citizenship" (ibid., p. 13).

Amendment 2 had drastic consequences for lesbians, gays, bisexuals, and transgendered people in Colorado. Not only did it eliminate the few "existing local ordinances that offered protections based on sexual orientation, but more importantly, it placed an absolute bar to the ability of gays, lesbians, and bisexuals to seek such protection in future" (Donovan, Wenzel, and Bowler 2000, 174). Interestingly, the passage of Amendment 2 meant that this newly created class of persons had only one recourse available to them: an appeal to the very same Colorado voters in the hope that they would pass yet another constitutional amendment, one overturning Amendment 2 (ibid.).

In response to Amendment 2, the lesbian and gay movements soon organized a massive national boycott of Colorado tourism and also began exploring their options for legal redress. Lesbian and gay citizens (including the tennis star Martina Navratilova and Denver city employee Richard Evans) challenged the constitutionality of Amendment 2, arguing in the Colorado courts that it denied equal protection. The Colorado Supreme Court supported this claim. It issued a ruling in *Evans v. Romer* favorable to lesbians and gays, stating in part that: "'the Equal Protection Clause of the Fourteenth Amendment to the United States Constitution protects a fundamental right to participate equally in the political process' and 'that any legislation or state constitutional amendment which infringes on this right by 'fencing out' an independently identifiable class of persons must be subjected to strict legal scrutiny'" (quoted in Donovan, Wenzel, and Bowler 2000, 174–75). The court rejected the argument that sexual orientation should denote a "suspect class"; instead, it "identified a fundamental right" to "'participate equally in the political process,' and then held Amendment 2 to a strict standard of judicial scrutiny" (ibid., p. 176).

In appealing the state Supreme Court decision to the U.S. Supreme Court, the state of Colorado argued that "the statute did not offend the Fourteenth Amendment because it did not deprive the gay community of anything" (Donovan, Wenzel, and Bowler 2000, 176). The state argued, as well, that Amendment 2 placed lesbians, gays, and bisexuals "on the same legal footing as all other citizens of Colorado" by denying "special rights" to them. If lesbians and gays needed any form of protection, they could access those general protections available to all Colorado citizens. Furthermore, the state claimed that "to preclude discrimination of gays on the part of employers and landlords was to in effect interfere with employers' and landlords' freedom of association and their free exercise of religion" (ibid.).

The conflicts in the Colorado Supreme Court over Amendment 2 had attracted considerable national attention, which was renewed when the U.S. Supreme Court chose to hear *Romer v. Evans*. This was the first lesbian and gay rights case that the Supreme Court had chosen to review since *Bowers v. Hardwick* in 1986. Chapter 3 has already indicated that lesbians and gays have "consistently been granted the lowest possible level of protection under the equal protection clause." A number of federal courts had interpreted the *Bowers* decision "as placing the Supreme Court's imprimatur on this lack of judicial protection" (Gertsmann 1999, 127). The plaintiffs in the *Romer* case were hopeful that the Supreme Court would change its position on lesbian and gay rights and issue the Christian Right an important defeat. With its 6-3 decision, the Supreme Court did not disappoint. In rejecting the state of Colorado's arguments, the majority wrote:

> In any event, even if, as we doubt, homosexuals can find some safe harbor in laws of general application, we cannot accept the view that Amendment 2's prohibition on specific protections does no more than deprive homosexuals of special rights. To the contrary, the amendment imposes a special disability upon those persons alone. Homosexuals are forbidden the safeguards that others enjoy or may seek without constraint. (Donovan, Wenzel, and Bowler 2000, 176)

The *Romer* decision is of crucial importance because of the message that it sent to the Christian Right and other antigay activists. The Court clearly rejected the central "special rights" argument put forth by proponents of antigay initiatives over the previous five years. In addition, it reaffirmed that when a class of citizens seeks protections from their government, it does not constitute a request for "special rights" (Donovan, Wenzel, and Bowler 2000, 178). This was a huge victory for the lesbian and gay movements and a defeat for the Christian Right and its supporters. And the victory was accomplished without the support of the Clinton administration, which inexplicably failed to file a friend of the court brief on behalf of the plaintiffs in the case.

Although the Christian Right still pursued antigay initiatives after *Romer*, clearly the ruling made it much more difficult to block lesbians and gays from appealing to legislatures for civil rights protections. Antigay activists have targeted a variety of policy areas with initiatives, recognizing that Donovan, Wenzel, and Bowler's empirical work indicates that "incremental" efforts aimed at reversing recent lesbian and gay advances in anti-discrimination laws are generally successful, while "nonincremental" policy changes, such as freezing existing laws or erecting barriers to lesbian and gay progress, are much less successful. Proposals that involve major departures from existing laws to penalize lesbians and gays are the final class of referendums; these are the least successful.

The Christian Right has organized to challenge gay adoptions through initiative petitions in a number of states, including Washington, but these petitions failed to qualify due to procedural difficulties. State affiliates of Focus on the Family organized contributors in mid 1999 to fund "action to stop the homosexual assault on schoolchildren, marriage, and society" (quoted in Donovan, Wenzel, and Bowler 2000, 180). A number of issues were at stake here, including whether same-sex marriage could be discussed in school curriculums, whether lesbian and gay clubs could be organized in public schools, and various policies that impinged on lesbian and gay adoption. Propositions opposing lesbian and gay marriage were referred to voters by state legislatures in Alaska and Hawaii in November 1998. If the Defense of Marriage Act (DOMA) laws had not been passed by state legislatures and Congress in 1997 and 1998, several lesbian and gay marriage initiatives might well have appeared on state ballots in 1998. As these and other examples suggest, the Christian Right continued to pursue initiative organizing after *Romer*. It soon proved adept, once again, at altering its tactics in response to the changing political, social, and legal landscape. And the victory of Amendment 2 was a reminder of the incredible resources available to the Christian Right, especially when compared to the paucity of national networks and limited financial resources available to the lesbian and gay movements. Bull and Gallagher (1996) argue that "such inadequacy left local activists to reinvent the same wheel time and again and proved to be one of the most enduring failures of the national gay movement" (p. 114). The structural and institutional advantages of the Christian Right would come together to throw the lesbian and gay movements on the defensive yet again in a number of arenas.

Curricular Battles

Given that schools have long been regarded as having important responsibilities for the moral development of youth, it is no surprise that the Christian Right has organized in communities throughout the United States to prevent the discussion of sexual orientation in school curriculums. These efforts have been generally effective, thus reinforcing the anti-lesbian and antigay climate that exists in virtually all American educational institutions. Lesbian and gay students are the targets of daily verbal harassment, and some are physically abused as well. Educational institutions reinforce the larger society's heterosexism by tolerating antigay jokes and harassment and by promoting heterosexual coupling (Button, Rienzo, and Wald 1997, 139). The Gay, Lesbian, and Straight Education Network (GLSEN), a national organization devoted to preventing antigay bias in schools, reports that these problems are pervasive. GLSEN estimates that in 1998, "80% of gay, lesbian, and bisexual youth were verbally attacked" and "that 33% of gay, lesbian, and bisexual students say they are not comfortable being out at school" (Meyer 1999, 34). Some estimates suggest that one-third of all suicides among adolescents involve teenagers who are struggling with how society treats their homosexuality (Bull and Gallagher 1996, 221).

In the 1990s, schools became an arena for the politics of lesbian and gays rights, as activists targeted school boards in an effort to persuade them to adopt curriculums that promote nonjudgmental discussions of homosexuality and safe-sex education within the context of AIDS. One educator, Karen Harbeck, believes that when homosexuality and education come together for public discussion, they provoke "one of the most publicly volatile and personally threatening debates in our national history" (Button, Rienzo, and Wald 1997, 148). The volatile 1992 debate over New York City's "Children of the Rainbow" multicultural curriculum provides plenty of evidence to support this claim. New York City emerged as a battleground between the Christian Right and the lesbian and gay grassroots movements when Joseph Fernandez, then chancellor of its school system, attempted to implement his "Children of the Rainbow" program. This curriculum was the "first-grade portion of the multicultural Rainbow Curriculum, which dealt with, among other issues, gay and lesbian families" (Bronski 1998, 133). Sexual orientation occupied a minor, but important, part of the entire plan; the curriculum was rooted in the assumption that the potential for homosexuality exists in students.

"Children of the Rainbow" articulated this assumption in the following way: "Teachers of first graders have an opportunity to give children a healthy sense of identity at an early age. Classes should include references to lesbians and gays in curricular areas and should avoid exclusionary practices by presuming a person's sexual orientation, reinforcing stereotypes, or speaking of lesbians and gays as 'they' or 'other.'" Two related books chosen for classroom use were *Heather Has Two Mommies* and *Daddy's Roommate* (ibid.). "Children of the Rainbow" and the broader multicultural Rainbow Curriculum received the support of former Mayor David Dinkins in addition to Chancellor Fernandez.

The Christian Right responded to this curricular initiative with disdain, however. New York's Roman Catholic Archdiocese and a coalition of right-wing community groups organized against it when the curriculum was still being developed and considered for adoption. The conservative Family Defense Council distributed a flyer that said, "We will not accept two people of the same sex engaged in deviant sex practices as 'family.' . . . In the fourth grade the Chancellor would demonstrate to pupils how to use condoms. . . . He would teach our kids that sodomy is acceptable but virginity is something weird" (quoted in Bronski 1998, 133). Ultimately, Fernandez lost his job as a result of the controversy generated by the Rainbow Curriculum, giving the Christian and antigay Right a major victory. The school board members who voted to remove him specifically objected to his "neglect of basic problems of the city's educational system like low reading and math scores and conditions in the schools [while he] concentrated his energies on a controversial social agenda." During a five-hour public hearing sponsored by the school board, "talk of condoms and homosexuals . . . dominated many of the speakers' comments" (Button, Rienzo, and Wald 1997, 148). Button, Rienzo, and Wald's interviews in various other communities revealed that the highly publicized Fernandez case had "a chilling effect on their . . . efforts to address sexual orientation issues and youth." The authors quote a Raleigh, North Carolina, school official as saying, "Controversy causes administration to go into denial—to pretend sexual orientation doesn't exist—and hope that nothing forces us to handle the issue. . . . I believe there are teachers who will talk with students one-on-one, but they don't feel like they can say anything about sexual orientation aloud in the classroom—they are out on a limb" (ibid., 149).

This timidity was apparent in other cities studied by the authors, including Iowa City and Cincinnati. To the extent that it is the norm in schools throughout the United States, it helps to reinforce the worst assumptions about lesbians and gays. In institutions where difficult issues are supposed to be examined with tolerance and respect for difference, lesbian and gay teachers remain closeted for fear of harassment, ridicule, and, even more seriously, loss of job. To the extent that the Christian and antigay Right continues to create a context for these sorts of attitudes, it challenges the fundamental tenets of the lesbian and gay liberation movements that are at the core of this book.

The Christian Right Targets Same-Sex Marriage

The battle over same-sex marriage provided another occasion for antigay groups to target lesbians and gays while mobilizing opposition at the grass roots. Chapter 3 discussed how same-sex marriage has been addressed by the legal process as well as by the President and Congress. We saw that the antigay Right organized in response to the 1993 *Baehr* and 1996 court of appeals decisions in the state of Hawaii. These decisions, which essentially endorsed same-sex marriage by ruling the Hawaii Marriage Law unconstitutional, led more than half of the states to enact some form of ban on same-sex marriages, largely as a result of the grassroots work of the Christian Right and its supporters. We have also seen how the President and Congress lent their support to the Christian Right's efforts when the virulently anti-lesbian and antigay 1996 Defense of Marriage Act (DOMA) was passed by Congress and signed into law by President Clinton. Clinton even championed his support of the measure on Christian radio during the fall 1996 presidential campaign; the ad was pulled after protests by lesbian and gay movement members. We have also seen that the antigay Right has responded to the Vermont Supreme Court's historic December 1999 decision, which mandates that lesbians and gays are entitled to the "common benefits and protections" that heterosexual couples already receive (Freiberg 2000, 1). Soon after the Vermont decision, legislators expressed considerable interest in prohibiting same-sex marriages in at least seven states.

The ability of the Christian Right to mobilize at the grass roots in response to lesbian and gay marriage raises important questions about whether securing same-sex marriage should be at the core of the lesbian and gay movements' political and social agenda. The Christian Right has been effective over the years in promoting the message that "Adam and Eve, not Adam and Steve" should be the norm in any decent society. The slogan has been used with considerable effect on Christian Right call-in shows and appears on protest signs at lesbian and gay rights marches. Sara Diamond believes that it has been particularly effective because "it captures the essence of what the Christian Right fears about homosexuals: that their unions, by definition, threaten biblical order and traditional gender relations" (Diamond 1998, 169). The slogan has also been effective because it targets a substantial element of society that assumes and celebrates heteronormativity.

The Christian Right's Campaign to "Cure" Lesbians and Gays

The Christian Right is composed of a variety of different organizations, which intersect with the lesbian and gay movements in unique ways. One initiative that received national attention in the mid 1990s was the "ex-gay movement," which boasts Exodus International as one of its leading organizations. A California-based umbrella group, Exodus International represents "some two hundred counseling ministries intent on convert-ing homosexuals out of their lifestyle" (Diamond 1998, 164). The polit-ical scientist John Green points out that Exodus International has an ambiguous relationship to groups that oppose lesbian and gay rights. Exodus International cooperates with such groups, but appears outwardly to be far less hostile to individual lesbians and gays (Green 2000, 126). In the summer of 1998, the ex-gay movement worked with Christian Right groups, including the Christian Coalition and the Family Research Council, to launch a high-profile, national campaign "aimed at portray-ing gay people as sick patients who could be 'healed' through prayer and counseling" (Andriote 1999, 410).

The campaign culminated in a national media blitz celebrating ex-gays. The movement took out full-page ads in the New York *Times* and other newspapers throughout the United States, more evidence of the Christian Right's enormous resources and ability to build coalitions rooted in hatred of those who challenge their views of morality. It is also a reminder that the lesbian and gay movements face multiple obstacles as they attempt to challenge a society that continues to reinforce and cele-brate narrow visions of heteronormativity.

Christian Radio

In recent years, the Christian Right has effectively used Christian radio to promote its antigay politics. Earlier in this chapter we discussed how Pat Robertson's *700 Club* television program has promoted his Christian Right agenda and built a network of supporters at the grass roots. James Dob-son is widely acknowledged as the nation's largest religious broadcaster after Robertson; he has used his radio commentaries to promote the agenda of the Christian Right, and specifically of his organization, Focus on the Family. In October 1998, Dobson learned of a syndicated newspaper col-umn written by Gannett News Service reporter Deborah Mathis that impli-cated him and other religious conservatives in the murder of University of Wyoming undergraduate Matthew Shepard. Dobson responded with a public commentary on his radio program, which is heard in millions of homes throughout the United States. (One reliable estimate suggests that Dobson's programs can be heard by 660 million people in some ninety-five countries; 3,023 broadcast facilities, "including some secular stations, carry Focus on the Family programming" [Johnson, 2000, p. 30].) As part of his message, Dobson encouraged his supporters to contact Mathis in protest; she quickly received thousands of calls. This is just one example of how Dobson has been successful in using his radio broadcasts for organizing purposes. Dobson's radio program is also identified as the vehicle that propelled Gary Bauer into the race for the 2000 Republican presidential nomination. Bauer is a Dobson protégé and has appeared on his radio show on a number of occasions.

Of course, Dobson is not alone in using radio to promote a conservative view of morality and an antigay message. Michael Reagan, the son of the former President, offers conservative radio commentary that reaches into forty-four states. In 1999 Reagan became the executive director of the Campaign for Working Families, which is an antigay political action committee that was associated for a time with the Family Research Council. Reagan's show has featured a number of antigay guests, including Randy Thomasson, "a leading proponent of the Knight initiative, the California ballot measure to ban recognition of gay marriages" (Johnson 2000, 31).

But perhaps the talk-radio host with the broadest visibility has been Dr. Laura Schlessinger, through her *Dr. Laura* show. Schlessinger's program, which is heard through 165 outlets that cover more than 90 percent of the United States, reaches 20 million listeners a week. Some fifty thousand people call her every day, though only about twenty-five actually get on the air. The New York *Times* has called her "the most-listened-to talk radio personality in the country" (Bronski 2000, 10). As a part of her homophobic attacks, she communicates this message regularly: "When God created Adam 'he didn't get Adam another guy. He didn't get Adam three guys. He got Adam a woman'" (Johnson 2000, 30). Schlessinger also encouraged her radio listeners and visitors to her Web site to protest Vermont's December 1999 decision on same-sex marriage by contacting Vermont state legislators in protest. She is particularly hostile to same-sex marriage, which she sees as "simply contrary to God's plan" (ibid.). And she claims that both science and God support her views of homosexuality: "If you're gay or lesbian, it's a biological error that inhibits you from relating normally to the opposite sex. The fact that you are intelligent, creative, and valuable is all true. The error is in your inability to relate sexually, intimately, in a loving way to a member of the opposite sex. It is a biological error." And she rejects the notion of lesbian and gay rights by arguing, "Rights? For sexual deviants ... there are no rights. That's what I'm worried about, with all the pedophilia and the bestiality and the sadomasochism and the cross-dressing. Is this all going to be 'rights' too, to deviant sexual behavior? Why does deviant sexual behavior get rights?" (Bronski 2000, 11).

The lesbian and gay movements have begun to fight back against Schlessinger. There is now an anti–Dr. Laura Web site, which has demanded that the Paramount company cancel her show. In the six months following its debut, the site received more than three million hits and organizers have planned other ways to target Dr. Laura. The Gay and Lesbian Alliance against Defamation (GLADD) arranged a winter 2000 meeting with her to discuss how her comments were creating a hostile climate for lesbians and gays. Because she largely rejected GLADD's arguments, the organization then met with Paramount executives to warn them that her inflammatory remarks are unacceptable. But GLADD was not satisfied with Paramount's tepid response or Schlessinger's lame apology, in which she claimed that lesbian and gay listeners probably misunderstood her: "Words that I have used in a clinical context have been perceived as judgment" (quoted in Bronski 2000, 11–12). Further challenges to Paramount and Dr. Laura's program continued through 2001.

The fact that the lesbian and gay movements recognize the importance of counter-organizing is integral to building an effective response to the efforts of the Christian Right and other antigay activists who use television and radio broadcasts as a vehicle for mobilizing supporters, building grassroots organizations, and communicating their narrow vision of morality. But as we have already seen, the Christian Right has considerable resource and network advantages here as well.

Conclusion and Implications

This chapter has made three broad arguments. First, the survey of the Christian Right's organizing efforts since the late 1970s indicates that it has been remarkably successful in adapting to changes in the political and social landscape. It has done particularly well in taking advantage of changing political opportunities under Presidents Ronald Reagan, George Bush, and Bill Clinton. As we have seen, the Christian Right has the advantage of well-developed local and national networks, as well as institutional and financial resources that dwarf those available to the lesbian and gay movements. Second, for the foreseeable future, the latter cannot hope to match the Christian Right's ability to organize at the grass roots. But the events of the past twenty-five years suggest that the lesbian and gay movements need to rethink their messages and strategies. More specifically, as I discuss in Chapter 6, they must develop their own sophisticated grassroots mobilizing and organizing strategies at the local and state levels. There are a number of barriers to doing so, not the least of which is a tendency for some sectors of the movements to look to our national organizations and national-level politics and policy for leadership. But we need a new conception of leadership, one that celebrates grassroots organizing in communities and states throughout the United States. Finally, this chapter has argued that the Christian Right has done particularly well in throwing the lesbian and gay movements on the defensive over the years, as the discussions of the Miami–Dade County ordinance, the Briggs initiative, the ban on military service, Colorado's Amendment 2, same-sex marriage, and battles over school curriculums suggest. The movements have too often found themselves reacting to the Christian Right rather than promoting an agenda of their own. This situation is unlikely to change anytime soon, although we might imagine a different kind of organizational strategy, one that attempts to build viable lesbian and gay movements at the grassroots and stresses the importance of political, social, and cultural change rooted in education. There is considerable evidence that the lesbian and gay movements already recognize the importance of such a strategy. Chapter 6 addresses these concerns in considerable detail.

6   Critical Reflections
on the Movements' Futures

Trying to find common ground for political mobilization among all these identities has become one of the most difficult tasks of what has come to be called
the gay rights movement.

—Robert Bailey

Getting specific is the prerequisite for a politics that is neither vanguardist nor
blandly pluralist, that recognizes differences as important and enduring and difficult and works not to erase or eliminate those differences but to weave the
threads that might link us.

—Shane Phelan

ALTHOUGH LIBERAL DEMOCRACY has guaranteed some lesbian
and gay rights, what are its limits? Is it possible for the lesbian and gay
movements to link identity concerns with a progressive coalition working on behalf of political, social, and economic change? What are the barriers to doing so? What might such a project look like in practice? Central to this book, these questions are at the core of this final chapter as
well. Our discussion thus far has provided an overview of several different strategies for pursuing political change, including the mainstream,
insider, assimilationist approaches that are most often associated with
electoral politics, interest-group liberalism, and legal-rights strategies.

As we have seen, the goal of equal rights is the centerpiece of the contemporary lesbian and gay rights movements' strategies. This rights-based
approach has dominated mainstream movement thinking from the early
years of the homophile movement to today's debates over the ban on military service and same-sex marriage. A minority group framework has
provided lesbians and gays with legitimacy by aligning them with other
identity-based movements, including the civil rights and women's movements. This narrow, rights-based perspective, rooted in identity politics,
has largely been unquestioned by the mainstream contemporary lesbian
and gay movements, especially those that dominate politics at the national
level. But this perspective, in and of itself, is far too limiting, as it often
ignores the economic and social inequalities that provide opportunities

for coalition building across class, racial, gender and workplace divides. It also fails to provide an effective challenge to the Christian Right's vast organizing efforts. This chapter discusses such issues as health care, income inequality, and child care, which are ripe for the kind of coalition building that would enable the contemporary lesbian and gay movements to transcend narrowly constructed identity politics. Building these coalitions is no easy task, but it is crucial to do so as we pursue a political strategy that embraces both cultural and political transformation. We will need to build long-term movements from the bottom up, and reject a top-down, elite-centered lesbian and gay politics. This strategy is what I call a radical democratic politics. It encourages lesbians and gays "to understand identity as less fixed and, therefore, a function of history and public discourse" (Lehr 1999, 12).[1] As it does so, this radical democratic conception both challenges and destabilizes "heterosexuality's claim to normalcy" (Herman 1994, 145). But this crucial goal cannot be accomplished by merely pursuing a narrow civil rights agenda; it requires a broad-based cultural strategy as well.

In order to make the case for a more progressive, coalition-based political program, it is important to discuss why a narrowly based identity politics is far too limiting if the goal is to challenge established views of heteronormativity that are often reflected in such public policy outcomes as the rejection of same-sex marriage and the military ban, as well as to challenge the messages and the vast organizing efforts of the Christian Right. The record of the interaction between the lesbian and gay movements and the Clinton administration, and the start of the presidency of George W. Bush, together provide an excellent opportunity to evaluate the limitations of the pluralist, insider approach to politics.

THE CLINTON RECORD ON LESBIAN AND GAY RIGHTS

The Promises and Disappointments

Bill Clinton's election to the White House in November 1992 provided the lesbian and gay movements with considerable optimism about the future. After twelve long years of Republican Party control of the White House, and the concomitant ascendancy of conservative notions of morality, lesbian and gay activists anticipated political and social conditions more favorable for the extension of lesbian and gay rights. After all, candidate Clinton had campaigned vigorously for lesbian and gay contributions and votes. He had promised to increase funding for HIV/AIDS, overturn the military ban, provide lesbians and gays with greater access to his administration than previous presidents had done, appoint openly lesbian and gay officials to his administration, support a gay civil rights bill, and issue an executive order that would bar discrimination on the basis of sexual orientation in all federal agencies.

We know that Clinton faced a number of barriers as he attempted to carry out his campaign promises: he had virtually no governing coalition, as he won with only 43 percent of the popular vote; his own Democratic Party was hardly united on whether lesbian and gay concerns should be on the policy agenda of the new administration; and he suffered from a very short honeymoon period that essentially collapsed in the wake of his attempt to overturn the military ban. Clinton disappointed lesbian and gay activists by failing to issue an executive order to eliminate the military ban. In addition, he was justifiably assailed for running an ad celebrating his signing of the Defense of Marriage Act (DOMA) on Christian radio stations during the 1996 presidential campaign, especially since he had criticized the authors of DOMA for attempting to inject such a volatile issue into the campaign. In the legal battle over Colorado's Amendment 2, the Clinton administration received considerable criticism when the Justice Department failed to file a friend-of-the-court brief on behalf of lesbian and gay groups that were seeking to have the measure declared unconstitutional. While it appears the decision not to act was taken by Attorney General Janet Reno, it clearly was not opposed by the President. When the Supreme Court issued its 1996 *Romer v. Evans* decision, which ruled Colorado's Amendment 2 unconstitutional, many lesbian and gay activists tempered their anger. But their willingness to do so speaks volumes about the mainstream lesbian and gay movements' interaction with the Clinton administration over time.

The discussion in Chapter 4 suggests that Clinton's record on HIV/AIDS policy was mixed. While he had promised during the campaign to rescind the Bush administration's rule that barred persons who were HIV-positive from entering the United States, even for a visit, he failed to provide the necessary leadership on the issue. In early 1993, Republicans approved an amendment to a Department of Health and Human Services authorization bill that converted the rule into a law. The Clinton administration spoke out against the amendment, but AIDS activists believed that the response was half-hearted. In the end, Clinton antagonized lesbian, gay, and AIDS activists by refusing to veto the HHS bill that contained the HIV ban (Chibbaro 1996a, 21).

The Clinton administration was also criticized for failing to "lift a nine-year-old ban on Federal financing for programs to distribute clean needles to drug addicts, even as the Government's top scientists certified that such programs did not encourage drug abuse and could save lives by reducing the spread of AIDS" (Stolberg 1998, A1). AIDS activists faulted the President for ignoring substantial evidence indicating that lifting the ban was the morally right and wise policy decision.

Finally, the Clinton administration's failure to overhaul the health care system meant that increasing numbers of Americans, many of whom are HIV positive or who have been diagnosed with AIDS, lack affordable health care. The fact that Clinton never seriously considered embracing comprehensive medical care was a particular disappointment to progressive members of the lesbian and gay communities and some AIDS activists.

Reflecting on Clinton's record at the start of his second term, one leading AIDS activist said that "Clinton is at risk of missing an opportunity in history." He pointed out that the Clinton administration could have done much more to increase the access of HIV-positive people and those diagnosed with AIDS to effective treatments. Yet he also gave the President high marks for using the presidency as a bully pulpit for addressing AIDS symbolically (personal interview, March 4, 1997). One example of this symbolism was Clinton's visit to the AIDS Quilt display in Washington, D.C. The fact that a leading gay AIDS activist would identify this as a central strength of the Clinton approach is a measure of how little Presidents Reagan and Bush accomplished in addressing AIDS. As this and other examples suggest, former President Clinton was the recipient of enormous generosity from leading members of the lesbian and gay movements during the course of his presidency. The overall Clinton record with respect to lesbian and gay concerns is also a reminder that the issue of homosexuality in American society is still characterized by considerable controversy and the lack of a clear social consensus.

The Clinton Administration's Accomplishments

While Clinton disappointed lesbian and gay activists by failing to issue an executive order to overturn the military ban, he did issue executive orders in three other cases, all of which extended lesbian and gay civil rights. The first, signed into law on August 3, 1995, "prohibits government agencies from denying security clearances to applicants solely on the basis of their sexual orientation." Clinton's action was the first time a President included a pro-lesbian and gay clause in an official presidential order (Chibbaro 1995b, 1).

Perhaps the most substantive accomplishment of the Clinton era with respect to lesbian and gay rights was his May 1998 executive order that banned antigay discrimination against federal civilian employees. Capping a forty-one-year effort to end federal workforce bias, Clinton's "action formally [added] sexual orientation to Executive Order 11478, which banned job discrimination against federal workers based on race, color, religion, sex, national origin, handicap and age" (Freiberg 1998, 1). Franklin Kameny, who was fired from his federal job in 1957 on grounds of homosexuality, hailed the decision: "It is a total victory which could not have been conceived when I was fired" (ibid., 29). Finally, Clinton issued an executive order that enabled lesbians and gays overseas to obtain asylum in the United States if they were the target of persecution.

Clinton also deserves credit for endorsing and lobbying the U.S. Senate for passage of the Employment Non-Discrimination Act (ENDA), a lesbian and gay civil rights bill, which was narrowly defeated. In doing so, he became the first President to back lesbian and gay civil rights legislation, which he did enthusiastically and publicly. The President also consistently opposed the state antigay ballot initiatives that increasingly appeared throughout the United States. Finally, when Senate Majority Leader Trent Lott compared homosexuality to alcoholism, kleptomania, and sex addiction, the White House joined lesbian and gay civil rights leaders in publicly repudiating his remarks.[2]

The Clinton administration also earned high marks from some for appointing openly lesbian and gay officials to the federal government. For example, Clinton created the first White House liaison to the gay community in June 1995, although his first appointee, Marsha Scott, immediately encountered criticism for being a heterosexual.[3] However, Clinton assuaged his critics when he chose an openly gay official at the Department of Labor, Richard Socarides, as the new White House liaison in June 1996.[4] Socarides was subsequently replaced by Julian Potter.

His other accomplishments were to use his presidential bully pulpit—giving speeches in which he supported lesbian and gay rights, and issuing gay-pride statements, gestures that no other U.S. President had offered. For example, Clinton's November 1997 speech to a $300,000 fund-raiser sponsored by the Human Rights Campaign (HRC) was the first delivered by a sitting President to a lesbian and gay rights organization. In that speech, the President renewed his support for ENDA, saying, "Being gay, the last time I thought about it seemed to have nothing to do with the ability to read a balance book, fix a broken bone or change a spark plug. Firing or refusing to hire people because they are gay is akin to discrimination based on race, religion, or gender. It is wrong and it should be illegal" (quoted in Baker 1997, 3.). Clinton's speech is also noteworthy for the publicity it received not only in the lesbian and gay press but in dailies throughout the United States. In this way, he helped to bring further attention to the concerns of the lesbian and gay civil rights movements.

IMPLICATIONS FOR THE LESBIAN AND GAY MOVEMENTS

Before I discuss how the experiences with Clinton might inform the future direction of the movements, it is important to recognize that the Clinton presidency afforded them the opportunity to interact with a President who articulated both verbal and occasional policy support for lesbians and gays. That it took so long for any President to do so says something about the previous occupants of the White House, as well as the political and cultural climate for discussing sexual orientation issues. But it is also a reminder that the lesbian and gay movements had little practical experience in dealing with an administration that was not openly hostile to their concerns. In light of this reality, we can understand why strategic mistakes might have been made as the movements interacted with the Clinton administration over various aspects of public policy, most notably the military ban, lesbian and gay marriage, and health care reform.

The Clinton experience has prompted some critical introspection regarding how the movements should interact with mainstream policy elites. The years of the Clinton presidency witnessed heightened fractiousness both within the lesbian and gay movements and in the larger society around lesbian and gay concerns. One movement leader complained bitterly to me that "our national organizations, such as the NGLTF and HRC wasted the first four years of the Clinton administration. We still don't have a comprehensive agenda" (personal interview, February 4, 1998). A comprehensive agenda has not yet emerged because of fundamental disagreements within the movements over strategy.

The mainstream movements were also guilty of celebrating the kind of access to power that the Clinton administration provided. But access is hardly a substitute for a seat at the table as an equal participant when public policy is formulated. All too often members of national organizations were assuaged by Clinton administration promises and rhetoric, as we have seen throughout this book. One national movement leader told me that, "Clinton has transformed this country for the better on gay and lesbian issues" (personal interview, February 5, 1997). But what does this mean in practice? That question often goes unanswered. Urvashi Vaid captured the essence of the problem when she wrote about the movements having achieved "virtual equality" by 1995: "In this state, gay and lesbian people possess some of the trappings of full equality but are denied all of its benefits. . . . In the state of virtual equality, gay and lesbian people are at once insiders, involved openly in government and public affairs to a degree never before achieved, and outsiders, shunned by our elected officials unless they need our money or votes in close elections" (Vaid 1995, 4). In the state of "virtual equality," we are mainstreamed and marginalized at the same time. Intoxicated by the trappings that come with access to those in power, many of our national leaders failed to challenge the Clinton administration's role in fostering "virtual equality." To the extent that they did not do so, they neglected to provide the leadership that we need to address broader cultural and structural inequalities. "Virtual equality" extends beyond the political sphere to the cultural and economic spheres as well, as when these leaders celebrate increased lesbian and gay visibility on television and access to a lesbian and gay marketplace.

If anything, the attention given to national-level policymaking, while important, often ignores the rich tapestry of grassroots organizing and mobilizing that is currently being done in communities throughout the United States. This much-needed work at the state and local levels can and must proceed regardless of who occupies the White House. This is one important lesson of the Clinton years. Our national organizations would be well advised to devote some of their resources to political work to fight the vast organizational network of the Christian Right at the state and local levels. After all, most people do not live in Washington, D.C. One example of such a grassroots effort is the National Gay and Lesbian Task Force's "Celebrating Our Families" campaign, which was launched in spring 1998, an organizational initiative rooted in addressing community concerns about family issues and building support for families that celebrate sexual difference. A second example is the "Equality Begins at Home" campaign, a series of coordinated actions on behalf of lesbian, gay, bisexual, and transgendered civil rights, which occurred during March 1999 in the capital cities of all fifty states and U.S. territories. The goal of this organizing initiative was to draw national attention to battles in state houses as well as to highlight state organizing challenges. This sort of organizing is crucial because it creates a context for the much-needed political, cultural, and educational change that is needed at all levels of society. How to translate this kind of organizing into concrete public policy that cuts across class, race, and gender divides is a crucial challenge for the contemporary lesbian and gay movements and is the focus of the final section of this chapter. But before we can propose such an organizing strategy, we must first see how it might be informed by the presidency of George W. Bush.

EARLY REFLECTIONS ON THE GEORGE W. BUSH PRESIDENCY

With the Supreme Court's December 11, 2000, decision in *Bush v. Gore,* the hand counting of Florida ballots was stopped and George W. Bush was handed the presidency, despite having lost the popular vote by more than half a million votes and won the Electoral College count by the narrowest of margins (271–266, with one abstention). The lesbian and gay movements were confronted with the reality of a conservative Republican entering the White House after eight years of Democratic rule. Exit polls conducted by the Voter News Service indicated that 4 percent of all voters in the 2000 elections had identified themselves as gay, and that Gore had received 70 percent of the gay vote, Bush 25 percent, and Ralph Nader (the Green Party candidate) 4 percent. Bush's 25 percent figure represented a slight improvement over Republican presidential candidate Bob Dole's showing in 1996 and a considerable increase over his father's in 1992.[5] Given the closeness of the election, lesbian and gay Republicans have claimed that Bush's ability to win the support of a quarter of lesbian and gay voters in such a close election provided the margin for his victory.[6]

The 2000 presidential campaign did not provide much evidence to suggest, however, that the Bush White House will be hospitable or responsive to the concerns of the lesbian and gay movements in substantive and meaningful ways. For example, at no time during the campaign did Bush or Vice President Dick Cheney speak out about HIV/AIDS in the United States or in Africa. This is hard to believe, given how the global AIDS crisis has exploded as a crucial international policy issue. Bush also failed to address any civil rights issue pertaining to the larger lesbian and gay movements, although media attention on Cheney's openly lesbian daughter, Mary, did force both her parents (her mother is former National Endowment for the Humanities director Lynne Cheney) to address the Republican Party's stance on lesbian and gay rights.[7] Despite this publicity, presidential candidate Bush remained largely silent on these issues.

The August 2000 Republican national convention in Philadelphia did attempt to showcase a more diverse and inclusive Republican Party, especially in terms of racial and ethnic diversity. Bush campaign officials gave Rep. Jim Kolbe (R-Arizona) the opportunity to speak at the convention; in doing so, he became the first openly gay speaker ever to address a Republican Party convention. And there was a contingent of eighteen openly gay delegates and alternate delegates at the convention (Chibbaro 2000, 1). In these ways, the 2000 convention managed to avoid the extreme conservative rhetoric and visible hostility to diversity that characterized the 1992 Republican Party national convention in Houston. But there was little of substance to encourage those lesbians and gays who embrace a rights-based or even broader legislative and cultural agenda.

Despite this attempt to reach out to gay Republicans at the Philadelphia convention, Bush managed to alienate the Log Cabin Republicans during the campaign. When *Meet the Press* host Tim Russert asked Bush in December 1999 whether he planned to meet with the Log Cabin Republicans, Bush said, "Oh, probably not." When Russert asked why not, Bush replied, "Well, because it creates a huge political scene. I mean, this is all—I am—I am—I am someone who is a uniter, not a divider. I don't believe in group thought, pitting one group of people against another. And all that does is kind of create a huge political, you know, nightmare for people" (quoted in Carlson 1999, 11). Bush had clearly stated that the Log Cabin Republicans were a divisive organization. In the end, Bush met with a group of gays who were called the "Austin 12," all of whom were carefully selected by Bush campaign officials.[8] Some of these officials were members of the Log Cabin Republicans, but they were chosen because of their loyalty to Bush, his campaign, and ultimately what they hoped would be his presidency.

Bush's attempt to distance himself from the Log Cabin Republicans revealed how far he would go to avoid antagonizing his Christian Right supporters, whose votes he desperately needed to win the 2000 election. The newly elected president was also undoubtedly aware that the Christian Right had caused his father considerable difficulty during his one-term presidency when they perceived him as compromising too much on conservative principles. George W. Bush clearly does not want to repeat the political mistakes made by his father.[9] Bush's attempts to appease the Christian Right also help to explain his discomfort with addressing lesbian and gay civil rights issues during the first year of his presidency. Slightly more than 70 percent of self-identified lesbian and gay voters (more than 2.8 million Americans) cast their ballots for Al Gore in the 2000 election, while Bush received the votes of more than 11 million religious conservatives (Bull 2001b, 25). These figures indicate that Bush owes his conservative religious base his loyalty, given their strong support for him in such a close election. The political scientist Robert Bailey captured the challenges confronting Bush well: "Gay rights is a no-win situation for Bush. If he aligns with the antigay right wing, the media will accuse him of bigotry. If he doesn't, he'll get attacked by conservatives" (quoted in Bull 2001c, 26).[10]

Bush's record as governor of Texas accurately presaged his 2000 campaign strategy and his likely response to lesbian and gay concerns as President: it showed no support for any issue pertaining to lesbian and gay rights. For example, he refused to adopt a non-discrimination policy for his own office that included sexual orientation. In addition, he has not stated his support for the Employment Non-Discrimination Act (ENDA). In 1999 he opposed adding a sexual-orientation provision to Texas hate crime laws, an issue that gained considerable attention after the brutal murder of James Byrd, an African American who was dragged to his death from the back of a pickup truck in Jasper, Texas. Byrd's family indicated support for an inclusive Texas hate-crimes statute, but Bush remained steadfast in his opposition. Bush also consistently supported the Texas state sodomy law, arguing that it reinforces "traditional values." In doing so, he challenged the legitimacy of lesbian and gay relationships.

He has also been unwavering in his opposition to lesbian and gay adoptions, saying "I'm against gay adoptions. I believe children ought to be adopted in families with a woman and a man who are married" (www.hrc.org, accessed November 3, 2000). As a presidential candidate, Bush continued to articulate these positions on issues of considerable importance to the lesbian and gay movements. He also indicated opposition to lesbians and gays serving openly in the military by supporting the current "don't ask, don't tell" policy. Finally, he has consistently opposed crucial HIV/AIDS prevention and education efforts, including those that provide information on the importance of "safe sex" to young Americans (www.hrc.org, accessed November 3, 2000).

Since assuming the presidency, Bush has done little to draw attention to lesbian and gay concerns. If anything, he has indicated his hostility by the appointment of former Senator John Ashcroft (R-Missouri) as Attorney General, the top law enforcement officer in the United States. As a member of the United States Senate, Ashcroft consistently voted in support of the Christian Right's positions when lesbian and gay issues came up for consideration. For example, he was one of only two members of the Senate Foreign Relations Committee who voted against former President Clinton's appointment of gay philanthropist James Hormel as ambassador to Luxembourg (Bull 2001b, 25). Bush's appointment of former Colorado Attorney General Gale Norton also did little to comfort the lesbian and gay movements since Norton was a vigorous defender of Colorado's Amendment 2, which would have eliminated all lesbian and gay rights laws in the state (Bull 2001c, 26). Bush also appointed Gen. Colin Powell, who had fought hard to keep the ban on lesbians and gays in the military, as Secretary of State. In addition, many lesbian, gay, women's, and civil rights groups expressed considerable consternation with Bush's first round of judicial nominees, judges who would be strategically placed throughout the judicial system to promote socially and economically conservative agendas.

Even before taking office, Bush indicated that he would eliminate the White House liaison to lesbians and gays, a position that was created by former President Clinton. Bush's fiscal year 2002 budget proposal called for a "$300 million increase in funding for AIDS research programs, modest increases in funding for HIV prevention efforts, and no increase at all for the Ryan White CARE Act program, which helps people with AIDS who have low incomes obtain medical treatment" (Chibbaro 2001a, 1). Lesbian and gay activists were hopeful that the Congress would rebuke Bush and his Christian Right supporters by increasing the overall funding levels for AIDS-related programs. They became even more optimistic when Democrats took control of the United States Senate in June 2001, with the announcement by Senator James Jeffords of Vermont that he was leaving the Republican Party to become an Independent. Jeffords's decision was a response to a Bush administration that he perceived had moved too far to the political right in its first months in office.[11] Bush further antagonized movement members when he announced in early June 2001 that he would not issue a proclamation naming June "Gay Pride Month," as Bill Clinton had previously done. In attempting to justify this decision, White House spokesman Scott McClellan said, "The president believes every person should be treated with dignity and respect but he does not believe in politicizing people's sexual orientation. That's a personal matter" ("White House Drops Gay Pride Month" 2001, 1B).

From the vantage point of the Log Cabin Republicans, however, there were some notable successes in the early months of the Bush administration. For example, former New Jersey governor Christie Todd Whitman was appointed head of the Environmental Protection Agency. Whitman had infuriated the Christian Right during her tenure as governor when she announced her opposition to the Boy Scouts' decision to ban openly gay members. And former Wisconsin governor Tommy Thompson (R-Wisconsin) was widely perceived to be a moderate on lesbian and gay concerns, despite his socially conservative position on other important issues of the day, as reflected in his state's restrictive welfare reform policies and his virulent opposition to abortion. The Log Cabin Republican national organization clearly played a role in preventing former Senator Dan Coats (R-Indiana) from becoming Bush's Secretary of Defense. Coats is known for his extreme opposition to lesbian and gay rights, which was clearly manifested in the debate over the military ban in 1993, when he took a lead in opposing any reform that would allow lesbians and gays to serve openly in the U.S. military. When Donald Rumsfeld, who was Bush's successful nominee as Secretary of Defense, announced early in his tenure that he had no intention of overturning the "don't ask, don't tell" policy and going back to pre-Clinton era policies, this was widely regarded as a "victory" by some of the more conservative members of the lesbian and gay movements. Rumsfeld further delighted his supporters when he announced the appointment of an openly gay business executive, Stephen Herbits, as a Pentagon hiring consultant. When Christian Right conservatives denounced the appointment, Rumsfeld defended his decision to hire Herbits (Chibbaro 2001b, 1). And the appointment of Scott Evertz as director of the White House Office of National AIDS Policy in April 2001 was widely viewed as a major victory, especially since the administration had stated just a month earlier that it was considering downsizing the office, eliminating the "AIDS czar," and staffing the office with personnel from the Department of

Health and Human Services. Interestingly, little attention was given to Evertz's fund-raising efforts for the Wisconsin Right to Life anti-abortion group prior to his Washington appointment. The fact that he was openly gay proved to be enough evidence for some of the Bush administration's sincerity in building meaningful bridges to the lesbian and gay community.[12]

What does all of this portend for the future of the lesbian and gay movements? And what are the implications of a conservative Bush presidency for progressive coalition building? First, it soon became clear that the lesbian and gay movements would no longer have direct access to the White House, a reality reinforced when President-elect Bush announced that he would eliminate the White House liaison to lesbians and gays. While Bush's decision appeared on the surface to be a negative development, it does not necessarily mean that the movements' organizing efforts at the federal level are irreparably damaged. This book has provided evidence to suggest that while the Clinton administration afforded national organization leaders plenty of access to the White House, this access did not translate into concrete influence over public policy decisions and outcomes. Perhaps Bush's decision will enable the larger movements to reconsider the limitations of mere access to the representatives of power and get on with the important business of organizing and building important political coalitions across the political system, especially at the state and local levels.

A hostile Bush presidency will remind leaders of the lesbian and gay movements that focusing the bulk of their organizing attention at the federal level may be a faulty political strategy. Major national organizations, such as the NGLTF and HRC, had already begun to recognize the importance of grassroots organizing by the second term of the Clinton presidency. Such efforts can then be used to pressure members of Congress when key votes on issues of importance to the movements come up for consideration. To the extent that a Bush White House can inspire even more attention to local and state organizing and policy efforts, then the lesbian and gay movements and their progressive supporters may be better off over the long term. Scarce resources that were once devoted to gaining access to the White House might be better spent in developing state and local education efforts and political strategies that challenge the Christian Right's vast organizing efforts and resources in communities throughout the United States.[13]

Second, George W. Bush's social conservatism and reactionary policies might inspire the larger lesbian and gay movements to overcome their tendencies toward fragmentation. The recognition of a common enemy might cause movement members to transcend areas of conflict to focus on issues where there is sufficient common ground for successful political organizing. The latter might include education around issues relevant to the movements, the passage of ENDA, grassroots programs aimed at prevention of hate-related violence, and the creation of humane HIV/AIDS policies at the local, national, and global levels. Of course, given the power of the Christian Right, all of these efforts will require the full resources of the movements and their allies. But opportunities for coalition building with other social movements, including local, national, and international human rights and civil rights groups, are perhaps more available now than they have ever been before. The great irony of the George W. Bush presidency may well be that as he embraces reactionary policies to mollify his Christian Right base, he provides the impetus for the lesbian and gay movements to challenge their assumptions about political organizing and priorities in ways that will revivify the movements for both the short and long term.

A STRATEGY FOR POLITICAL, SOCIAL, AND CULTURAL CHANGE

The central weakness of a narrowly construed rights-based strategy for political and legal change is that it ignores the broader cultural transformation of society that is the proper goal of any meaningful liberation movement. The ultimate goal is to force a culture to reexamine and rethink its attitudes, beliefs, and values regarding sexual orientation. Dennis Altman summarizes the challenge well: "The gay movement must be concerned not just with specific legal and electoral battles, but also with the far broader and more amorphous ways in which homophobia is maintained through a complex structure of institutions, values, and often unconscious prejudices" (Altman 1982, 130–31). The lesbian and gay movements have confronted the problem of narrow reformist thinking before, as Martin Duberman points out:

> Indeed, by 1974 the gay movement in general was heading into the same set of interlocking dilemmas that have characterized protest movements throughout our history. How to prevent a radical impulse from degenerating into reformist thinking? How to mobilize a constituency for substantive change when most of the members of that constituency prefer to focus energies on winning certain limited concessions, like civil rights legislation, and show little interest in joining with other dispossessed groups to press for systemic social restructuring? (Duberman 1999, 278–79)

The analysis presented in this book suggests that, for the most part, the contemporary lesbian and gay movements embraced a reformist, civil rights strategy for political change in the Clinton era. We were more satisfied with access to people in positions of power than with questioning what such people can and should do for those at the margins of society. We also seem to have accepted mere access to the powerful as a worthwhile objective, in place of the much more crucial goal of participating in public policy decision making. Michael Warner offers a depressing but accurate picture of how the lesbian and gay movements at the national level were transformed for the worse in the 1990s: "Its [movement politics'] public face is now dominated by a small group of media celebrities, connected to a network of big-money politics that revolves around publicity consultants and campaign professionals and litigators" (Warner 1999, 67). A number of other factors fundamentally altered the lesbian and gay movements in the Clinton era, including the increased centralization of lesbian and gay politics in Washington, D.C., the decline of direct-action activism, and the creation of "highly capitalized lifestyle magazines as the movement's principal public venue," which have helped to foster a politics characterized by media celebrity (ibid., 145). These developments have all worked to encourage the contemporary lesbian and gay movements to retreat from the radical chapters of their histories and embrace a reformist, assimilationist politics that generally eschews meaningful cultural and structural change.

Further, this political mainstreaming has not led to the kind of gains that its adherents often champion. For example, some celebrate "the end of AIDS" even when the drugs prompting this "celebration" are too costly for all but a few, and even though little is known about the long-term use of these drug cocktails.[14] In addition, when we speak of "the end of AIDS," we essentialize a hideous epidemic, one that continues to escalate in many countries throughout the world, not to mention among our own African-American and Hispanic communities in the United States. Homophobic initiatives continue to proliferate at the local, state, and federal levels, as the Christian Right's antigay efforts continue unabated. The campaign to repeal sodomy statutes has largely stalled, and the "Don't Ask, Don't Tell" policy has been an abysmal failure. Increasing numbers of lesbians and gays, often enduring harassment and the threat of exposure, are being discharged from the military.[15] The same-sex marriage campaign did nothing to prevent the Defense of Marriage Act, "and, for the first time, the codification into state and federal law of the heterosexuality of marriage" (Warner 1999, 128). President Clinton, the "friend" of lesbians and gays, signed both "Don't Ask, Don't Tell" and the Defense of Marriage Act into law, in effect enshrining homophobia as a national policy (Warner 1999, 128–29). And when it came time for the lesbian and gay movements to organize at the grass roots to pressure President Clinton and members of Congress, they were not able to do so. Julian Potter, who served as field organizer for the Campaign for Military Service, a coalition of groups that attempted to persuade President Clinton and Congress to lift the ban on lesbians and gays in the military, identified a crucial problem still facing the lesbian and gay movements: "What dawned on all of us was that there essentially was no visible grass roots from which to build support for a national initiative. There were lots of gay bars but few statewide gay organizations or local community centers to draw upon. We had little experience in playing partisan politics. We were thrown into the limelight in not a very flattering way" (Bull 2000a, 17).

Potter's experience demonstrates the importance of building a movement from the bottom up in order to mobilize the citizenry and hold elites accountable. If the movements fail to transcend narrow rights-based initiatives and broaden their overall agenda for change, they will continue to endure such ugly defeats as those over the military ban and same-sex marriage.[16]

This depressing state of affairs calls for a return to a more radical conception of democratic citizenship, one that embraces political, social, cultural, and economic change informed from the grass roots. This is the only kind of broad-based strategy that will enable the lesbian and gay movements to respond effectively to the antigay distortions of the Christian Right. At the core of this strategy is the importance of coalition building—both across organizations within the lesbian and gay movements (inter-movement cooperation) and across movements that have common interests with our own (intra-movement cooperation). In a participatory democracy, citizens are no longer passive consumers but active and willing, politically engaged human beings who link their own individual interests with a larger community of people.[17] Rights are not merely extended but are made more inclusive.[18] The ultimate goal is to reconceptualize what it is to be an American, to challenge what Audre Lorde has called the American norm: someone who is "white, thin, male, young, heterosexual, christian, and financially secure." It is important to do so because "this mythical American norm" is socially constructed and is the locus of considerable power and privilege in American society (Lorde 1984, 116). No single political strategy can begin to accomplish this goal; multiple strategies for political, social, cultural, and economic transformation are at the core of this radical democratic conception of politics.

There are three possible strategic directions that the movements might pursue. First, many advocate an exclusive focus on lesbian and gay rights, specifically on such narrowly defined issues as same-sex marriage and the military ban. This position dominated the mainstream movements' thinking during the decade of the 1990s. Second, some believe that the lesbian and gay movements should work to end discrimination and prejudice in its many forms. The third position, which is associated with a radical conception of democratic citizenship, argues for a common progressive movement, for building bridges across movements for economic, feminist, and racial justice, and for lesbian and gay liberation (Vaid 1995, 303). This latter position is central to the analysis in this book. Underlying this perspective is a commitment to political organizing that recognizes the untapped potential of lesbians and gays and their straight allies in America's communities—a potential that must be mobilized around political and cultural issues that bridge identities if the Christian Right and the corporate/capitalist Right are to be challenged successfully. The challenge is to reframe the strategy and the substantive message of the lesbian and gay movements and ultimately to transcend a narrow civil rights approach. But how can this be accomplished while also showing respect for the diverse identities that compose the contemporary lesbian and gay movements? This is the question that we probe in the remainder of this chapter.

Coalition Politics

If our goal is to move beyond a narrow focus on identity politics, we have two possible options. The first is what Urvashi Vaid calls "the coalition-around-an-issue strategy," which involves working with people who share interests and common purpose around the same issues. The second option is much more ambitious because it requires people to create a "common movement" (Vaid 1995, 303). The "coalition-around-an issue strategy" could lead to the recognition of common ground, which is the precursor to a common movement, whereby individuals come together to talk about issues of interest and strategies for working toward common goals that have been identified through participatory democratic processes. Vaid poses three important questions that should be asked by organizers at the outset of any campaign or political project: "How does this issue affect different populations within the gay and lesbian community? Can we build coalitions with the non-gay community around this issue? How can we educate the different segments of our community on the direct way this project or campaign affects them?" (ibid.).

Beyond these questions, the movements need to identify the kinds of issues that will foster the building of both short- and long-term alliances that are rooted in a radical democratic politics. Coalitions have surely been the catalyst behind virtually all of the movements' legislative victories, including the Americans with Disabilities Act, the Hate Crimes Statistics Act, the Ryan White AIDS Care Act, the local laws that lesbian and gay activists have passed working with other community members, and the antigay referendums that have been defeated throughout the United States (Vaid 1997, 7). The importance of coalition building certainly has not been lost on those who are concerned with national-level policy-making. For example, Tom Sheridan, a former high-ranking official at the AIDS Action Council, explains its importance: "Coalition politics is effective because it's the hardest to get people to do. The Hill really respects it because they figure that if you can get up here with a coalition that big and that diverse and have everyone agreeing on something, you must have hit something" (quoted in Andriote 1999, 230). A central goal of radical democratic politics is to build permanent coalitions around political strategies and concrete public policies that cut across race, class, and gender divides, coalitions that will be ready to respond to the Christian Right's distortions in all political arenas. What issues might inspire individuals to work together to build a common movement?

A challenge to class-based hierarchy both within the lesbian and gay movements and in the larger society. Addressing class-based hierarchy requires a recognition that ameliorating the inequalities that emanate from the unequal distribution of property, wealth, and income is of utmost importance.[19] These class-based hierarchies are reproduced in the lesbian and gay communities and are reinforced by a capitalist market economy that offers the allure of a lesbian and gay market niche. But as we know, this market niche is only available to those who can afford to participate.

The 1999 San Francisco mayoral race between incumbent Willie Brown and openly gay challenger Tom Ammiano offers some evidence that class-based issues are important to voters. Ammiano mounted a successful write-in campaign just three weeks before the November general election and forced a runoff with Brown. Ammiano was able to do so by embracing a progressive political agenda that rejected narrow identity politics. He called for "open honest government, campaign finance reform, neighborhood empowerment/anti-chain stores, public transit, affordable housing, and compassion for the homeless" (Hill 2000, 8).

One political analyst believes that "his campaign provided hope and inspiration not only to those left out of the economic boom, but also to those who have gotten a piece of it but are nonetheless troubled by things like secretive WTO proceedings, fast-track NAFTA deals, and local machine politics funded by Silicon Valley and big developers" (Hill 2000, 8). While Ammiano lost in the runoff election, his ability to mobilize lesbian and gay voters and progressive straights into a political coalition suggests a strategy for other candidates and communities wishing to build coalitions with those who share common class-based interests.

Environmental justice. One way that we can build coalitions across communities of people who share common interests is to organize around environmental concerns. The future of the planet is important to us all, regardless of our identities. One organization that is doing superb coalition building in this regard is the Labor/Community Strategy Center, headquartered in Los Angeles. A multiracial center for policy and strategy development and for political organizing, it is representative of progressive grassroots organizations that attempt to link class-based concerns with our environmental future. The center has focused on the auto, oil, petrochemical, and tire industries, and all factories that use and emit dangerous chemicals, pushing for democratic control over their basic production decisions.

In its attempt to build coalitions around these concerns, the center has approached groups who are affected by corporate decisions that damage the environment—workers in factories and offices, students, women, members of various minority communities, white working people, farm laborers working with pesticides on a daily basis, and inner-city residents who face groundwater contamination and air pollution (Rimmerman 1997, 85–86). The lesbian and gay movements can borrow strategies for community-based organizing from successful environmental-justice organizations, such as the Labor/Community Strategy Center. In doing so, the movements can build coalitions with those committed to environmental justice around both environmental and social justice concerns.

Wage inequalities, universal childcare, and union organizing. A study published jointly by the AFL-CIO and the Institute for Women's Policy Research revealed that women earned 74 cents on the dollar compared with men doing the same full-time work.[20] While the pay gap between the sexes has slowly begun to erode over the past twenty years, it is unacceptable that women make considerably less than men who perform the same full-time jobs. Equitable living wages are important for everyone, not just for the white men who have typically enjoyed economic and institutional privilege in American society.

In addition to fair wages, comprehensive, high-quality childcare is also desperately needed to support working parents and their children. As more lesbians and gays become parents, the importance of this issue will become more obvious. The workplace understandably became an important activist site for lesbians and gay men in the 1980s and 1990s, given "the centrality of work in most people's lives and because of the blatantly discriminatory policies encountered on the job" (Hunt 1999, 2).

Important workplace issues—benefits, hiring, firing, promotions, leaves of absence, perks, pensions, harassment, education initiatives, and even violence—continue to "be shaped to discriminate against sexual minorities in ways that can be economically and psychologically harmful" (Hunt

1999, 2). These issues are obviously of importance to all workers, but lesbians and gays have been particular targets of discrimination. If all of these crucial workplace issues are to be addressed seriously, then coalitions will need to be built among workers with the support of active labor union organizing.[21]

Affirmative action and campaigns to remedy structural inequalities in inner-city schools. As Chapter 2 points out, gender and racial inequalities have been reproduced within the lesbian and gay movements. In few of our most prominent national organizations are African Americans and Hispanics well represented in leadership positions. The movements are largely dominated, at least at the national level, by white middle- and upper-class men and women. Before the movements can build coalitions around ethnic and racial issues, they must first challenge the marginalization of African Americans, Hispanics, and other minorities. Supporting aggressive affirmative action in the workplace and in educational institutions is one avenue for serious coalition building. A second is to address the structural inequalities that pervade inner-city schools, where disadvantaged minority children are often concentrated. The poverty of resources in these schools, when compared to their largely white suburban counterparts, means that children in the inner city begin the race for success in American life well behind those who are more privileged. Until these structural inequalities are addressed and challenged, they will continue to be reproduced. It is in the interest of lesbians and gays to work with others to organize on behalf of specific public policies that will ameliorate these inequalities.

Comprehensive medical care. "Comprehensive medical care will never happen in the United States. As a result, we need to be much more pragmatic about how we approach health care" (personal interview, February 5, 1997). That is the view of one member of the national movement's elite class. The pragmatism to which this person refers characterized the Clinton White House's health-care reform efforts in the administration's first term. When Bill Clinton took office in January 1993, some thirty-nine million Americans lacked adequate medical insurance. As I write this in the spring of 2001, that number has ballooned to forty-four million. It is in the interest of the lesbian and gay movements to support comprehensive medical care in light of HIV/AIDS and the exorbitant costs of the medicines people depend on in order to survive.

The political scientist Robert Bailey reports in his study of the 1992 presidential exit poll that health care was "the top policy priority among lesbian and gay voters across the country. The gay and lesbian sample also approved of higher taxes for health care. Only jobs and economic issues competed with health policy as a strong issue for gay men and lesbians." At the time of the 1994 midterm elections, a Voter News Service exit poll found that "the gay and lesbian sample again ranked health care as their top policy priority among the choices provided" (Bailey 1999, 119). These findings support the claim that lesbians and gays would be willing to join a coalition committed to bringing about comprehensive medical care in the United States.

How might we pay for comprehensive health care? Coalitions of citizens' groups can challenge the federal government to reduce federal spending for costly and unneeded weapons systems and direct these monies to develop a system of national health insurance. This will not be easy, given the realities of a well-entrenched military/industrial complex. Such a plan will also require a substantial, progressive tax increase that would place the financial burden on those who can best afford it. We also need to finance further research and support for women's health issues, including breast, cervical, and ovarian cancers.

Comprehensive government responses to HIV/AIDS, especially resources for education, prevention, and treatment. Cathy Cohen's important work on AIDS among African Americans is a reminder that this disease has had devastating consequences for many communities. With this in mind, we need support for a new AIDS movement, one that recognizes that AIDS is a global problem and that also takes into account the specific needs of lesbians, gay men, African Americans, poor people, and others who are marginalized in American society.[22]

This new AIDS movement requires a society that refuses to stigmatize sex, but instead provides accessible information about safer sex practices.[23] We need a new AIDS movement that organizes on behalf of legalizing and financing the distribution of clean needles in inner cities throughout the United States. If these public-policy goals are to be achieved, they will need the support of coalitions of diverse individuals committed to humane AIDS policies. But they will also need the support of the mainstream lesbian and gay movements who appear to have lost interest in AIDS in recent years, as same-sex marriage and the military ban have dominated their agenda.

The movements need to support those lesbian and gay institutions that were created in the midst of the epidemic's major infection wave in the 1980s. We need to do the following: distribute information about HIV/AIDS prevention; organize to challenge discrimination; pressure federal, state, and local governments around AIDS-related issues; and provide the changing supports that become necessary as people who are HIV-positive live longer, thanks to their access to new medical advances. As we build coalitions with others around HIV/AIDS, we must work to insure that more people have access to the information and drugs associated with these medical advances.[24]

Hate crimes legislation. While this book was being written, the brutal murders of two gay men—Matthew Shepard and Billy Jack Gaither—received considerable public attention. Their murders were particularly heinous. In October 1998 Shepard was brutally beaten and tied to a fence post outside Laramie, Wyoming. Then, with a fractured skull, he was left all night in near-freezing temperatures. In February 1999 Gaither was beaten to death in Sylacauga, Alabama, and his body burned. Shepard's murder, in particular, prompted a national debate over the merits of a federal hate-crimes law called the Hate Crimes Prevention Act, which would afford federal agencies jurisdiction over bias incidents. This crime also appears to have galvanized the lesbian and gay movements and their straight allies around federal hate-crimes legislation, but the reality is that hundreds of lesbians, gays, bisexuals, and transgendered people (as well as people suspected of falling into these categories) have been the targets of bias-related crimes over the years, often with little response from the police, government officials, schoolteachers and principals, or community leaders.

A number of natural coalitions can be built around hate-related violence, such as lesbians and gays with battered women and civil rights groups. To the extent that these groups fail to work together and instead organize themselves according to their separate identities, there will be no long-lasting coalition to address the sources of hate crimes. Hate-crimes legislation at the federal, state, and local levels is an important symbolic gesture, but most forms of the legislation address the issue *after* a crime has been committed. What is desperately needed is a long-term coalition to explore how the sources of hate crimes can be targeted before they occur. Many of these conversations are already occurring in communities throughout the United States, but the problem also needs the formal involvement of educators. Their research-based insights into the roots of bias crimes can help communities devise appropriate responses, and they can also push for curricular innovations in schools that emphasize diversity and tolerance.

Education for difference. As we saw in Chapter 5, in the discussion of the Christian Right's organizing efforts, education is a major cultural and political battleground, and conflicts will continue there for the foreseeable future. The task for lesbian and gay movements is to build broad support for diversity education, including on lesbian and gay issues. There is little hope that the movements can tackle a project of this size without support from other interested groups. But if framed appropriately, education that seeks to promote understanding and respect for difference should cut cross divisions of class, race, and identity.

The Christian Right is well ahead of the movements in challenging education-for-difference efforts in many communities throughout the United States. Local school boards in some communities have been stacked with candidates supported by the Christian Right, making them morally and culturally conservative. This is the reality that the movements must face if they hope to reach out and build coalitions with others who have been the targets of hate and discrimination. The importance of education cannot be overestimated. While winning passage of civil rights, anti-discrimination, or hate-crime laws may provide some tangible benefits for lesbians and gays, these measures will not challenge prejudices and fears that are deeply rooted (Bronski 1998, 247). Properly trained and committed educators are in the best position to do so.

Support for lesbian and gay youth issues. One of the most serious issues facing the lesbian and gay movements is the problem of teen suicide. One Canadian study "claims to provide the most compelling proof to date of a link between homosexuality and youth suicide, concluding that gay and bisexual males are nearly 14 times more at risk than their heterosexual contemporaries of making a serious attempt on their own lives" (King 1996, 41). As Chapter 5 pointed out, lesbian and gay youth are often subjected to considerable harassment in school. A significant number report having been physically assaulted as well.[25] There is a connection between the harassment faced by lesbian and gay youth in their schools and suicide. Once again, these issues need a committed coalition of groups to come together to discuss how to best protect and promote the well-being of all our youth, but certainly that of lesbian and gay youth, who, although they are particularly at risk, are often ignored in social policy.

A number of organizations already represent the interests of lesbian, gay, bisexual, and transgendered youth. At the national level, there is the National Youth Advocacy Coalition (NYAC) which was formally established in 1994. It attempts to educate members of Congress and other decision makers on youth-related issues. NYAC also pushes other organizations to "develop the capacity to represent the concerns of gay, lesbian, bisexual, and transgendered youth" (personal interview with NYAC staff member, March 4, 1997). All too often the national organizations discussed in this book largely ignore youth. Since its creation in 1994, NYAC has worked on a number of youth-related issues: supporting student groups in high school and even on some college campuses; supporting students who have been harassed in schools; fighting against federal funding cuts in programs that benefit youth; working on suicide issues in the context of mental health services; addressing youth substance abuse; supporting youth-related HIV education and treatment programs; and addressing youth homelessness (personal interview, March 4, 1997).

All of these important issues deserve a much higher profile in the contemporary lesbian and gay movements. While hundreds of local and regional organizations exist at the grassroots to provide social and educational services to lesbian and gay youth, many lack the resources to provide services at the level they are needed. In addition, in many small towns and rural communities throughout the United States, these crucial resources are nonexistent. This set of issues poses a unique opportunity for the lesbian and gay movements to build coalitions with others around the importance of providing basic services and support for all of our youth.

The Employment Non-Discrimination Act (ENDA). The vast majority of lesbians and gay men can be fired for their sexual orientations, despite the fact that eleven states and many cities now outlaw job discrimination. There is a need for federal legislation, such as ENDA, that bans discrimination in employment based on sexual orientation. Support and publicity for this legislation serves an important symbolic purpose, as well, because it highlights the reality that employment discrimination exists. Despite the fact that the legislation was defeated by the U.S. Senate in 1996 by the narrowest of margins (50–49), ENDA will probably not pass in this increasingly conservative political climate. The prospects for the passage of ENDA certainly did not improve with the election of George W. Bush. Bush has consistently opposed ENDA because he believes, erroneously, that it provides "special treatment."

This is an issue where lesbians and gays can build an effective coalition with other civil rights groups, while recognizing that how the issue is framed will determine the American public's support. Gregory B. Lewis and Marc A. Rodgers have studied both demographic and attitudinal sources of support for lesbian and gay employment rights. They conclude that

> Americans support the concept of equal rights more than they favor laws to enforce them, especially when they are asked to expand legal coverage rather than just to support existing laws. If the debate over gay employment protections can be framed as simply preventing employment discrimination, gay rights supporters should garner majority support, but opponents have frequently been able to reframe the issue around morality or to focus attention on the occupations where public distrust is greatest, especially elementary school teachers. Defusing fears of gay teachers will

be a key issue in winning employment protections for gay and lesbian people in all occupations. (Lewis and Rogers 1999, 139)

These findings suggest that passage of ENDA will require a broad-based coalition of civil rights activists to come together to educate the public about the importance of this legislation and to rally support around a basic civil rights issue. In the meantime, the lesbian and gay movements may need to work with coalitions of civil rights supporters at the state and local level in order to combat job discrimination based on sexual orientation.

Support for freedom of choice. For most lesbians and gay men, there is an important connection between promoting abortion rights and promoting the movements' rights-based agenda. That connection is rooted in the constitutional right to privacy—that the government should not interfere with an individual's right to personal reproductive and sexual choices. This is an issue that obviously cuts across race, class, gender, and sexual orientation.

A campaign to overturn the military ban. This book has already discussed the military ban in considerable detail. By its very nature, the ban makes use of federal government policy to enforce the ugliness of the closet. For this and many other reasons, it must be overturned. This issue, like all of the others discussed here, needs to be connected to a framework for broader cultural change, one that transcends narrowly circumscribed identity politics.

A campaign to eliminate sodomy laws. At this time, four states—Texas, Arkansas, Kansas, and Oklahoma—still have same-sex sodomy laws; twelve more ban sodomy for both opposite- and same-sex couples. The same-sex sodomy laws that are on the books are enforced arbitrarily, as two Texas citizens can attest. In 1998 Houston police burst into the apartment of John Geddes Lawrence, where he and Tyron Garner were having sex in Lawrence's bedroom. Both men were arrested and held in jail for over twenty-four hours. Fortunately, Texas's Fourteenth Circuit Court of Appeals ruled 2–1 in June 2000 that the 1860 sodomy statute "violates the state constitution's equal rights protections" ("A Sodomy Law's Last Stand" 2000, p. 13).

It is hard to believe that in the twenty-first century such laws remain on the books and that police arrest citizens for having sex in the privacy of their own homes. The lawyers at the Lambda Legal Defense and Education Fund deserve considerable credit for doing the tough legal work on behalf of Lawrence and Garner. But the broader movements need to be building coalitions with others to challenge the sodomy laws.

What the above agenda attempts to do is to place basic civil rights goals within a broader radical democratic framework for political, cultural, and economic change. The key to building coalitions around these and other issues is to focus on commonalities rather than differences, but to do so in a way that celebrates respect for difference. As the next section makes clear, this will be a challenging goal to reach. A number of barriers will have to be acknowledged, confronted, and ultimately overcome.

Barriers to Building a Common Movement

First and foremost, a narrow, rights-based organizing strategy is supported by the political, cultural, and economic ethos of American society, as enshrined in the Bill of Rights and the Constitution, which upholds the importance of protecting *individual* rights. We are socialized to think in terms of protecting the individual's right to life, liberty, and happiness—often defined in ways that emphasize the acquisition of private wealth. An identity politics that embraces narrow civil rights goals, such as same-sex marriage or overturning the ban on lesbians and gays in the military, reinforces the primacy of the individual. And in fact, there are practical advantages to a narrowly circumscribed, identity-based organizing strategy, as writer and activist Suzanne Pharr suggests. These include " 'clarity of focus in tactics and strategies, self-examination and education apart from the dominant culture' and the 'development of solidarity and group bonding. Creating organizations based on identity allows us to have visibility and collective power, to advance concerns that otherwise would never be recognized because of our marginalization within the dominant society' " (quoted in Vaid 1995, 286).

Pharr's analysis goes a long way toward explaining why narrow identity politics will continue to dominate the mainstream lesbian and gay movements' strategic thinking, despite the setbacks of the Clinton era. The platform agenda for the 2000 Millennium March (see Appendix B) suggests that this narrow, rights-based strategy, which is rooted in an essentialist model of organizing, is deeply embedded in the mainstream lesbian and gay movements' thinking. Notice that only a few of the issues that I identify above—hate crimes legislation, ENDA, the military ban, youth issues, and abortion rights—appear on the 2000 march agenda. Instead, the organizers imposed a number of narrow, rights-based goals on the march agenda without much internal debate, which is testimony to how hierarchical the policy process is, how removed it is from ordinary movement members, and how far away the lesbian and gay movements are from the broad political and cultural agenda that I am advocating in this book.

But there are other serious barriers as well. The celebration of the lesbian and gay consumer in a thriving lesbian and gay market is a serious obstacle to achieving the kind of radical democratic politics that I champion in this book. We already know that most celebrate the thriving lesbian and gay market as a sign of progress and economic success. And the advertising industry has reinforced the positive aspects of these economic developments by bombarding the lesbian and gay community with ads that tout "the political rewards of consumption" (Chasin 2000, xviii). Those who celebrate this "progress" fail to consider the negative consequences of these economic developments for political organizing.

Chapter 4 attempted to account for the apparent decline in the movements' use of direct-action, outsider politics in recent years. The most provocative, interesting, and perhaps persuasive explanation is that lesbian and gay consumerism arose in response to the combined influences of capitalist market economies, advertising, and the growth of lesbian and gay communities that organize themselves around this market-driven imperative. The consumer market, by its very nature, reinforces the politics of privatism and thus deters citizens from participating in the public sphere, which a radical democratic politics requires. In other words, when citizens are more interested in shopping and accessing the new lesbian and gay market niche, they often lack the critical facility, not to mention the time, to connect their private activities with the larger public sphere.

The lesbian and gay market niche also reinforces the narrow form of identity politics that undermines the ability of the movements to build the political coalitions that are necessary to respond to the Christian Right's campaigns of hatred and distortion. In her insightful book *Selling Out: The Gay and Lesbian Movement Goes to Market,* Alexandra Chasin articulates this problem convincingly:

> Constituted by marketing, identified by and through participation in gay and lesbian for-profit and nonprofit institutions, gay men and lesbians have reason to appreciate both the movement and the market that produce and reproduce gay culture. Rights are absolutely necessary, and they are clearly won through identity-based practices. But identity-based movement and market activity—while indispensable and inevitable on both individual and group levels—ultimately promote sameness, leaving difference vulnerable to appropriation and leaving it in place as grounds for inequality. If liberal rights and the rights of the consumer are the best possible outcomes of the partnership between identity politics and identity-based consumption, that is because they leave the structures of capitalism untouched. Progressive coalitions that focus on economic injustice may address those structures. They serve a diverse constituency, including gay men and lesbians. They dislocate the myth that private consumption can ever do the work of progressive political action. (Chasin 2000, 244)

If one accepts Chasin's analysis, the central problem becomes how to foment this progressive impulse when the market imperative plays such an important role in capitalist societies and in the lives of individual citizens. How might this critique be articulated and, more importantly, heard, in a society that celebrates consumer niches and markets? Educators obviously have a vital role to play, but to make the case for education erroneously assumes that teachers are unaffected by the prevailing political, economic, and cultural ideology. The movements' leaders in politics and the press might help foster critical self-reflection about these issues as well. But the reality is that the mainstream lesbian and gay movements, with their overwhelming emphasis on the importance of gaining access to power and to markets, are a major impediment to achieving a radical democratic politics.

And even if such a critical counter-organizing effort were successful, what is the likelihood that lesbian and gay movements could successfully mobilize a citizenry that has been socialized to conceive of politics as a largely passive activity? The available evidence provides a mixed response to this important question. Americans vote less often than citizens in other liberal democracies around the world.[26] I have argued elsewhere that citizens fail to participate in the electoral arena because they do not see the link between their vote and the decisions made by those who hold power in the American policy process.[27] But fortunately, some citizens do participate in politics through a variety of alternative channels, such as town meetings and protest politics. It is this participatory impulse that must be tapped if a radical democratic politics is to evolve. As students of democratic theory and democratic practice have made clear, however, the barriers to a fully developed radical democratic challenge to liberal democracy are considerable.[28]

Finally, as we have seen repeatedly throughout this book, the lesbian and gay movements are highly fragmented across identities and subject to conflicting and multiple cross-pressures. Given this reality, how can they build a coherent agenda, one that reflects agreement on a common political and cultural strategy? And if the movements cannot agree on a coherent agenda, how can we expect them to build the coalitions needed to address the issues we have discussed? As Kenneth Sherrill points out, "to the degree that there is any gay agenda in the United States, it is for equality, and freedom from discrimination and violence. A more sophisticated agenda would require a level of collective identity among gay people not found anywhere in the world" (Sherrill 1996, 473).[29]

In the face of these realities, how can I or other activists, scholars, and educators promote such a strategy? First, in order to build a truly democratic social movement, it is important that the larger movements not accept a narrowly focused identity politics without debate. The movements need to discuss and debate current and future strategies. The ideas in this book have been presented with that goal in mind. Second, we must recognize that a broader cultural and political strategy was embraced by the Gay Liberation Front in the early 1970s and had considerable support throughout the 1970s and into the 1980s. I would argue that some of that same support is present today, especially given the failure of the narrow civil rights, identity-politics perspective. Third, there is also the possibility that more people will become dissatisfied with the rights-based political strategy as we continue to lose battles with the Christian Right over key policy initiatives. Finally, I am hopeful that more activists will recognize what Urvashi Vaid calls an "an even more fundamental" problem of identity-based organizing: the idea "that there is something at once singular and universal that can be called gay or lesbian or bisexual or even transgendered identity." The movements cannot assume an essentialist perspective, given the diversity of people and identities that compose them. Our identities are hardly unitary or fixed; they are informed by our economic status, gender, geographic location, history, race, and other aspects of our lives. In other words, our identities are, if anything, socially constructed (Vaid 1995, 286–87).

Basic Rights Oregon

While these are certainly formidable obstacles to building a progressive political and cultural movement, there is reason for optimism in the kind of grassroots, coalition-based organizing that has occurred and is currently taking place in various states and localities. We should not be surprised that the state and local levels are the locus of considerable progressive organizing, given a 1999 NGLTF survey of the fifty states, which found a significant increase in state legislation affecting lesbians and gays. In 1999 there were 472 bills, compared to 160 in 1996. The majority of these were gay-hostile. It is no surprise, too, that state and local grassroots organizers have become increasingly frustrated that the bulk of the movements' resources reside at the national level, with organizations such as HRC (Ireland 1999, 11).

One organization that deserves considerable movement support is Basic Rights Oregon (BRO), a progressive grassroots group of the kind that signals a new direction for the lesbian and gay movements. A key organizer told me that "one of the organization's highest priorities is building coalitions with others" (telephone interview, June 26, 2000). The organization showed enormous progressive leadership with its Voter File Project, "a coalition with labor, environmental and pro-choice organizations that in the past three years has pooled lists and resources to identify over half a million voters for Election Day get-out-the-vote drives (out of a voting population of some 2 million)" (Ireland 1999, 11). How does the Voter File Project work in practice? Each participating group retains control of its own lists, but "a steering committee meets regularly to discuss which candidates and referendums to support or oppose, and members share money and resources to keep the voter file updated and to expand it." The list contains some 125,000 gay-friendly voters. As a result, BRO has the same kind of clout in the state as the union movement. Asked about her organization's political influence, BRO's former executive director, Jean Harris, responds, "Why do you think [U.S. Senator] Ron Wyden supports marriage equality for lesbians and gays?" (quoted in Ireland 1999, 11).

Harris's question confirms the effectiveness of BRO's organizational efforts and points to a possible future direction for movement organizing. One of the most compelling features of BRO's organizing strategy is that "it is always looking for ways to build coalitions with others to organize against the Christian Right and to support progressive causes" (telephone interview, June 26, 2000). The organization's support for same-sex marriage is part of a broader agenda for political, social, and cultural change. Same-sex marriage is just one of the many issues on which BRO builds coalitions with others. For example, the organization developed a year-round Fair Workplace Project campaign in 1995, which entailed working with corporations to develop nondiscriminatory personnel policies. Over four hundred corporations, including Nike and Hewlett Packard, have signed onto this project. BRO has also worked to mobilize and train civil rights volunteers, organizations, and employees, a project that transcends narrowly focused identity politics.

BRO has been a model of how to organize against the Christian Right through its work tracking the antigay efforts of Lon Mabon's Oregon Citizens' Alliance (OCA) and the Oregon Christian Coalition (OCC). In 2000 the OCA secured enough signatures to place its "Student Protection Act" on the November ballot. BRO did an excellent job in publicizing the nature of the act and what it would do to openly lesbian and gay teachers (see Appendix C). Through the Internet and door-to-door canvassing, the organization worked furiously organizing against this initiative, as its June 23, 2000, "Weekly Update" e-mail to subscribers suggested:

We are revving up our campaign to defeat the OCA in November. The campaign team is doing outreach at PRIDES across the state, running door to door canvasses to identify pro-gay voters and educate voters about the initiative, and recruiting our supporters, like you, to become part of the campaign. If you see OCC or OCA members gathering signatures, and if they leave their petitions unattended, write down the names of the signature gatherers listed on the sheet. Report this to Basic Rights Oregon—unattended position sheets will be thrown out when the OCA/OCC file their signatures. (E-mail to author, from Basic Rights Oregon's *Weekly Update,* June 26, 2000)

The organization specifically targeted "queer" youth activists as it attempted to mobilize against the Christian Right's efforts (see Appendix D). Recognizing the importance of BRO's work, the HRC and NGLTF lent financial and grassroots training support (telephone interview, June 26, 2000). While BRO is certainly comfortable with a rights-based strategy, as its name suggests, it provides a compelling model for a form of state and local organizing that embraces outsider politics and recognizes the importance of building coalitions with others in order to promote a progressive political and cultural agenda while also challenging the Christian Right's continued assault on sexual minorities. BRO's outstanding grassroots organizing was rewarded on November 7, 2000, when the referendum on the Student Protection Act was defeated by Oregon voters by a margin of 53–47 percent. Similar grassroots organizations exist throughout the United States. What all of them desperately need are some of the resources that have been accumulated over the years by national organizations, such as HRC, through their extensive fundraising networks.

REFLECTIONS ON THE FUTURE

The lesbian and gay movements face several immediate and long-term challenges. First, this book has argued that if the movements are to be successful, they must develop an extensive grassroots network in all fifty states, one that can be mobilized when needed to respond to reactionary Christian Right initiatives and to hold national lawmakers accountable as well.

There is evidence that the national lesbian and gay organizations have finally begun to recognize the importance of supporting state and local organizers with resources, education, and training. The importance of all of these efforts should not be underestimated.

Second, the lesbian and gay movements must reframe issues in ways that link narrow civil rights concerns with broader political, cultural, and economic strategies for change. Needed are continuing efforts to challenge race, gender, and economic hierarchies within the movements themselves as well as in the larger society. If this latter goal is to be accomplished successfully, it will require cooperation within and between progressive movements and serious efforts to transcend narrow identity politics while also respecting the diverse identities encompassed by the movements.

Third, education at all levels is crucial to challenge the socially constructed notion that heterosexuality is normative. Teachers need to afford students the opportunity to confront sexual-orientation issues in historical, political, social, cultural, and economic contexts. For this to happen, teachers will also need to be properly trained to discuss these issues given a society that celebrates heterosexuality in all of its forms.

The Christian Right will certainly organize against any educational efforts that challenge the heterosexual paradigm. With this in mind, the lesbian and gay movements must work with others to build the coalitions needed to promote and protect an honest and open educational climate.

It should come as little surprise that a teacher concludes his book by talking about the importance of education. At the end of my Sexual Minority Movements and Public Policy course, which I have taught at Hobart and William Smith Colleges for several years, my students always ask what they can do to engage the issues raised in the course, which are also the issues that I have discussed throughout this book. They want to do something about these concerns and insist on a discussion of strategy in the last class meeting. With their help, I try to tease out possible directions for individuals who want to do something in response to the course materials. Two concrete possibilities often emerge from our discussions. First, individuals can challenge individual acts of homophobia, cowardice, and misunderstanding as they go about their daily lives among family members, friends, and co-workers. To do so in a society that celebrates heterosexuality is unmistakably an act of courage and resistance. But the analysis in this book suggests that an individual response is not enough, given the enormity of the task facing the contemporary lesbian and gay movements. What is also needed is an approach that encourages citizens to work with others to challenge heterosexuality's claim to normalcy. This requires political organizing, cultural change, and individual and collective acts of courage and resistance. The goal cannot merely be to let us into established societal structures and institutions, but instead it must be to inspire thoughtful reflection regarding how lesbians, gays, bisexuals, and those who are transgendered can challenge those structures that help to define what it means to be an American. This book has been written with these goals in mind.

Appendix A

Platform of the 1993 March on Washington for Lesbian, Gay, and Bi Equal Rights and Liberation

ACTION STATEMENT PREAMBLE TO THE PLATFORM

The Lesbian, Gay, Bisexual and Transgender movement recognizes that our quest for social justice fundamentally links us to the struggles against racism and sexism, class bias, economic injustice and religious intolerance. We must realize if one of us is oppressed we all are oppressed. The diversity of our movement requires and compels us to stand in opposition to all forms of oppression that diminish the quality of life for all people. We will be vigilant in our determination to rid our movement and our society of all forms of oppression and exploitation, so that all of us can develop to our full human potential without regard to race, religion, sexual orientation/identification, identity, gender and gender expression, ability, age or class.

THE MARCH DEMANDS

1. We demand passage of a Lesbian, Gay, Bisexual, and Transgender civil rights bill and an end to discrimination by state and federal governments including the military; repeal of all sodomy laws and other laws that criminalize private sexual expression between consenting adults.
2. We demand massive increase in funding for AIDS education, research, and patient care; universal access to health care including alternative therapies; and an end to sexism in medical research and health care.
3. We demand legislation to prevent discrimination against Lesbians, Gays, Bisexuals and Transgendered people in the areas of family diversity, custody, adoption and foster care and that the definition of family includes the full diversity of all family structures.

From "What Are Lesbian and Gay Rights" as it appears in *Gay and Lesbian Politics: Sexuality and the Emergence of a New Ethic* by Mark Blasius. Reprinted by permission of Temple University Press. © 1994 by Temple University. All Rights Reserved.

4. We demand full and equal inclusion of Lesbians, Gays, Bisexuals and Transgendered people in the education system, and inclusion of Lesbian, Gay, Bisexual and Transgender studies in multicultural curricula.
5. We demand the right to reproductive freedom and choice, to control our own bodies, and an end to sexist discrimination.
6. We demand an end to racial and ethnic discrimination in all forms.
7. We demand an end to discrimination and violent oppression based on actual or perceived orientation/identification, race, religion, identity, sex and gender expression, disability, age, class, AIDS/HIV infection.

PLATFORM DEMANDS AND RELATED ITEMS

1. We demand passage of a Lesbian, Gay, Bisexual and Transgender civil rights bill and an end to discrimination by state and federal governments including the military; repeal of all sodomy laws and other laws that criminalize sexual expression between consenting adults.

    Passage of "The Civil Rights Amendment Act of 1991" (HR 1430 and S574).

    Repeal of Department of Defense directive 1332.14.

    Repeal of laws prohibiting sodomy, cross-gender expression (dress codes) or non-coercive sexual behavior between consenting adults.

    Amendment of the Code of Federal Regulations to recognize same-sex relationships.

    Passage of the Equal Rights Amendment.

    Implementation of, funding for and enforcement of the Americans with Disabilities Act of 1991.

    Passage and implementation of graduated age-of-consent laws.

2. We demand massive increase in funding for AIDS education, research, and patient care; universal access to health care including alternative therapies; and an end to sexism in medical research and health care.

    The provision of responsive, appropriate health care for people with disabilities, deaf and hard of hearing people.

    Revision of the Centers for Disease Control definition of AIDS to include infections particular to women.

    Implementation of the recommendation of the National AIDS Commission immediately.

    A massive increase in funding for AIDS education, research and care—money for AIDS, not for war. This money should come from the defense budget, not existing social services.

    An increase in funding and research to provide an independent study of HIV infection in women, People of Color, Bisexuals, Heterosexuals, children, and women to women transmission.

Access to anonymous testing for HIV.

No mandatory HIV testing.

A cure for AIDS.

The development and legalization of a national needle exchange program.

Free substance abuse treatment on demand.

The redefinition of sexual re-assignment surgeries as medical, not cosmetic, treatment.

The provision of appropriate medical treatment for all transgendered people in prisons and hospitals.

An increase in funding and research for chronic illness, including breast, ovarian, and other cancers particular to women.

The right of all people with chronic illness, including HIV/AIDS, to choices in medical treatment as well as the right to end such treatment.

3. We demand legislation to prevent discrimination against Lesbians, Gays, Bisexuals and Transgendered people in the areas of family diversity, custody, adoption and foster care and that the definition of family includes the full diversity of all family structures.

The recognition and legal protection of a whole range of family structures.

An end to abuse and exploitation of and discrimination against youth.

An end to abuse and exploitation of and discrimination against older/old people.

Full implementation of the recommendations contained in the report of the Health and Human Services Task Force on Youth Suicide.

Recognition of domestic partnerships.

Legalization of same sex marriages.

4. We demand full and equal inclusion of Lesbians, Gays, Bisexuals and Transgendered people in the educational system, and inclusion of Lesbian, Gay, Bisexual and Transgender studies in multicultural curricula.

Culturally inclusive Lesbian, Gay, Bisexual and Transgender Studies program; and information on abortion, AIDS/HIV, childcare and sexuality at all levels of education.

Establishment of campus offices and programs to address Lesbian, Gay, Bisexual and Transgender students' special needs.

The ban of all discriminatory ROTC programs and recruiters from learning institutions.

An end to discrimination at all levels of education.

5. We demand the right to reproductive freedom and choice, to control our own bodies, and an end to sexist discrimination.

The right to control our own bodies.

Unrestricted, safe and affordable alternative insemination.

An end to sterilization abuse.

That access to safe and affordable abortion and contraception be available to all people on demand, without restriction and regardless of age.

That access to unbiased and complete information about the full range of reproductive options be available to all people, regardless of age.

6. We demand an end to racial and ethnic discrimination in all forms.

Support for non-racist policies and affirmative action.

An end to institutionalized racism.

Equal economic opportunity and an end to poverty.

Full reproductive rights, improvement of pre-natal services, availability of alternative insemination for Lesbians and Bisexual women of color.

Repeal all 'English Only' laws and restore and enforce bilingual education.

Repeal all discriminatory immigration laws based on race and HIV status.

A commitment to ending racism, including internalized racism, sexism and all forms of religious and ethnic oppression in our communities and in this country.

An end to the genocide of all the indigenous peoples and their cultures.

Restoration of the self-determination of all indigenous people of the world.

7. We demand an end to discrimination and violent oppression based on actual or perceived sexual orientation/identification, race, religion, identity, sex and gender expression, disability, age, class, AIDS/HIV infection.

An end to anti-Semitism.

An end to sexist oppression.

An end to discrimination against people with disabilities, deaf and hard of hearing people.

An end to discrimination based on sexual orientation in all programs of the Boy Scouts of America.

An end to economic injustice in this country and internationally.

And end to discrimination against prisoners with HIV/AIDS.

An end to discrimination against people with HIV/AIDS, and those perceived as having HIV/AIDS.

An end to consideration of greater dysphoria as a psychiatric disorder.

An end to hate crimes including police brutality, rape and bashing.

An end to censorship.

Appendix B

The Millennium March Agenda: A Status Update

ONE OF THE primary objectives of the Millennium March[1] is to rally the GLBT community around a common political agenda. However, the process by which that agenda is established has been the subject of much controversy, and there is no single set of priorities about which all March participants agree. Here is a brief update on some of the issues most frequently proposed to be part of the March agenda:

HATE CRIMES LEGISLATION

Hate crimes laws provide harsher sentences for violent crimes motivated by bias based on gender, ethnicity, religion, or physical disability. In 22 states and Washington, D.C., sexual orientation is also a protected category. But the federal hate Crimes Prevention Act is stalled in Congress—partly because it includes protection for gay men and lesbians.

RIGHT TO MARRY

It is not possible for gay or lesbian couples to get married legally anywhere in the United States. But there has been significant progress toward meaningful civil unions in recent months. Vermont's House and Senate passed a law that would extend many of the rights of marriage to same-sex couples. And the rabbis of Reform Judaism voted in March to recognize and conduct same-sex unions in their synagogues. However, the U.S. Congress and 31 states have passed "defense of Marriage" acts that attempt to permanently restrict marriage to opposite-sex couples.

EMPLOYMENT NON-DISCRIMINATION

Although 11 states and many cities outlaw job discrimination based on sexual orientation, the vast majority of gay men and lesbians can be fired because of their sexuality. The federal Employment Non-Discrimination Act was voted down by the Senate in 1996 by a narrow 50–49 margin

191

and never made it to the floor of the House. House Minority leader Dick Gephardt, D-MO, has promised to introduce it if Democrats retake control of the House, and Al Gore has pledged his support. George W. Bush opposes ENDA as "special treatment."

MILITARY SERVICE

Until the 1993 passage of "Don't Ask, Don't Tell," gay men and lesbians were officially banned from the U.S. Armed Forces. Now they are only excluded if they are open about their sexuality. Most reports have concluded that DADT has worsened harassment for gay and lesbian servicemembers. Al Gore, both Clintons, and many prominent Democrats now believe that DADT has failed and that gay men and lesbians should be allowed to serve openly and equally.

LESBIAN HEALTH ISSUES

Historically, the practice of medicine has been based on an understanding of male anatomy. Women's health was an early, pressing concern of the feminist movement, and in the past decade, lesbians have organized to focus attention on their own specific health needs. Lesbians are less likely to seek health care (especially gynecological exams) than other women, and they are at higher risk for breast, cervical and ovarian cancers because they are less likely to have children by age 30. A 1999 study by the National Academy of Science concluded that extensive research into lesbian health is still desperately needed.

AIDS/HIV

HIV has not been receiving as much attention from the gay and lesbian community as it once did. Recently introduced drugs have greatly extended the life expectancies of HIV-positive people—at least those who can afford the medications. Funding for AIDS research continues to be approved each year by Congress, but many believe the money is insufficient. Outside the gay and lesbian community, the biggest area of concern is Africa, where HIV prevention and treatment are still woefully inadequate.

LGBT PEOPLE OF COLOR

Misunderstood by both those who share their skin color and those who share their sexual preference, LGBT people of color—while always judged first and foremost by race—often feel caught between two worlds. The controversy over lack of diversity surrounding this March on Washington proved that this double exclusion has not gone away.

ADOPTION RIGHTS

In every state except Florida, it is legal for gay men or lesbians to adopt children. Until 1990, however, only one parent was typically recognized by the government. Now about half of the states allow "second parent adoptions"—the granting of joint parental responsibility to two unmarried people. There is no federal legislation on the issue, though some organizations are challenging gay adoption bans as unconstitutional.

LGBT AGING ISSUES

Gay culture has always privileged youth, but life goes on well past the hedonistic twenties and thirties. As the population in general is living longer, so are we. Senior gays and lesbians face unique challenges, both legal—such as rights of succession—and social, such as meeting people and growing older without the support of children.

LGBT YOUTH ISSUES

Gay and lesbian adolescents and teens have always been one of the most vulnerable groups to anti-gay prejudice. They are at a higher risk for suicide and are believed to have higher rates of drug and alcohol abuse. However, an increasing number of gay teens are coming out early in life and are fighting to make their schools a safe place for their peers. Of particular note has been the increasing number of gay-straight alliances formed in high schools—a move that has received praise from many teachers' organizations, but that has drawn criticism from "pro-family" groups. At least one school district has banned extracurricular student groups altogether, since barring gay-straight alliances alone would be considered discriminatory.

OVERTURNING ANTI-GLBT LAWS

The passage of California's anti-same-sex marriage Knight Initiative has galvanized the gay community to work against homophobic legislation across the country. The biggest priorities currently are similar "Defense of Marriage" laws in 31 states, as well as Florida and Utah's laws that create obstacles for gay families.

RIGHT TO PRIVACY/CHOICE

Many gay men and lesbians see a connection between reproductive freedom and gay rights. Both are based on the principle that the government should not—and indeed cannot, because of the constitutional right to privacy—pass laws that interfere in personal sexual and reproductive choices.

GLOBAL GLBT ISSUES

The United States falls somewhere in the middle of the spectrum with respect to gay rights. Many countries—most notably, western European nations and Australia—are considered more progressive socially and politically on gay issues. Gay and lesbian activists are working on strengthening connections among countries to move the agenda along on a global scale.

Appendix C

Another Divisive Anti-Gay Initiative from the OCA:
Bringing Discrimination into Oregon's Schools

What Would the So-Called "Student Protection Act" Actually Do?

The OCA has misleadingly called their initiative the "Student Protection Act." In fact, this discriminatory measure will not "protect" anyone.

Depending on how this initiative is interpreted:

✗   **Good teachers could be fired, just because they are openly gay or lesbian.**

✗   **Counseling or support programs for gay or lesbian students would be banned.**

✗   **Books and materials written by gays or touching on homosexual ideas, culture or famous gay people would be removed and banned unless they specifically condemned gays. Examples could include works by Plato and Walt Whitman, and books such as "The Color Purple."**

✗   **HIV/AIDS education and other health related classes would be jeopardized, denying students the information they need to make responsible choices.**

Here is the actual text of the initiative:

Certified Ballot Title: **Prohibits Public School Instruction Encouraging, Promoting, Sanctioning Homosexual, Bisexual Behaviors**

AN ACT: *Relating to the instruction in ethics and morality. Referred to as the "Student Protection Act"*

BE IT ENACTED BY THE PEOPLE OF THE STATE OF OREGON:

Section 1, ORS 336.067 is amended to read (new section):

(e) Sexual Orientation as it relates to homosexuality and bisexuality, is a divisive subject matter not necessary to the instruction of students in public schools. Notwithstanding any other law or rule, the instruction of behaviors relating to homosexuality and bisexuality shall not be presented in a public school in a manner which encourages, promotes or sanctions such behaviors.

Section 2, ORS 659.155 is amended to read (new section):

(l) Any public elementary or secondary school determined by the Superintendent of Public Instruction or any community college determined by the Commissioner for Community College Services to be in noncompliance with provisions of ORS 336.067 (e) or ORS 659.150 and this section shall be subject to appropriate sanctions, which may include withholding of all or part of state funding, as established by rule of the State Board of Education.

As in the past, the OCA's initiative is as dangerous for what it <u>doesn't</u> say. It doesn't define what is meant by homosexuality and bisexuality being "presented." Neither does it define "encourages, promotes or sanctions." And it is certainly not even-handed: it is conspicuously silent on schools offering anti-gay materials.

The OCA's latest anti-gay initiative would bring anti-gay discrimination into every Oregon school. It's unnecessary, unfair, and tramples Oregon's tradition of fairness and respect for basic rights.

BASIC RIGHTS OREGON
ADDRESS P.O. Box 40625 Portland, OR 97240 **PHONE** 503.222.6151 **FAX** 503.236.6686

Reprinted by permission of Basic Rights Oregon.

Appendix D

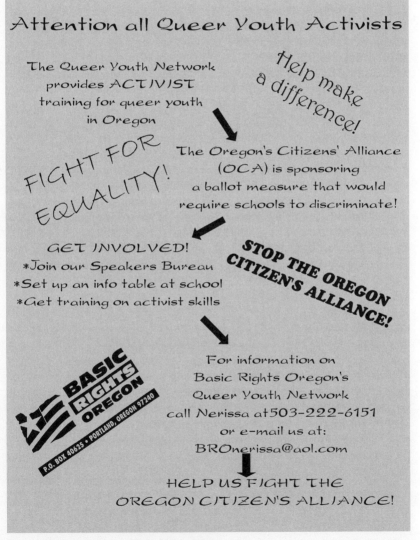

Attention all Queer Youth Activists

The Queer Youth Network
provides ACTIVIST
training for queer youth
in Oregon

Help make
a difference!

FIGHT FOR
EQUALITY!

The Oregon's Citizens' Alliance
(OCA) is sponsoring
a ballot measure that would
require schools to discriminate!

GET INVOLVED!
*Join our Speakers Bureau
*Set up an info table at school
*Get training on activist skills

STOP THE OREGON
CITIZEN'S ALLIANCE!

BASIC RIGHTS OREGON
P.O. BOX 40625 • PORTLAND, OREGON 97240

For information on
Basic Rights Oregon's
Queer Youth Network
call Nerissa at 503-222-6151
or e-mail us at:
BROnerissa@aol.com

HELP US FIGHT THE
OREGON CITIZEN'S ALLIANCE!

Reprinted by permission of Basic Rights Oregon.

Notes

CHAPTER ONE

The Franklin Kameny quote used as the epigraph for Chapter 1 appears in Loughery 1998, pp. 442–43.

1. As this book will make clear, the so-called lesbian and gay movement is composed of a diversity of groups and individuals, and in it we see the convergence of a wide range of identities. Judging it inappropriate to collapse this rich diversity into a unitary discussion, I will refer to the lesbian and gay *movements* in the plural throughout this book. I place "lesbian" first in acknowledgment of the reality that women continue to occupy a position of structural inequality in the larger society.

2. It is also important to recognize that the interests of lesbians and gay men are not the same, especially in a country where "American women working full time still earn an average of 74 cents for each dollar earned by men, according to a new report published jointly by the AFL-CIO and the Institute for Women's Policy Research (IWPR) in Washington" (Barko 2000, 61). For a discussion of the implications of this report and "the other gender gap," see Barko 2000, pp. 61–64.

3. I acknowledge Martin Duberman's discussion of this important distinction in his essay "Feminism and Gay Men," in Duberman 1999, p. 286.

4. The political-science theory associated with this perspective is the democratic theory of elitism. Elitists argue that too much citizen participation will destabilize the political and economic system. For classic statements of this perspective, see Schumpeter 1950 and Huntington 1975, pp. 59–118. For a good critique of this perspective, see Bachrach 1971.

5. bell hooks describes marginalization in this way: "To be in the margin is to be part of the whole but outside the main body" (hooks 1984, i).

6. Yet it is also important to point out that many gays, lesbians, and bisexuals do not suffer from the kind of "advanced marginalization" that Cathy Cohen identifies with African Americans. Cohen contends that "In this contradictory political context, more African Americans still lack the political, economic, and social resources necessary to participate actively in decision-making that significantly influences and structures their lives" (Cohen 1999, 9).

7. David A. Snow has done some of the most important work on the construction of social movement frames. See, for example, Snow 1992.

8. For an excellent discussion of the concept of power as it relates to the lesbian and gay movements and the Christian Right, see Wald 2000b. The theme of power is central to the entire collection of essays.

9. As Sidney Tarrow has pointed out, some movements combine institutional and extra-institutional action. This is certainly true of ACT UP, which embraced unconventional politics in the form of "zaps" and "die-ins" while also pursuing the lobbying and the coordinating of committees that one typically associates with insider politics. See Tarrow 1998, p. 209, for a brief discussion of this kind of movement politics.

10. See McAdam 1982 for a fine overview of the political-process approach to social movements. See also Tarrow 1998, pp. 18–19, for a good discussion of the development of the political-process model.

11. Annamarie Jagose offers an excellent discussion of the distinction between essentialist and social-constructionist views of sexual identity: "To a certain extent, debates about what constitutes homosexuality can be understood in terms of the negotiation between so-called essentialist and constructionist positions. Whereas essentialists regard identity as natural, fixed and innate, constructionists assume identity is fluid, the effect of social conducting and available cultural models for understanding oneself. 'Essentialists hold that a person's sexual orientation is a culture-independent, objective and intrinsic property,' writes Edward Stein, 'while social constructionists think it is culture-dependent, relational and, perhaps, not objective.' Essentialists assume that homosexuality exists across time as a universal phenomenon which has a marginalised but continuous and coherent history of its own. Constructionists, by contrast, assume that because same-sex sex acts have different cultural meanings in different historical contexts, they are not identical across time and space" (Jagose 1996, 8–9).

12. For a good discussion of the weaknesses of new-social-movement theory, see Adam, Duyvendak, and Krouwel 1999, pp. 4–5.

13. This discussion of a rights-based strategy is based on the superb discussion in Blasius 1994, pp. 131–78.

14. Urvashi Vaid defines "virtual equality" in the following way: "In this state, gay and lesbian people possess some of the trappings of full equality but are denied all of its benefits. We proceed as if we enjoy real freedom, real acceptance, as if we have won lasting changes in the laws and mores of our nation. In the state of virtual equality, gay and lesbian people are at once insiders, involved openly in government and public affairs to a degree never before achieved, and outsiders, shunned by our elected officials unless they need our money or votes in close elections" (Vaid 1995, 4).

15. The Lambda Legal Defense and Education Fund is discussed in Chapter 3, when the legal-rights strategy is examined critically.

CHAPTER TWO

The quote from Urvashi Vaid used as the epigraph for Chapter 2 appears in Vaid 1995, p. 34.

1. See Chauncey 1994.
2. See Bérubé 1990.
3. See D'Emilio 1983.
4. See Adam 1995.

5. The name "Mattachine" was first used by medieval masked singers. Hay and his cofounders used this name to suggest that homosexuals were also invisible.

6. This pioneering lesbian group was "named for a woman who was thought to be Sappho's contemporary" (Cruikshank 1992, 68).

7. Besides being the chief organizer of the Washington, D.C., Mattachine Society, in 1971 Kameny also became the first openly gay candidate to run for a seat in Congress. He won only 1.6 percent of the vote in his effort to become the first congressional delegate representing the District of Columbia. But despite low voter support, his candidacy was an important one, especially to assimilationists, because it suggested that doors were opening, albeit slowly and slightly, for lesbians and gays to enter into the mainstream electoral process. In addition to his 1971 campaign, Kameney coined the national rallying cry "Gay is Good!" For a good discussion of the various roles that Kameny played within the broader movements, see Streitmatter 1995, pp. 57–62.

8. Members of the Mattachine Society and the Daughters of Bilitis held an historic demonstration at the White House on May 29, 1965. The demonstrations included ten men and three women. The group held signs, including one reading, "Governor Wallace Met with Negroes, Our Government Won't Meet with Us." A second White House demonstration in October 1965 drew thirty-six protesters (Raben 1998, 278).

9. The analysis here borrows from Urvashi Vaid's thoughtful discussion of these issues in Vaid, 1995, p. 57.

10. See, for example, Doug Ireland's scathing critique of HRC's endorsement in Ireland 1999, pp. 11–17.

11. For example, an October 1996 article on the organization, which appeared in the *Washington Blade*, was titled "NGLTF's Identity Crisis" (Freiberg 1996, 1, 31, 33).

12. For a good discussion of the problems faced by the Leadership Forum, see Whitfield 2000, pp. 1, 27.

13. For a good overview of the meeting between George W. Bush and representatives from the Log Cabin Republicans, see Cassels 2000, pp. 1, 12.

14. Regarding "non-connected" PACs, political action committee expert Robert Biersack explains, "some PACs . . . are formed independently to influence the electoral process. These are known as 'nonconnected' PACs. They are formed by individuals who care about specific issues or government policies and seek to promote their views by organizing groups that directly lobby members of Congress. PACs formed by these nonconnected, ideological, or issue groups must pay for their overhead using voluntary contributions. Moreover, these and other groups that are organized primarily for political purposes do not receive the same tax advantages as other charitable organizations. As a result, many issue-oriented groups create several organizations, some of which can receive tax-exempt contributions for public education and other purposes, and others, including PACs, that are primarily political. Nonconnected PACS have the same limits on contributions to candidates, but they may seek contributions from any individual, not just group members. It is these committees that have popularized the direct-mail solicitation techniques that fill America's mailboxes" (Biersack 1994, 5).

15. For a more fully developed discussion of these constraints, see Cohen 1999, p. 338.

16. For a good discussion of how the movements ignore these broader issues, see Duberman, "Racism in the Gay Male World," in Duberman 1999, p. 345.

CHAPTER THREE

The quote from Kevin M. Cathcart used as an epigraph for Chapter 3 appeared in a letter to the editor of the New York *Times*, Sept. 18, 1996, p. A24. The quote from Alexis de Tocqueville comes from his *Democracy in America*, ed. Phillips Bradley, 2 vols. (New York: Vintage, 1954).

1. I will not attempt a comprehensive history of lesbian and gay legal status since that status continues to change over time, and also varies from state to state. As we will see later in this chapter, this dynamic legal process is very much rooted in our system of separation of powers and federalism, which refers to the balance of powers between the federal and state governments.

2. For an excellent discussion of the values associated with classical liberalism and liberal democracy, see Macpherson 1976.

3. For an excellent case study of the importance of lesbian community building in the Buffalo, New York, bar culture from 1940 to 1960, see Davis and Kennedy 1993.

4. Jim Kepner claims that J. Edgar Hoover issued the order to confiscate the October 1954 issue of the magazine "because Hoover had been accused in the prior issue of 'One' of sleeping with Clyde Tolson, his driver and bodyguard" (Cain 1993, 9).

5. For a full discussion of the legal cases that provide a broad context for the Court's 1986 *Bowers v. Hardwick* decision, see the excellent review in Pacelle 1996, pp. 208–13.

6. The lesbian and gay movements were also understandably angered when Justice Lewis Powell, Jr., who cast the deciding vote in the *Bowers* case, informed a group of law students that he had changed his vote at the last minute, after reviewing the case for less than half an hour. The legal scholar John C. Jeffries, Jr., reports that Powell very reluctantly took sides in this case. Since he could not find a "middle ground," he voted for retaining the status quo. See Jeffries 1994.

7. Gertsmann defines "suspect classes" as those groups "that are so powerless or despised that they cannot effectively participate in the pluralistic political process." As a result, they need to be strongly protected by the courts (Gertsmann 1999, 27).

8. It is important to recognize that the lesbian and gay movements did not choose to take the *Bowers* case to the U.S. Supreme Court; Georgia attorney general Michael Bowers did. The movements actually won in Georgia's Eleventh Circuit Court, and the state of Georgia appealed to the Supreme Court. I am grateful to Patricia Cain for reminding me of this important point (e-mail communication to author, Sept. 3, 2000).

9. For a good discussion of the limitations of the courts as policy makers, see Cain 2000, pp. 5–9.

10. For an excellent discussion of school-desegregation barriers, see the essays in Orfield, Eaton, and the Harvard Project on School Desegregation 1996.

11. See, for example, Salokar 1997.

12. The discussion that follows borrows heavily from several earlier works that I have published that address President Clinton's promise and failed attempt to overturn the military ban. See Rimmerman 1996a, 1996b, 1998b, and 2000.

13. See Rimmerman 1993, p. 17, for a more fully developed discussion of these important issues.

14. In July 1993 President Clinton proposed "Don't Ask, Don't Tell" as a compromise policy. It contained the following provisions:

1. Military recruiters are barred from asking whether prospective enlistees are gay or lesbian.
2. Homosexual conduct is forbidden both on-base and off-base.
3. Homosexual conduct is defined as including the following behaviors:
   a. same-sex intercourse
   b. public acknowledgment of homosexuality
   c. an attempt at a same-sex marriage
   d. same-sex hand-holding or kissing
4. Permissible actions include the following:
   a. telling a spouse, attorney, or member of the clergy about your homosexuality
   b. associating with openly gay and lesbian people
   c. going to a gay or lesbian bar
   d. marching in a gay pride march in civilian clothes
5. Military personnel found to have engaged in homosexual conduct may be discharged.
6. Military officials may not initiate an inquiry to determine if an enlistee is gay or lesbian, but if they suspect, based on "articulable facts," that a person has engaged in prohibited activity, they may investigate to verify their suspicion.
7. Military personnel may not "out" suspected gays and lesbians capriciously and without evidence, and any attempt at blackmailing a suspected gay or lesbian member of the armed forces may be punished with a dishonorable discharge, a two-thousand-dollar fine, and a one-year jail term. (Reproduced from Bull 1993, 24)

Clinton's proposal was subsequently modified by Senator Sam Nunn (D-Georgia). The Nunn proposal "included a statement that homosexual conduct is incompatible with military service; it expressly permitted questioning recruits about sexual orientation; it provided no examples of off-base conduct that might be permitted; and it omitted the Clinton policy's stated objective of enforcing sodomy laws equally for heterosexuals and homosexuals—all of this using language carefully crafted to immunize the new policy as much as possible from judicial challenge" (Rayside 1998, 230). Even though Nunn's proposed policy was much more restrictive than Clinton's, announced several days before, the Clinton administration signaled its approval. Congress then sent Nunn's version, in the form of an amendment to a major budget bill, to the White House on November 17, 1993, where it was signed without ceremony by President Clinton (ibid., 231). Until that point, the ban had been enforced through an executive order, which could at least be changed through a presidential directive. The codification meant that any change to Nunn's policy would require action by the full Congress. In addition, the congressional version stated that lesbians and gays have no constitutional right to serve in the armed forces. The final element of Nunn's plan is precisely what Bill Clinton had hoped to challenge by overturning the military ban through an executive order (Rimmerman 1998b, 259).

15. Concrete examples of these policies are Clinton's commitment to welfare reform associated with workfare, support for the death penalty, and a willingness to question the overall effectiveness of the 1960s Great Society programs.

16. Urvashi Vaid develops this critique (Vaid 1995, p. 386).

17. Osburn and Benecke 1996. For a good review of the application of the current military policy, see D'Amico 2000.

18. It is important to remember that the Cammermeyer case was a challenge to the old military policy regarding lesbians and gays, the policy in effect when Bill Clinton assumed the presidency in January 1993.

19. For a fine discussion of how the courts have addressed this distinction, see Jacobson 1996.

20. For a good discussion of how the campaign for same-sex marriage has become institutionalized within the broader lesbian and gay movements, see Warner 1999, especially p. 85.

21. For a full discussion of Ettlebrick's perspective, see Ettlebrick 1997, pp. 817–18.

22. For a good overview of her position, see Hunter 1995b.

23. The Supreme Court of Hawaii listed some of the benefits to those who are married in its *Baehr v. Lewin* decision: "1. a variety of state income tax advantages, including deductions, credits, rates, exemptions, and estimates; 2. public assistance from and exemptions relating to the Department of Human Services; 3. control, division, acquisition, and disposition of community property; 4. rights relating to dower, curtesy, and inheritance; 5. rights to notice, protection, benefits, and inheritance under the Uniform Probate Code; 6. award of child custody and support payments in divorce proceedings; 7. the right to spousal support; 8. the right to enter into premarital agreements; 9. the right to change of name; 10. the right to file a nonsupport action; 11. post-divorce rights relating to support and property division; 12. the benefit of the spousal privilege and confidential marital communications; 13. the benefit of the exemption of real property from attachment or execution; 14. the right to bring a wrongful death action," as quoted in Warner 1999, pp. 117–18.

24. Robert Bailey provides a succinct and thoughtful overview of what constitutes domestic partnership: "The term domestic partnership covers many different concepts. Generally, it refers to the conferring of legal status to cohabiting partners in same-sex or unmarried opposite-sex partners. Obviously, no city can grant any legal status beyond its own authorization by state law. So typically the options available to localities are 'marriage-like' entitlements: a neutral partnership registry, a set of fringe benefits for the domestic partners of public employees, and specific family or spouse entitlements that can be granted by the local

government. Among these are bereavement leave and family/paternity/maternity leave offered by contract to the partner of civil servants and public employees" (Bailey 1999, 309).

25. For an excellent overview of the historical and contemporary context for the debate over same-sex marriage, see Dolkart 1998, pp. 316–18. The following discussion borrows from Dolkart's thoughtful discussion of the central legal issues involved.

26. *Baker v. Nelson; Jones v. Hallahan; Singer v. Hara.*

27. I am grateful to Patricia Cain for reminding me of this important point (e-mail communication with author, Sept. 3, 2000).

28. The following states do not recognize same-sex marriages (in parentheses is the year such non-recognition was adopted): Alabama (1998), Arizona (1996), Arkansas (1997), Delaware (1996), Florida (1997), Georgia (1996), Idaho (1996), Illinois (1996), Indiana (1997), Iowa (1998), Kansas (1996), Kentucky (1998), Louisiana (1996), Maine (1997), Michigan (1996), Minnesota (1997), Mississippi (1997), Missouri (1996), Montana (1997), North Dakota (1997), Oklahoma (1996), South Carolina (1996), South Dakota (1996), Tennessee (1996), Utah (1995), Virginia (1997), Washington (1998). This information is from Eskridge 1999, pp. 362–71.

29. For a good overview of the background of the President's decision to sign DOMA, see Purdum 1996.

30. Sullivan argues that same-sex marriage is a crucial goal for the lesbian and gay movements to champion because "marriage, under any interpretation of American constitutional law, is among the most basic civil rights." He rejects "civil unions" of the kind embraced by Vermont's state legislature because they continue to promote stigmatization. For a thoughtful overview of these arguments, see Sullivan 2000.

CHAPTER FOUR

The quote from Paula Treichler used as an epigraph for Chapter 4 comes from Treichler 1999, p. 98. Michael Callen is quoted in Rofes 1990, pp. 13–14.

1. For further discussion of how unconventional politics has been used in these diverse arenas, see Rimmerman 1997.

2. For an excellent discussion of the Stonewall rebellion and its consequences, see Duberman 1993.

3. The political scientist Matthew Moen offers this analysis of the relationship between the New Right and the Christian Right: "New-Right leaders Richard Viguerie, Paul Weyrich, and Howard Phillips, in particular, actively spawned a host of overlapping organizations in the mid-1970's, a tactic that those political mentors both realized vis-a-vis the Christian Right and passed on to its politically inexperienced leaders" (Moen 1992, 67). For a full discussion of the relationship between the New Right and the Christian Right, see Moen 1992.

4. President Gerald Ford's announcement of the swine flu program was an exception. For a discussion of the federal government's responses to swine flu and Legionnaire's disease, see Foreman 1994, and Perrow and Guillen 1990.

5. For a fine discussion of Koop's efforts to address AIDS in meaningful ways, see Koop 1991.

6. For a critique of the belief that an AIDS czar is even needed, see Foreman 1994.

7. In his thoughtful book, *Political Language: Words that Succeed, Policies that Fail* (1977), the political scientist Murray Edelman discusses how presidents appoint commissions as a way to deflect attention from substantive policy responses. I believe that Reagan's appointment of the Watkins AIDS Commission provides evidence to support Edelman's claim.

8. In his fine book on AIDS, John-Manuel Andriote points out that the AIDS Action Council's board members became very interested in hiring Jean McGuire as the organization's first executive director when they found out that she had two children. McGuire told Andriote in a personal interview that the board member who contacted her "was trying to impress on me how important they felt it was not to have a gay image of AIDS Action Council. And a woman with two kids who was committed to this issue despite the fact that so many people affected by it are gay . . ." As it turned out, McGuire got the job despite the fact that she identified herself privately as bisexual. She was never asked about her sexual orientation in the interview; today she lives with a female partner. See Andriote 1999, pp. 228–29.

9. For an excellent discussion of the de-gaying and re-gaying of AIDS, see Peter Scott 1997, pp. 305–27.

10. See Watney 1994, pp. 145–47, for an interesting discussion of the regaying of AIDS throughout Europe.

11. Mass's May 18, 1981, article, "Disease Rumors Largely Unfounded," "was the first mention of the disease in any publication at all" (Alwood 1996, 212). The article commented, "Last week there were rumors that an exotic new disease had hit the gay community in New York. Here are the facts. From the New York City Department of Health, Dr. Steve Phillips explained that the rumors are for the most part unfounded. Each year, approximately 12 to 24 cases of infection with a protozoa-like organism, pneumocystis carinii, are reported in New York City area. The organism is not exotic; in fact, it's ubiquitous. But most of us have a natural or easily acquired immunity" (ibid.).

12. David Colby and Timothy Cook examined nightly news coverage of AIDS by NBC, ABC, and CBS in the period 1982–89 and concluded that "authoritative sources, especially within the Reagan administration, made few efforts to call attention to AIDS, and the dramatic accident that alerted the media to AIDS did not occur until 1985 with the revelation of the illness of Rock Hudson" (Colby and Cook 1991, 246).

13. For an illuminating discussion of why certain elements of the lesbian and gay press failed to address AIDS adequately in the early years, see Streitmatter 1995, chapter 9.

14. For a fine discussion of how the gay community was forced to take ownership of AIDS in the face of governmental indifference, see Siplon 1999.

15. Kramer's frustration with the lack of a serious response to AIDS by policy elites and members of the gay community first manifested itself in his impor-

tant essay "1,112 and Counting," originally published in the March 14–27, 1983, issue of the New York *Native* and reprinted in every major lesbian and gay newspaper throughout the United States. The article's opening lines catch the reader's attention immediately: "If this article doesn't scare the shit out of you, we're in real trouble. If this article doesn't rouse you to anger, fury, rage, and action, gay men may have no future on this earth. Our continued existence depends on just how angry you can get." The article is reprinted in its entirety in Kramer 1994, pp. 33–51.

16. For his full critique of GMHC, see Kramer 1994, pp. 100–139.

17. For an overview of the theory of participatory democracy, see Rimmerman 1997.

18. The CDC definition is important because it has served as a filter "through which eligibility for AIDS-related government benefits must often pass" (Arno and Feiden 1992, 200). In the early years of the epidemic especially, women were often ineligible for important entitlement programs because their HIV-related infections were not included in the official CDC definition. For example, infections of the reproductive organs and genital tract are often associated with HIV, but in the early years they were not included in the CDC's definition of AIDS. Further, the clinical trials needed to determine what medical treatments women need were not adequately funded during this time (ibid.).

19. As Nancy E. Stoller (1997) points out in her excellent discussion of women in AIDS organizations, women have had important roles from the beginning. She observes, "although AIDS has struck men in higher numbers than women, women have been among the ill since the beginning. They have also been involved as caretakers, educators, physicians, public health officials, and community activists. As a diverse social group linked by gender in an epidemic in which gender and sexuality are key, women, and lesbians in particular, have played powerful symbolic, sexual, and social roles" (Stoller 1997, 177).

20. For excellent discussions of how ACT UP connects art, photography, and politics in important ways, see Crimp 1988, Crimp with Rolston 1990, and Sadownick 1990.

21. For a good discussion of the mainstream media's coverage of ACT UP protests, see Streitmatter 1995, p. 288.

22. For a good discussion of the Lesbian Avengers, see Schulman 1994, pp. 279–319.

23. Unlike ACT UP, which had clear connections to the direct-action practices of past movements, TAG had no real precedent in civil rights, feminist, or lesbian and gay rights activism. For further discussion of this claim, see Harrington 1997, p. 277.

24. The companies are: The Pharmaceutical Manufacturers' Association of South Africa; Alcon Laboratories (S.S.) (Proprietary) Limited; Bayer (Proprietary) Limited; Bristol-Myers Squibb (Proprietary) Limited; Byk Madaus (Proprietary) Limited; Eli Lilly (South Africa) (Proprietary) Limited; Glaxo Wellcome (South Africa) (Proprietary) Limited; Hoechst Marion Roussel Limited; Ingelheim Pharmaceuticals (Proprietary) Limited; Janssen-Cilag Pharmaceutica (Proprietary) Limited; Alundbeck South Africa (Proprietary) Limited; Merck (Proprietary) Limited; Msd (Proprietary)

Limited; Novartis South Africa (Proprietary) Limited; Novo Noridsk (Proprietary) Limited; Pharmacia and Upjohn (Proprietary) Limited; Rhone-Poulenc Rorer Sothafrica (Proprietary) Limited; Roche Products (Proprietary) Limited; Schering (Proprietary) Limited; S. A. Scientific Pharmaceuticals (Proprietary) Limited; SmithKline Beecham Pharmaceuticals (Proprietary) Limited; Universal Pharmaceuticals (Proprietary) Limited; Wyeth (Proprietary) Limited; Zeneca South Africa (Proprietary) Limited; Bayer Ag; Boehringer-Ingelheim International; Boehringer-Ingelheim Kg; Bristol-Myers Squibb Company; Byk Gulden Lombergschemische Fabrik; Dr. Karl Thomae; Eli Lilly and Company; F. Hoffman-LaRoche Ag; Merck, Merck and Company, Inc.; Rhone-Poulenc Rorer S.A.; SmithKline Beecham; Oliver Cornish (Getty and Michael Botkin's Ghost, Survive Writers Pool 2001, 20).

25. For a good discussion of the October 14, 1979, National March on Washington for Lesbian and Gay Rights, see Clendinen and Nagourney 1999, pp. 403–5, 407–9, and 414–15.

26. In its final version, passed by the Senate by a vote of 94–2, the Helms Amendment stated that, "none of the funds made available under this Act to the Centers for Disease Control shall be used to provide AIDS education, information, or prevention materials and activities that promote or encourage, directly, homosexual sexual activities. . . . Education, information, and prevention activities and materials paid for with funds appropriated under this Act shall emphasize—(1) abstinence from sexual activity outside a sexually monogamous marriage (including abstinence from homosexual activities); and (2) abstinence from the use of illegal intravenous drugs" (King 1993, 120).

By a vote of 368–47, the House of Representatives adopted a motion that instructed "House members of the House-Senate Conference Committee to accept the Senate language of the Helms amendment. Democrats voted for this resolution by a 196–46 margin; Republicans voted for it by a 172–1 margin" (Sherrill 1993, 117). Congress finally overturned the Helms amendment in 1992, "after the American Civil Liberties Union and the Center for Constitutional Rights filed a legal challenge based on the first amendment" (King 1993, 121).

27. For a thoughtful critique of this appropriation of another movement's style, see Keith Boykin 1996, chapter 2, "Are Blacks and Gays the Same?"

28. See Appendix A for the full platform of the 1993 March on Washington.

29. For a fine overview of Frank's role in the 1993 debate over the military ban, see Rayside 1996.

30. Keith Boykin (2000, pp. 89–91) offers an important analysis of how the voices of African-American lesbians, gays, bisexuals, and transgendered people were excluded from the march planning process.

31. For an excellent discussion of the debates surrounding the closure of public sex establishments, see Dangerous Bedfellows 1996.

32. See Warner 1999, pp. 24–33, for his insightful discussion of "the hierarchies of shame," and chapter 4 for a full discussion of the Giuliani administration's crackdown in New York City.

33. See also Badgett 1995, 1997a, and 1997b.

34. See Chasin 2000 for a superb discussion of the issues raised by this question. I will address Chasin's arguments in some detail in Chapter 6, when I exam-

ine the consequences of this identity-based market strategy for the future of the lesbian and gay movements.

CHAPTER FIVE

The quote from Matthew Moen used as an epigraph for Chapter 5 appears in Moen 1992, p. 9. The quote from Didi Herman comes from Herman 1997, pp. 68–69.

1. This important question is also at the core of Didi Herman's *The Antigay Agenda* (1997, p. 6).

2. My discussion here is built on Sara Diamond's excellent overview and analysis in *Not by Politics Alone* (1998, p. 5).

3. For further discussion of these issues, see Epstein 1999, p. 46, and Rayside 1998.

4. Conservative activists Howard Phillips and Paul Weyrich joined Viguerie as leaders of the emerging "New Right."

5. For an excellent overview and discussion of the Miami–Dade County ordinance battle, see Loughery 1998, pp. 371–88. See also Clendinen and Nagourney 1999, pp. 291–311.

6. Clendinen and Nagourney report that even in liberal Seattle, "a police officer had easily gathered the signatures needed to put the city's gay rights ordinance before voters in November" (1999, p. 382).

7. For a more thorough discussion of Cameron's views, see Bull and Gallagher 1996, pp. 26–29.

8. Urvashi Vaid claims that Bush received considerable support from lesbian and gay voters in the 1988 general election. I am uncomfortable making such a claim in the absence of empirical evidence for this conclusion. Exit-poll data on lesbian and gay voters first became available in the 1990 midterm elections. For discussions of exit-poll data for lesbians and gays, see Hertzog 1996 and Bailey 1999.

9. While this chapter's focus is the Christian Right, it is important to point out that the decade of the 1990s witnessed the emergence of a visible gay Right as well. It was composed of neoconservatives, such as Andrew Sullivan, "who repudiated sexual radicalism and sought to reduce the gay movement's struggle for the establishment of equal rights in the public realm" (Epstein 1999, 67); traditional conservatives, such as Bruce Bawer, who were particularly hostile to the increased visibility of "queer politics"; and the Log Cabin Republican club, discussed in Chapter 2. For a brief discussion of these developments, see Epstein 1999, p. 67. Interested readers should also see the following primary sources: Bawer 1993, Sullivan 1995, Sullivan 1998, and Tafel 1999.

10. Sara Diamond explains how *The Gay Agenda* became an important vehicle for mobilizing antigay sentiment during the military debate: "Emerging seemingly out of nowhere, Ty and Jeannette Beeson of the Antelope Valley Springs of Life Church in Lancaster, California, suddenly made headlines with their nationwide promotion of 'The Gay Agenda,' a twenty-minute video featuring scenes from gay pride marches and interviews with antigay doctors, all to the effect that

gays threaten social stability. 'The Gay Agenda' made its debut during the 1992 anti-gay rights ballot initiative campaigns in Oregon and Colorado. But soon after the controversy over gays in the military broke out, Pat Robertson broadcast 'The Gay Agenda' for the one million viewers of his 700 Club program. Anti-gay military officers showed 'The Gay Agenda' at prayer breakfasts and Bible-study meetings. The film was an effective piece of propaganda in the campaign, led by Christian broadcasters in early 1993, to flood Congress with phone calls against lifting the ban" (Diamond, 1998, p. 159).

11. A spokesperson for the Human Rights Campaign Fund pointed out that while his organization could generate a maximum of thirty-five thousand letters on behalf of overturning the ban, Pat Robertson's Christian Coalition had the resources to consistently generate over a hundred thousand. This is just one indicator of the Christian Right's enormous resource advantage. See Lehring 1996, p. 284.

12. At the time these events were unfolding, I was working as an American Political Science Association Congressional Fellow in the office of Senator Tom Daschle (D–South Dakota). My personal observations confirm Rayside's analysis. Senator Daschle's office received many phone calls from South Dakotans protesting Clinton's proposal to overturn the ban and very few, if any, phone calls in support of his efforts.

13. Lou Sheldon's contribution to the rhetoric of hate is his declaration that homosexuality is " 'deviant' and contrary to medical standards, 'a developmental disorder' " (Bull and Gallagher 1996, 84). Sheldon proved himself to be remarkably adept at exploiting the positions of conservative white Christians, and he appealed to African Americans who were increasingly irritated by rhetoric that equated lesbian and gay activism to the civil rights movement. He produced a forty-five-minute video, *Gay Rights, Special Rights,* that showed clips from Martin Luther King, Jr.'s famous "I Have a Dream" speech, and then contrasted that event with the 1993 Gay and Lesbian March on Washington "by interviewing only white participants." By January 1994 Sheldon estimated that he had sold almost forty-five thousand copies of the $19.95 video (ibid., 171). Sheldon and his organization received national publicity and thus legitimacy in August 1995, when then House Speaker Newt Gingrich agreed to permit congressional hearings that examined Sheldon's "allegation that gay activists were proselytizing in the nation's public schools" (ibid., 256).

14. For a good overview of Dobson's Focus on the Family and the power of his organization, see Johnson 2000, pp. 30–31.

15. For an excellent discussion of the battle over the Oregon initiative, see Bull and Gallagher 1996, chapter 3. Lon Mabon, the head of the Oregon Citizens Alliance, used the "special rights" argument with considerable effectiveness in 1988.

16. Bull and Gallagher provide further analysis confirming the effectiveness of the "special rights" argument: "Moreover, by emphasizing that gays were not a 'legitimate' minority recognized by the federal government but instead were seeking minority status based on behavior that most found offensive, Colorado for Family Values could salve the conscience of voters concerned that they were taking a stand against civil rights" (Bull and Gallagher 1996, p. 113).

17. For a review of some of these public opinion polls and their findings, see Gertsmann 1999, pp. 99–102.

18. While the "special rights" argument was integral to the Christian Right's victory in Colorado, it was not the only argument used to persuade Colorado voters to support Amendment 2. For example, former Senator William Armstrong (R-Colorado) wrote in a Colorado for Family Values letter that lesbians and gays were "pleasure-addicted," and had "no use for the traditional family, for traditional moral standards, or for traditional religion" (Bull and Gallagher 1996, 114). Bull and Gallagher identify three components to the Christian Right's characterization of lesbians and gays as "destructive and harmful to society": (1) lesbians and gays are "licentious and promiscuous, . . . their practices abhorrent and perverse"; (2) homosexuality and pedophilia are so closely related that they are essentially synonymous; and (3) gays pose "a health threat to and financial drain on the rest of the population" as a result of AIDS (ibid., 114–15).

CHAPTER SIX

The quote from Robert Bailey used as an epigraph for Chapter 6 comes from Bailey 1999, p. 54. The quote from Shane Phelan appears in Phelan 1994, p. 40.

1. In this final chapter, I build on Valerie Lehr's (1999) notion of a radical democratic politics.

2. See Chibbaro 1998 for a discussion of the White House's response.

3. For articles examining the Scott appointment, see Billard 1995 and Moss 1995b.

4. For an overview of the Socarides appointment, see Chibbaro 1996b.

5. In 1992 Bill Clinton received 72 percent of the gay vote, George Bush père 14 percent, and Ross Perot 14 percent. In 1996 Clinton received 66 percent of the gay vote, Bob Dole 23 percent, and Perot 7 percent (Log Cabin Republicans, 2001). Some have questioned such figures, arguing that lesbian and gay voters are not likely to report their sexual orientations to pollsters. For this reason, the 4–5 percent turnout figures that has been cited for lesbians and gays (the so-called "gay vote") in the 1992, 1996, and 2000 elections may underestimate the number of lesbians and gays who actually vote in any given election.

6. Such claims conveniently ignore the many ways in which the 2000 presidential election has been contested, as well as the reality that in its narrow 5–4 decision in *Bush v. Gore,* the Supreme Court essentially handed Bush the White House.

7. For a good discussion of the issues raised by the media's coverage of Mary Cheney, see Sarah Wildman, "Hiding in Plain Sight," *The Advocate,* Sept. 12, 2000, pp. 26–30.

8. The "Austin 12" included several prominent party members: former Rep. Steve Gunderson (R-Wisconsin); David Catania, a Washington, D.C., city councilman; Brian Bennett, who had served as chief of staff to former Rep. Bob Dornan (R-California); Log Cabin Republicans official Carl Schmid; Scott Evertz, a Wisconsin native who had close ties to the new Secretary of Health and Human Services, former Wisconsin Governor Tommy Thompson, and who was eventually chosen to be the Bush administration's AIDS czar; and Donald Capoccia, a New York real estate developer and confidant of New York Republican Governor George E. Pataki. Charles Francis, a conservative gay Republican with close ties to Bush, helped to arrange the meeting. He is also the founder of the "gay-straight"

Republican Unity Coalition, which hosted campaign events for candidate Bush "and is now the main gay interest group with access to the Administration" (Clendinen 2001a, 72) For a good discussion of Francis's role as a conduit between the Bush administration and gay Republicans, see Dudley Clendinen, "Dubya's Gay Friend," *Out*, June 2001, p. 72, and Shawn Zeller, "A New GOP 'Tone' on Gay Rights?" *National Journal*, May 26, 2001, pp. 1582–83.

9. I am grateful to Steven Lee for reminding me of the importance of this explanation for understanding George W. Bush's interactions with the Christian Right as both a presidential candidate and once he assumed the presidency.

It did not take long for President Bush to be assailed by a Washington, D.C.–based antigay group. The Culture and Family Institute issued a May 31, 2001, report that attacked Bush's record for his first hundred days in office. Specifically, it criticized his failure to "reverse the pro-homosexual agenda of his predecessor, Bill Clinton" (quoted in Chibbaro 2001, 20). The organization claims that Bush's support for what it calls the "gay Republican agenda" has infuriated "Christians and other pro-family Americans." The report lists examples to support the organization's claim that Bush has supported pro-gay policies:

- By appointing a "homosexual activist" to head the White House AIDS office;
- By failing to overturn "a single Clinton executive order dealing with homosexuality";
- By continuing Clinton administration initiatives seeking to strengthen Pentagon measures against antigay harassment in the military;
- By appointing a "homosexual activist and gays-in-the-military crusader" as a temporary consultant to Secretary of Defense Donald Rumsfeld;
- And by supporting an application by the International Lesbian and Gay Association to obtain non-governmental organization status at the United Nations. The group says a middle-level U.S. official at the U.N. "spoke in favor" of ILGA's application before a U.N. agency (ibid.).

10. For an excellent discussion of how lesbian and gay rights issues might have been pivotal in the 2000 presidential election, see Robert Dreyfuss, "The Double-Edge Wedge," *The American Prospect*, August 28, 2000, pp. 23–31.

11. For a good discussion of George Bush's proposed FY 2002 AIDS budget and the response of AIDS advocates, see Bob Roeher, "Gay Man Named to Head AIDS Office," *Bay Area Reporter*, April 12, 2001, p. 13.

12. For a good discussion of the Evertz appointment, see Elizabeth Becker, "Gay Republican Will Run White House AIDS Office," *New York Times*, April 9, 2001, p. A13.

13. For a good discussion of local organizing activities in the first six months of the Bush presidency, see Chris Bull, "Going Local," *The Advocate*, June 19, 2001, pp. 33–36.

14. One estimate is "that the cost of combination therapy that includes protease inhibitors and other antivirals can range up to $14,000 a year, excluding the costs of drugs to prevent opportunistic infections and expensive services such as viral load tests, which typically cost about $200.00" (Andriote 1999, 378). Providing access to information about these new drugs is also a critical issue in the AIDS service-

delivery process. For a discussion of these and other issues pertaining to the development of protease inhibitors and other antivirals, see Andriote 1999, pp. 378–80.

15. See Osburn and Benecke 1996, chapter 9. These authors issue a yearly report on the implementation of "Don't Ask, Don't Tell, Don't Pursue" under the auspices of their organization, the Servicemembers Legal Defense Network (SLDN). Based in Washington, D.C., SLDN "is the sole national legal aid and watchdog organization for those targeted by the military's new policy on homosexuals, and the only means currently available to document abuses" (Osburn and Benecke 1996, 250). For a good overview of the implementation of the policy over time, see D'Amico 2000.

16. The political scientist Michael Goldfield points out that the African-American civil rights movement faced similar problems, which undermined its long-term success. Goldfield argues that two important elements, which were part of organizing in the 1930s and 1940s, were missing from the 1960s-era movement. First, he claims, "the exclusive focus on rights led the movement largely to gloss over those class issues that were at the root of problems faced by poor and working-class African-Americans. Second . . . the main missing link from the struggles of the 1960s—in good part a consequence of the contradictory resolution of the 1930s turning point—was the organized labor movement" (Goldfield 1997, p. 295). For a good discussion of these and other issues pertaining to the African-American civil rights movement, see Goldfield 1997.

17. For further discussion of this participatory democratic spirit, see Rimmerman 1997.

18. For a discussion of rights within the context of radical democratic politics, see Lehr 1999, pp. 95–96.

19. There is considerable evidence to indicate that since about the 1980s, disparities in the distribution of income and wealth in the United States have widened. One excellent source for 1998 data on the distribution of wealth, debts, and income is Henwood 2000.

20. For a more fully developed discussion of this study and its implications, see Barko 2000.

21. For an excellent cross-national study of labor unions in comparative perspective, see Hunt 1999b.

22. For a more fully developed and nuanced discussion of the need to transcend identity politics in response to HIV/AIDS, see Cohen 1999.

23. For an important discussion of these issues, see Warner 1999.

24. For a good discussion of these issues, see Gagnon and Nardi 1997, p. 13.

25. The Gay, Lesbian, Straight Education Network (GLSEN) has collected survey data regarding the lesbian/gay experience in schools. These data provide plenty of empirical evidence to support the claim that lesbian and gay students (and those suspected of being so) face hostile environments in many of the nation's schools. The following data gathered by GLSEN appeared in Bronski 1999, p. 16:

- 97 percent of students in public high schools in Massachusetts reported regularly hearing homophobic remarks from their peers in a 1993 report of the Massachusetts Governor's Commission on Gay and Lesbian Youth;
- 53 percent of the students reported hearing anti-gay remarks made by school staff;

- 46 percent of gay, lesbian, and bisexual students reported in a 1997 Massachusetts Youth Risk Behavior Study they attempted suicide in the past year compared to 9 percent of their peers;
- 22 percent were in a fight that resulted in receiving medical attention compared to 3 percent of their peers;
- gay students are three times as likely to have been threatened with a weapon at school than their peers during the previous 12 months, according to Youth Risk Behavior surveys done in Massachusetts and Vermont;
- 28 percent of gay youths drop out of high school altogether, according to a U.S. Department of Health and Human Services study.

GLSEN's goal is make America's schools safe for all youth. They have focused on four major fronts: (1) a fight for new laws that would extend equal protection to all students regardless of sexual orientation; (2) efforts to change the attitudes of those who influence daily life in schools—"from public policy leaders in Washington, DC to state superintendents to local school board members"; (3) providing materials that can help train teachers about lesbian, gay, bisexual, and transgendered issues in ways that help stop harassment and violence; (4) organizing for change by strengthening grassroots activism (GLSEN 2000 fundraising and information letter, p. 3). GLSEN's national organization is located in New York City; it has eighty-five chapters nationwide.

26. Voter participation rates in selected democracies are as follows: Australia (1993), 90 percent; Austria (1986), 87 percent; Canada (1988), 75 percent; East Germany (1990), 93 percent; France (1988), 81 percent; Hungary (1990), 64 percent; Italy (1991), 85 percent; Japan (1993), 75 percent; South Korea (1992), 79 percent; Switzerland (1987), 46 percent; United States (1996), 49 percent. These figures appear in Miroff, Seidelman, and Swanstrom 1995, p. 120.

27. See Rimmerman 1997.

28. See Macpherson 1976, Pateman 1970, Mansbridge 1980, Mathews 1999, Paget 1990, and Putnam 2000.

29. In her book *Solidarity of Strangers: Feminism after Identity Politics*, the political theorist Jodi Dean develops the concept of "reflective solidarity" as one possible way to overcome these sorts of obstacles. Dean describes reflexive solidarity this way: "Without certain foundations or traditions capable of bringing us together, reflection itself has to become the basis of our shared connection. Because political contestation in contemporary democracies includes cultural representations as well as social obligations, there is no solution or final answer to the proper configuration of identity and democracy. All we have left is reflective solidarity—a solidarity rooted in our ability to connect with each other through contestation and critique. We have to accept our interconnections even as we question them" (Dean 1996, 74). For a discussion of issues pertaining to justice and difference, see Young 1990.

Appendix B

1. The source for the march agenda was <www.planetout.com/pro/specials/mmow>, accessed August 13, 2000.

References

Adam, Barry D. 1995. *The Rise of a Gay and Lesbian Movement.* Rev. ed. New York: Twayne Publishers.

Adam, Barry D., Jan Willem Duyvendak, and André Krouwel. 1999. "Introduction." In *The Global Emergence of Gay and Lesbian Politics: National Imprints of a Worldwide Movement.* Philadelphia: Temple University Press.

Altman, Dennis. 1982. *The Homosexualization of America, the Americanization of the Homosexual.* New York: St. Martin's Press.

Alwood, Edward. 1996. *Straight News: Gays, Lesbians, and the News Media.* New York: Columbia University Press.

Anderson, Scott. 1994. "A Monumental March in Washington." In *Long Road to Freedom:* The Advocate *History of the Gay and Lesbian Movement,* ed. Mark Thompson. New York: St. Martin's Press.

Andriote, John-Manuel. 1999. *Victory Deferred: How AIDS Changed Gay Life in America.* Chicago: University of Chicago Press.

Arno, Peter S., and Karyn L. Feiden. 1992. *Against the Odds: The Story of AIDS, Drug Development, Politics, and Profits.* New York: Harper and Collins.

Bachrach, Peter. 1971. *The Theory of Democratic Elitism: A Critique.* Boston: Little Brown.

Badgett, M. V. Lee. 1995. "The Wage Effects of Sexual Orientation Discrimination." *Industrial and Labor Relations Review* 48, no. 4 (July).

———. 1997a. "Thinking Homo/Economically." In *A Queer World,* ed. Martin Duberman, pp. 467–76. New York: New York University Press.

———. 1997b. "Vulnerability in the Workplace: Evidence of Anti-Gay Discrimination." *Angles: The Policy Journal of the Institute for Gay and Lesbian Strategic Studies* 2, no. 1 (September).

———. 1998. *Income Inflation: The Myth of Affluence among Gays, Lesbian, and Bisexual Americans.* New York: NGLTF Policy Institute.

Baer, Denise L., and David A. Bositis. 1993. *Politics and Linkage in a Democratic Society.* Englewood Cliffs, N.J.: Prentice Hall.

Bailey, Robert W. 1999. *Gay Politics, Urban Politics: Identity and Economics in the Urban Setting.* New York: Columbia University Press.

Baker, Peter. 1997. "Echoing Truman on Race, Clinton Calls for Gay Rights." *International Herald Tribune,* November 10, p. 2.

Barko, Naomi. 2000. "The Other Gender Gap." *The American Prospect,* June 19–July 3, pp. 61–64.

Bawer, Bruce. 1993. *A Place at the Table: The Gay Individual in American Society.* New York: Poseidon Press.

Becker, Elizabeth. 2001. "Gay Republican Will Run White House AIDS Office." New York *Times*, April 9, p. A13.

Bérubé, Allan. 1990. *Coming Out Under Fire: The History of Gay Men and Women in World War II*. New York: Free Press.

Biersack, Robert. 1994. "Introduction." In *Risky Business? PAC Decisionmaking in Congressional Elections*, ed. Robert Biersack, Paul S. Herrnson, and Clyde Wilcox. Armonk, N.Y.: M. E. Sharpe.

Billard, Betsy. 1995. "Shooting Straight." *The Advocate*, July 25, pp. 26–28.

Blasius, Mark. 1994. *Gay and Lesbian Politics: Sexuality and the Emergence of a New Ethic*. Philadelphia: Temple University Press.

Blasius, Mark, and Shane Phelan, eds. 1997. *We Are Everywhere: A Historical Sourcebook of Gay and Lesbian Politics*. New York: Routledge.

Boykin, Keith. 1996. *One More River to Cross: Black and Gay in America*. New York: Anchor Books.

———. 2000. "Where Rhetoric Meets Reality: The Role of Black Lesbians and Gays in 'Queer' Politics." In *The Politics of Gay Rights*, ed. Craig A. Rimmerman, Kenneth D. Wald, and Clyde Wilcox. Chicago: University of Chicago Press.

Brewer, Sara, David Kaib, and Karen O'Connor. 2000. "Sex and the Supreme Court: Gays, Lesbians, and Justice." In *The Politics of Gay Rights*, ed. Craig A. Rimmerman, Kenneth D. Wald, and Clyde Wilcox. Chicago: University of Chicago Press.

Bronski, Michael. 1998. *The Pleasure Principle: Sex, Backlash, and the Struggle for Gay Freedom*. New York: St. Martin's Press.

———. 1999. "Littleton, Movies, and Gay KIDS." *Z Magazine*, July/August, pp. 12–16.

———. 2000. "Dr. Laura: Moral Dominatrix." *Z Magazine*, May, pp. 10–12.

Brudnoy, David. 1997. *Life Is Not a Rehearsal*. New York: Doubleday.

Bull, Chris. 1993. "Broken Promise." *The Advocate*, August 27, p. 24.

———. 1999. "Still Angry after All These Years." *The Advocate*, August 17, pp. 17–20.

———. 2000a. "Home in the White House." *The Advocate*, March 14.

———. 2000b. "More Military Maneuvers." *The Advocate*, February 1.

———. 2001a. "Going Local." *The Advocate*, June 19, pp. 33–36.

———. 2001b. "Same Players, New Game." *The Advocate*, February 27, pp. 24–25.

———. 2001c. "Uncharted Waters." *The Advocate*, January 30, pp. 24–26.

Bull, Chris, and John Gallagher. 1996. *Perfect Enemies: The Religious Right, The Gay Movement, and the Politics of the 1990s*. New York: Crown.

Burkett, Elinor. 1995. *The Gravest Show on Earth: America in the Age of AIDS*. Boston: Houghton Mifflin.

Button, James W., Barbara A. Rienzo, and Kenneth D. Wald. 2000. "The Politics of Gay Rights at the State and Local Level." In *The Politics of Gay Rights*, ed. Craig A. Rimmerman, Kenneth D. Wald, and Clyde Wilcox. Chicago: University of Chicago Press.

———. 1997. *Private Lives, Public Conflicts: Battles over Gay Rights in American Communities*. Washington, D.C.: Congressional Quarterly Press.

Cain, Patricia. 1993. "Litigating for Lesbian and Gay Rights: A Legal History." *Virginia Law Review* 79: 1551–1641.

———. 2000. *Rainbow Rights: The Role of Lawyers and Courts in the Lesbian and Gay Civil Rights Movement*. Boulder, Colo.: Westview Press.

Cannon, Lou. 1991. *President Reagan: The Role of a Lifetime*. New York: Simon and Schuster.

Carlson, Tucker. "Log Cabin Blues." 1999. *The Weekly Standard*, December 20, pp. 11–12.

Cassels, Peter. 2000. "Bush Meeting with Gay GOP: Stagecraft or Statesmanship?" *Bay Windows*, April 20, pp. 1, 12.

Chasin, Alexandra. 2000. *Selling Out: The Gay and Lesbian Movement Goes to Market*. New York: St. Martin's Press.

Chauncey, George. 1994. *Gay New York*. New York: Basic Books.

Chibbaro, Lou, Jr. 1995a. "Bob Dole Tells Log Cabin: No Thanks." *The Washington Blade*, September 1.

———. 1995b. "Clinton: Being Gay is 'Not a Security Risk.'" *The Washington Blade*, August 4.

———. 1996a. "The Clinton Quandary." *The Washington Blade*, November 1.

———. 1996b. "White House Gay Liaison Named." *The Washington Blade*, June 21, p. 1.

———. 1998. "White House Chides Lott for Statements." *The Washington Blade*, June 1998, pp. 1, 14.

———. 2000. "We Shut Them Out." *Washington Blade*, August 2, pp. 1, 16.

———. 2001a. "Activists Concerned about Proposed Spending Levels." *Washington Blade*, April 13, pp. 1, 26.

———. 2001b. "Gay Pentagon Aide Draws Ire from Right." *Washington Blade*, April 20, pp. 1, 18.

———. 2001c. "Group Denounces Bush." *Washington Blade*, June 1, p. 20.

Clendinen, Dudley. 2001a. "Dubya's Gay Friend." *Out*, June, p. 72.

———. 2001b. "Going to Extremes." *Out*, June, pp. 68–72, 118–26.

Clendinen, Dudley, and Adam Nagourney. 1999. *Out for Good: The Struggle to Build a Gay Rights Movement in America*. New York: Simon and Schuster.

Cohen, Cathy J. 1999. *The Boundaries of Blackness: AIDS and the Breakdown of Black Politics*. Chicago: University of Chicago Press.

Colby, David C., and Timothy E. Cook. 1991. "Epidemics and Agendas: The Politics of Nightly News Coverage of AIDS." *Journal of Health Politics, Policy and Law* 16, no. 2 (Summer): 215–49.

Crimp, Douglas, ed. 1988. *AIDS: Cultural Analysis, Cultural Activism*. Cambridge: Cambridge University Press.

Crimp, Douglas, with Adam Rolston. 1990. *AIDS Demographics*. Seattle: Bay Press.

Cruikshank, Margaret. 1992. *The Gay and Lesbian Liberation Movement*. New York: Routledge.

D'Amico, Francine. 2000. "Sexuality and Military Service." In *The Politics of Gay Rights*, ed. Craig A. Rimmerman, Kenneth D. Wald, and Clyde Wilcox. Chicago: University of Chicago Press.

Dangerous Bedfellows. 1996. "Introduction." In *Policing Public Sex: Queer Politics and the Future of AIDS Activism,* ed. Dangerous Bedfellows. Boston: South End Press.

Darnovsky, Marcy, Barbara Epstein, and Richard Flacks. 1995. "Introduction." In *Cultural Politics and Social Movements,* ed. Marcy Darnovsky, Barbara Epstein, and Richard Flacks. Philadelphia: Temple University Press.

Davis, Madeline, and Elizabeth Lapovsky Kennedy. 1993. *Boots of Leather, Slippers of Gold: The History of a Lesbian Community.* New York: Routledge.

Dean, Jodi. 1996. *Solidarity of Strangers: Feminism after Identity Politics.* Berkeley: University of California Press.

DeBold, Kathleen, ed. 1994. *Out for Office: Campaigning in the Gay Nineties.* Washington: Gay and Lesbian Victory Fund.

D'Emilio, John. 1983. *Sexual Politics, Sexual Communities: The Making of a Homosexual Minority in the United States, 1940–1970.* Chicago: University of Chicago Press.

———. 1992. *Making Trouble: Essays on Gay History, Policies, and the University.* New York: Routledge.

———. 2000. "Cycles of Change, Questions of Strategy: The Gay and Lesbian Movement after Fifty Years." In *The Politics of Gay Rights,* ed. Craig A. Rimmerman, Kenneth D. Wald, and Clyde Wilcox. Chicago: University of Chicago Press.

Diamond, Sara. 1989. *Spiritual Warfare: The Politics of the Christian Right.* Boston: South End Press.

———. 1995. *Roads to Dominion: Right-Wing Movements and Political Power in the United States.* New York: Guilford Press.

———. 1998. *Not by Politics Alone.* New York: Guilford Press.

Dolkart, Jane. 1998. "Law." In *St. James Press Gay and Lesbian Almanac,* ed. Neil Schlager. Detroit: St. James Press.

Donovan, Todd, Jim Wenzel, and Shaun Bowler. 2000. "Direct Democracy and Gay Rights Initiatives after Romer." In *The Politics of Gay Rights,* ed. Craig A. Rimmerman, Kenneth D. Wald, and Clyde Wilcox. Chicago: University of Chicago Press.

Dreyfuss, Robert. 2000. "The Double-Edge Wedge." *The American Prospect,* August 28, pp. 23–31.

Duberman, Martin. 1993. *Stonewall.* New York: Dutton.

———. 1999. *Left Out: The Politics of Exclusion/Essays/1964–1999.* New York: Basic Books.

Eagles, Charles. 1986. "Introduction." In *The Civil Rights Movement in America,* ed. Charles Eagles. Jackson: University Press of Mississippi.

Edelman, Murray. 1977. *Political Language: Words that Succeed, Policies that Fail.* New York: Academic Press.

Epstein, Steven. 1996. *Impure Science: AIDS, Activism, and the Politics of Knowledge.* Berkeley: University of California Press.

———. 1999. "Gay and Lesbian Movements in the United States: Dilemmas of Identity, Diversity, and Political Strategy." In *The Global Emergence of Gay and Lesbian Politics: National Imprints of a Worldwide Movement,* ed. Barry

D. Adam, Jan Willem Duyvendak, and Andre Krouwel. Philadelphia: Temple University Press.

Escoffier, Jeffrey. 1998. *American Homo: Community and Perversity.* Berkeley: University of California Press.

Eskridge, William. 1999. *Gaylaw: Challenging the Apartheid of the Closet.* Cambridge: Harvard University Press.

Ettlebrick, Paula. 1997. "Since When Is Marriage a Path to Liberation?" In *Sexuality, Gender, and the Law,* ed. William N. Eskridge and Nan D. Hunter. New York: Foundation Press.

Foreman, Christopher. 1994. *Plagues, Products, and Politics: Emergent Public Health Hazards and National Policymaking.* Washington, D.C.: Brookings Institution.

Freiberg, Peter. 1996. "With Success Comes Scrutiny." *Washington Blade,* August 23.

———. 1998. "President's Order Protects Workers." *Washington Blade,* June 5, pp. 1, 29, 31.

———. 2000a. "Vermont's Legislature Grapples with Choices." *Washington Blade,* January 21, p. 1.

———. 2000b. "Victory in Vermont." *Washington Blade,* April 28, pp. 1, 51, 53.

Gagnon, John A., and Peter M. Nardi. 1997. "Introduction." In *In Changing Times: Gay Men and Lesbians Encounter HIV/AIDS,* ed. Martin Levine, Peter M. Nardi, and John A. Gagnon. Chicago: University of Chicago Press.

Gallagher, John. 1996. "Speak Now." *The Advocate,* June 11.

———. 2000. "Separate but Equal." *The Advocate,* February 1.

Gamson, Joshua. 2000. "Whose Millennium March?" *The Nation,* April 17, pp. 16–20.

Gertsmann, Evan. 1999. *The Constitutional Underclass: Gays, Lesbians, and the Failure of Class-Based Equal Protection.* Chicago: University of Chicago Press.

Getty, Jeff, and Michael Botkin's Ghost, Survive AIDS Writers Pool. 2001. "An Old-Fashioned Demo." *Bay Area Reporter,* March 8, p. 20.

GLSEN Fundraising and Information Newsletter. 2000. New York: Gay, Lesbian, and Straight Education Network.

Goldfield, Michael. 1997. *The Color of Politics: Race and the Mainsprings of American Politics.* New York: New Press.

Golebiowska, Ewa A., and Cynthia J. Thomsen. 1999. "Group Stereotypes and Evaluations of Individuals: The Case of Gay and Lesbian Political Candidates." In *Gays and Lesbians in the Democratic Process: Public Policy, Public Opinion, and Political Representation,* ed. Ellen D. B. Riggle and Barry Tadlock. New York: Columbia University Press.

Green, John C. 2000. "Antigay: Varieties of Opposition to Gay Rights." In *The Politics of Gay Rights,* ed. Craig A. Rimmerman, Kenneth D. Wald, and Clyde Wilcox. Chicago: University of Chicago Press.

Haider-Markel, Donald P. 1997. "From Bullhorns to PACS: Lesbian and Gay Politics, Interest Groups and Policy." Ph.D. diss., University of Wisconsin–Milwaukee.

_____. 1999. "Creating Change—Holding the Line: Agenda Setting on Lesbian and Gay Issues at the National Level." In *Gays and Lesbians in the Democratic Process,* ed. Ellen D. B. Riggle and Barry L. Tadlock. New York: Columbia University Press.

Harrington, Mark. 1997. "Some Transitions in the History of AIDS Treatment Activism: From Therapeutic Utopianism to Pragmatic Praxis." In *Acting on AIDS: Sex, Drugs, and Politics,* ed. Joshua Oppenheimer and Helena Reckitt. London: Serpent's Tail.

Henwood, Doug. 2000. "Wealth News." *Left Business Observer,* no. 94, May 5, pp. 3, 5.

Herman, Didi. 1994. *Rights of Passage: Struggles for Lesbian and Gay Equality.* Toronto: University of Toronto Press.

_____. 1997. *The Antigay Agenda: Orthodox Vision and the Christian Right.* Chicago: University of Chicago Press.

_____. 2000. "The Gay Agenda Is the Devil's Agenda: The Christian Right's Vision and the Role of the State." In *The Politics of Gay Rights,* ed. Craig A. Rimmerman, Kenneth D. Wald, and Clyde Wilcox. Chicago: University of Chicago Press.

Hertzog, Mark. 1996. *The Lavender Vote: Lesbians, Gay Men, and Bisexuals in American Electoral Politics.* New York: New York University Press.

Hill, Steven. 2000. "San Francisco Mayoral Race." *Z Magazine,* February, p. 17.

hooks, bell. 1984. *Feminist Theory: From Margin to Center.* Boston: South End Press.

Hunt, Gerald. 1999a. "What Can be Done? Sexual Diversity and Labor Unions in Perspective." In *Laboring for Rights: Unions and Sexual Diversity Across Nations,* ed. Gerald Hunt. Philadelphia: Temple University Press.

_____, ed. 1999b. *Laboring for Rights: Unions and Sexual Diversity Across Nations.* Philadelphia: Temple University Press.

Hunt, Ronald J. 1999. *Historical Dictionary of the Gay Liberation Movement: Gay Men and the Quest for Social Justice.* Lanham, Md.: Scarecrow Press.

Hunter, Nan D. 1995a. "Identity, Speech, and Equality." In Lisa Duggan and Nan D. Hunter, *Sex Wars: Sexual Dissent and Political Culture.* New York: Routledge.

_____. 1995b. "Marriage, Law, and Gender: A Feminist Inquiry." In Lisa Duggan and Nan D. Hunter, *Sex Wars: Sexual Dissent and Political Culture,* pp. 107–22. New York: Routledge.

Huntington, Samuel P. 1975. "The United States." In *The Crisis of Democracy,* ed. Michel Crozier, Samuel P. Huntington, and Joji Watnanuki, pp. 59–118. New York: New York University Press.

Ireland, Doug. 1999. "Rebuilding the Gay Movement." *The Nation,* July 12, pp. 11–17.

Jacobson, Peter D. 1996. "Sexual Orientation and the Military: Some Legal Considerations." In *Out in Force: Sexual Orientation and the Military,* ed. Gregory M. Herek, Jared B. Jobe, and Ralph M. Carney. Chicago: University of Chicago Press.

Jagose, Annamarie. 1996. *Queer Theory: An Introduction.* New York: New York University Press.

Jay, Karla. 1999. *Tales of the Lavender Menace*. New York: Basic Books.

Jeffries, John C. 1994. *Justice Lewis F. Powell, Jr.* New York: Scribner.

Johnson, Hans. 2000. "Onward Christian Soldiers." *The Advocate,* February 15, pp. 30–31.

Johnston, Hank, Enrique Larana, and Joseph R. Gusfeld. 1994. "Identities, Grievances, and New Social Movements." In *New Social Movements,* ed. Hank Johnston, Enrique Larana, and Joseph R. Gusfeld. Philadelphia: Temple University Press.

Kaiser, Charles. 1997. *The Gay Metropolis 1940–1996.* New York: Houghton Mifflin.

Kayal, Philip M. 1993. *Bearing Witness: Gay Men's Health Crisis and the Politics of AIDS.* Boulder: Westview Press.

Keen, Lisa. 1997. "Court Calls Military Policy 'Degrading and Deplorable.'" *Washington Blade,* July 4, pp. 1, 23.

———. 1999a. "Court 'Punts' on Marriage." *Washington Blade,* December 12, p. 1.

———. 1999b. "Vermont's 'Step Forward.'" *Washington Blade,* December 24, p. 1.

Keen, Lisa, and Suzanne B. Goldberg. 1998. *Strangers to the Law: Gay People on Trial.* Ann Arbor: University of Michigan Press.

King, Edward. 1993. *Safety in Numbers.* London: Cassell.

King, Mike. 1996. "Suicide Watch." *The Advocate,* November 12, pp. 41–44.

Koop, C. Everett. 1991. *The Memoirs of America's Family Doctor.* New York: Random House.

Kramer, Larry. 1994. *Reports from the Holocaust: The Story of an AIDS Activist.* Rev. ed. New York: St. Martin's Press.

Lehr, Valerie. 1999. *Queer Family Values.* Philadelphia: Temple University Press.

Lehring, Gary L. 1996. "Constructing the 'Other' Soldier: Gay Identity's Military Threat." In *Gay Rights, Military Wrongs: Political Perspectives on Lesbians and Gays in the Military,* ed. Craig A. Rimmerman. New York: Garland.

Lewis, Gregory B., and Jonathan L. Edelson. 2000. "DOMA and ENDA: Congress Votes on Gay Rights." In *The Politics of Gay Rights,* ed. Craig A. Rimmerman, Kenneth D. Wald, and Clyde Wilcox. Chicago: University of Chicago Press.

Lewis, Gregory B., and Marc A. Rogers. 1999. "Does the Public Support Equal Rights for Gays and Lesbians?" In *Gays and Lesbians in the Democratic Process,* ed. Ellen D. B. Riggle and Barry L. Tadlock. New York: Columbia University Press.

Log Cabin Republicans. 2001 (January 22). "The Gay Vote 2000." Available from www.lcr.org, accessed May 21, 2001.

Lorde, Audre. 1984. *Sister Outsider: Essays and Speeches.* Freedom, Calif.: Crossing Press.

Loughery, John. 1998. *The Other Side of Silence: Men's Lives and Gay Identities: A Twentieth Century History.* New York: Henry Holt.

Lowi, Theodore J. 1979. *The End of Liberalism.* 2d ed. New York: Norton.

Macpherson, C. B. 1976. *The Life and Times of Liberal Democracy.* Oxford: Oxford University Press.

Mansbridge, Jane J. 1980. *Beyond Adversary Democracy.* New York: Basic Books.

Mathews, David. 1999. *Politics for People: Finding a Responsible Public Voice.* 2d ed. Urbana: University of Illinois Press.

Mayer, Margit, and Roland Roth. 1995. "New Social Movements and the Transformation to Post-Fordist Society." In *Cultural Politics and Social Movements,* ed. Marcy Darnovsky, Barbara Epstein, and Richard Flacks. Philadelphia: Temple University Press.

McAdam, Doug. 1982. *The Political Process and the Development of Black Insurgency.* Chicago: University of Chicago Press.

———. 1994. "Culture and Movements." In *New Social Movements: From Ideology to Identity,* ed. Enrique Larana, Hank Johnston, and Joseph Gusfield. Philadelphia: Temple University Press.

Meyer, Lisa. 1999. "Hostile Classrooms: The State of Hate." *The Advocate,* April 13.

Miroff, Bruce, Raymond Seidelman, and Todd Swanstrom. 1995. *The Democratic Debate.* Boston: Houghton Mifflin.

Moen, Matthew C. 1992. *The Transformation of the Christian Right.* Tuscaloosa: University of Alabama Press.

———. 1996. "The Evolving Politics of the Christian Right." *PS: Political Science and Politics* (September): 461–64.

Morris, Aldon D. 1984. *The Origins of the Civil Rights Movement: Black Communities Organizing for Change.* New York: Free Press.

Moss, J. Jennings. 1995a. "The Czar Trip." *The Advocate,* December 12, pp. 22–28.

———. 1995b. "Picking Up the Pieces." *The Advocate,* October 31, pp. 25–27.

———. 1996. "Where Have All the Radicals Gone?" *The Advocate,* December 10, pp. 45–48.

Nardi, Peter M., and John H. Gagnon. 1997. "Introduction." In *In Changing Times: Gay Men and Lesbians Encounter AIDS,* ed. Martin P. Levine, Peter M. Nardi, and John H. Gagnon, pp. 171–89. Chicago: University of Chicago Press.

Nichols, Jack. 1996. *The Gay Agenda.* Amherst, N.Y.: Prometheus Books.

O'Bryan, Will. 2001. "Arizona Lifts Sodomy Ban." *Washington Blade,* May 11, p. 1.

Odets, Walt. 1996. "Why We Stopped Doing Primary Prevention for Gay Men in 1985." In *Policing Public Sex,* ed. Dangerous Bedfellows, pp. 115–40. Boston: South End Press.

Oppenheimer, Joshua. 1997. "Movements, Markets, and the Mainstream: Gay Activism and Assimilation in the Age of AIDS." In *Acting on AIDS: Sex, Drugs, and Politics,* ed. Joshua Oppenheimer and Helena Reckitt. London: Serpent's Tail.

Orfield, Gary, Susan E. Eaton, and the Harvard Project on School Desegregation. 1996. *Dismantling Desegregation: The Quiet Reversal of Brown v. Board of Education.* New York: New Press.

Osburn, C. Dixon, and Michelle M. Benecke. 1996. "Conduct Unbecoming Continues: The First Year Under 'Don't Ask, Don't Tell, Don't Pursue.' " In Craig

A. Rimmerman, ed., *Gay Rights, Military Wrongs: Political Perspectives on Lesbians and Gays in the Military.* New York: Garland.

Pacelle, Richard. 1996. "Seeking Another Forum: The Courts and Lesbian and Gay Rights." In Craig A. Rimmerman, ed., *Gay Rights, Military Wrongs: Political Perspectives on Lesbians and Gays in the Military.* New York: Garland.

Paget, Karen. 1990. "Resurgence at the Grassroots?" *The American Prospect,* Summer, pp. 115–28.

Panem, Sandra. 1988. *The AIDS Bureaucracy.* Cambridge, Mass.: Harvard University Press.

Pateman, Carole. 1970. *Participation and Democratic Theory.* Cambridge: Cambridge University Press.

Perrow, Charles, and Mauro F. Guillen. 1990. *The AIDS Disaster: The Failure of Organizations in New York and the Nation.* New Haven: Yale University Press.

Phelan, Shane. 1994. *Getting Specific: Postmodern Lesbian Politics.* Minneapolis: University of Minnesota Press.

Plano, Jack C., and Milton Greenberg. 1986. *The American Political Dictionary.* 7th ed. New York: Holt, Rinehart, and Winston.

Purdum, Todd S. 1996. "Gay Rights Groups Attack Clinton on Midnight Signing." *New York Times,* September 22, 1996, p. A16.

Putnam, Robert D. 2000. *Bowling Alone: The Collapse and Revival of American Community.* New York: Simon and Schuster.

Raben, Robert. 1998. "Politics." In *St. James Press Gay and Lesbian Almanac,* ed. Neil Schlager. Detroit: St. James Press.

Rayside, David. 1996. "The Perils of Congressional Politics." In *Gay Rights, Military Wrongs: Political Perspectives on Lesbians and Gays in the Military,* ed. Craig A. Rimmerman. New York: Garland.

———. 1998. *On the Fringe: Gays and Lesbians in the Political Process.* Ithaca, N.Y.: Cornell University Press.

Riggle, Ellen D. B., and Barry L. Tadlock, eds. 1999. *Gays and Lesbians in the Democratic Process.* New York: Columbia University Press.

Rimmerman, Craig A. 1993. *Presidency by Plebiscite: The Reagan-Bush Era in Institutional Perspective.* Boulder, Colo.: Westview Press.

———. 1994. "New Kids on the Block: The WISH List and the Gay and Lesbian Victory Fund in the 1992 Elections." In *Risky Business? PAC Decisionmaking in Congressional Elections,* ed. Robert Biersack, Paul S. Herrnson, Clyde Wilcox. Armonk, N.Y.: M. E. Sharpe.

———. 1996a. "Introduction." In *Gay Rights, Military Wrongs: Political Perspectives on Lesbians and Gays in the Military,* ed. Craig A. Rimmerman. New York: Garland.

———. 1996b. "Promise Unfulfilled: Clinton's Failure to Overturn the Military Ban on Lesbians and Gays." In *Gay Rights, Military Wrongs: Political Perspectives on Lesbians and Gays in the Military,* ed. Craig A. Rimmerman. New York: Garland.

———. 1997. *The New Citizenship: Unconventional Politics, Activism, and Service.* Boulder: Westview Press.

———. 1998a. "ACT UP." In *Encyclopedia of AIDS,* ed. Raymond A. Smith. Chicago: Fitzroy Dearborn.

———. 1998b. "Military." In *St. James Press Gay and Lesbian Almanac,* ed. Neil Schlager. Detroit: St. James Press.

———. 1998c. "U.S. Congress." In *Encyclopedia of AIDS,* ed. Raymond A. Smith. Chicago: Fitzroy Dearborn.

———. 1998d. "U.S. Presidency." In *Encyclopedia of AIDS,* ed. Raymond A. Smith. Chicago: Fitzroy Dearborn.

———. 1999. "The Gay and Lesbian Victory Fund Comes of Age: Reflections on the 1996 Elections." In *After the Revolution: PACs, Lobbies, and the Republican Congress,* ed. Robert Biersack, Paul S. Herrnson, and Clyde Wilcox. Needham Heights, Mass.: Allyn and Bacon.

———. 2000. "A 'Friend' in the White House?" In *Creating Change: Sexuality, Public Policy, and Civil Rights,* ed. John D'Emilio, William B. Turner, and Urvashi Vaid. New York: St. Martin's Press.

Rist, Darrell Yates. 1989. "AIDS as Apocalypse: The Deadly Costs of an Obsession." *The Nation,* February 13.

Roehr, Bob. 2001. "Gay Man Named to Head AIDS Office." *Bay Area Reporter,* April 12, p. 13.

Rofes, Eric. 1990. "Gay Lib vs. AIDS: Averting Civil War." *Outlook,* no. 8 (Spring).

Rom, Mark Carl. 2000. "Gays and AIDS: Democratizing Disease?" In *The Politics of Gay Rights,* ed. Craig A. Rimmerman, Kenneth D. Wald, and Clyde Wilcox. Chicago: University of Chicago Press.

Rosenberg, Gerald. 1991. *The Hollow Hope: Can Courts Bring About Social Change?* Chicago: University of Chicago Press.

Roundy, Bill. 2000. "Vermont Ruling Triggers New Marriage Ban Effort." *Washington Blade,* January 21, p. 27.

Sadownick, Douglas. 1990. "ACT UP Makes a Spectacle of AIDS." *High Performance* (Spring): 26–31.

Salokar, Rebecca Mae. 1997. "Beyond Gay Rights Litigation: Using a Systemic Strategy to Effect Political Change in the United States." *Gay and Lesbian Quarterly* 3: 385–415.

Saslow, James M. 1994. "'A Gentle, Angry People' Came from Everywhere." In *Long Road to Freedom: The Advocate History of the Gay and Lesbian Movement,* ed. Mark Thompson. New York: St. Martin's Press.

Schmitt, Eric. 1995. "Judge Overturns Pentagon Policy on Homosexuals." *New York Times,* March 31, p. A1.

Schneider, Beth E., and Nancy E. Stoller. 1995. "Introduction: Feminist Strategies of Empowerment." *Women Resisting AIDS: Feminist Strategies of Empowerment,* ed. Beth E. Schneider and Nancy E. Stoller. Philadelphia: Temple University Press.

Schulman, Sarah. 1994. *My American History: Lesbian and Gay Life during the Reagan/Bush Years.* New York: Routledge.

Schumpeter, Joseph. 1950. *Capitalism, Socialism, and Democracy.* 3d ed. New York: Harper and Row.

Scott, James. 1990. *Domination and the Arts of Resistance: Hidden Transcripts.* New Haven: Yale University Press.

Scott, Peter. 1997. "White Noise: How Gay Men's Activism Gets Written Out of AIDS Prevention." In *Acting on AIDS: Sex, Drugs, and Politics,* ed. Joshua Oppenheimer and Helena Reckitt. London: Serpent's Tail.

Sherrill, Kenneth. 1993. "On Gay People as a Politically Powerless Group." In Marc Wolinsky and Kenneth Sherrill, eds., *Gays and the Military: Joseph Steffan versus the United States.* Princeton: Princeton University Press.

———. 1996. "The Political Power of Lesbians, Gays, and Bisexuals." *PS: Political Science and Politics* 29, no. 3 (September): 469–73.

Shilts, Randy. 1987. *And the Band Played On: Politics, People, and the AIDS Epidemic.* New York: St. Martin's Press.

Siplon, Patricia. 1999. "A Brief History of the Political Science of AIDS Activism." *PS: Political Science and Politics* 32, no. 3 (September): 578–79.

Smith, Anna Marie. 1997. "The Centering of Right-Wing Extremism through the Construction of an 'Inclusionary' Homophobia and Racism." In *Playing with Fire: Queer Politics, Queer Theories,* ed. Shane Phelan. New York: Routledge.

Smith, Miriam. 1999. *Lesbian and Gay Rights in Canada: Social Movements and Equality-Seeking, 1971–1995.* Toronto: University of Toronto Press.

Smith, Rhonda. 1998a. "Forum Picks New Director." *Washington Blade,* February 20.

———. 1998b. "New Executive Director Resigns." *Washington Blade,* May 29.

Snow, David A. 1992. "Master Frames and Cycles of Protest." In *Frontiers in Social Movement Theory,* ed. Aldon D. Morris and Carol McClurg Mueller. New Haven: Yale University Press.

"A Sodomy Law's Last Stand." 2000. *The Advocate,* July 18, p. 13.

Stein, Arlene. 1995. "Sisters and Queers: Decentering Lesbian Feminism." In *Cultural Politics and Social Movements,* ed. Marcy Darnovsky, Barbara Epstein, and Richard Flacks. Philadelphia: Temple University Press.

Stein, Edward. 1999. *The Mismeasure of Desire: The Science, Theory, and Ethics of Sexual Orientation.* New York: Oxford University Press.

Stolberg, Sheryl Gay. 1998. "Clinton Decides Not to Finance Needle Program." *New York Times,* April 21, p. A1.

Stoller, Nancy A. 1995. "Lesbian Involvement in the AIDS Epidemic: Changing Roles and Generational Differences." In *Women Resisting AIDS: Feminist Strategies of Empowerment,* ed. Beth E. Schneider and Nancy E. Stoller. Philadelphia: Temple University Press.

———. 1997. "From Feminism to Polymorphous Activism: Lesbians in AIDS Organizations." In *Changing Times: Gay Men and Lesbians Encounter HIV/AIDS,* ed. Martin P. Levine, Peter M. Nardi, and John H. Gagnon, pp. 171–89. Chicago: University of Chicago Press.

Strasser, Mark. 1997. *Legally Wed: Same-Sex Marriage and the Constitution.* Ithaca, N.Y.: Cornell University Press.

Streitmatter, Rodger. 1995. *Unspeakable: The Rise of the Gay and Lesbian Press in America.* Boston: Faber and Faber.

Sturgeon, Noël. 1995. "Theorizing Movements: Direct Action and Direct Theory." In *Cultural Politics and Social Movements*, ed. Marcy Darnovsky, Barbara Epstein, and Richard Flacks. Philadelphia: Temple University Press.

Sullivan, Andrew. 1995. *Virtually Normal: An Argument about Homosexuality*. New York: Alfred A. Knopf.

————. 1998. *Love Undetectable: Notes on Friendship, Sex, and Survival*. New York: Alfred A. Knopf.

————. 2000. "State of the Union: Why 'Civil Union' Isn't Marriage." *The New Republic*, May 8, pp. 18–23.

Tafel, Richard. 1999. *Party Crasher: A Gay Republican Challenges Politics as Usual*. New York: Simon and Schuster.

Tarrow, Sidney. 1994. *Power in Movement: Social Movements, Collective Action, and Politics*. Cambridge: Cambridge University Press.

————. 1998. *Power in Movements and Contentious Politics*. 2d ed. Cambridge: Cambridge University Press.

"Task Force Report." 1998 (Spring). Washington, D.C.: National Gay and Lesbian Task Force.

Taylor, Verta, and Nancy E. Whittier. 1992. "Collective Identity in Social Movement Communities." In *Frontiers in Social Movement Theory*, ed. Aldon D. Morris and Carol McClurg Mueller. New Haven: Yale University Press.

Teal, Donn. 1995. *The Gay Militants*. New York: St. Martin's Press.

Thompson, Mark, ed. 1994. *Long Road to Freedom*: The Advocate *History of the Gay and Lesbian Movement*. New York: St. Martin's Press.

Toner, Robin. 1999. "Gay Republican Cleaves to the Party Despite a Bush Snub." New York *Times*, November 29, p. A14.

Toobin, Jeffrey. 1999. *A Vast Conspiracy: The Real Story of a Sex Scandal That Nearly Brought Down a President*. New York: Random House.

Treichler, Paula. 1999. *How to Have Theory in an Epidemic: Cultural Chronicles of AIDS*. Durham, N.C.: Duke University Press.

Trice, Elliott R. 1998. "Organizations." In *St. James Press Gay and Lesbian Almanac*, ed. Neil Schlager. Detroit: St. James Press.

Vaid, Urvashi. 1995. *Virtual Equality: The Mainstreaming of Gay and Lesbian Liberation*. New York: Anchor Books.

————. 1997. "Coalition as Goal, Not Process." *Gay Community News* 22, no. 4 (Spring): 6–9.

Wachtell, Lipton, Rosen, and Katz [law firm]. 1993. "Motion for Summary Judgment of Joseph Steffan." In *Gays and the Military: Joseph Steffan versus the United States*, ed. Marc Wolinsky and Kenneth Sherrill, pp. 3–39. Princeton, N.J.: Princeton University Press.

Wald, Kenneth. D. 2000. "The Context of Gay Politics." In *The Politics of Gay Rights*, ed. Craig A. Rimmerman, Kenneth D. Wald, and Clyde Wilcox. Chicago: University of Chicago Press.

Warner, Michael. 1999. *The Trouble with Normal: Sex, Politics, and the Ethics of Queer Life*. New York: Free Press.

Washington Blade. 1997. "A Look at the Largest Gay Political Organizations." December 12.

Watney, Simon. 1994. *Practices of Freedom: Selected Writings on HIV/AIDS.* Durham, N.C.: Duke University Press.

——. 1997. "The Political Significance of Statistics in the AIDS Crisis: Epidemiology, Representation, and Regaying." In *Acting on AIDS: Sex, Drugs, and Politics,* ed. Joshua Oppenheimer and Helena Reckitt. London: Serpent's Tail.

"White House Drops Gay Pride Month." 2001. *Ithaca Journal* (Ithaca, N.Y.), June 2, p. 1B.

Whitfield, LeRoy. 2000. "Black Gays Focus on Accountability." *Washington Blade,* February 25, pp. 1, 27.

Wieseltier, Leon. 1993. "Covenant and Burling." *New Republic,* February 1, p. 77.

Wilcox, Clyde. 1992. *God's Warriors: The Christian Right in Twentieth-Century America.* Baltimore: Johns Hopkins University Press.

——. 1996. *Onward Christian Soldiers? The Religious Right in American Politics.* Boulder: Westview Press.

Wilcox, Clyde, and Robin M. Wolpert. 1996. "President Clinton, Public Opinion, and Gays in the Military." In *Gay Rights, Military Wrongs: Political Perspectives on Lesbians and Gays in the Military,* ed. Craig A. Rimmerman. New York: Garland.

Wildman, Sarah. 2000. "Hiding in Plain Sight." *The Advocate,* September 12, pp. 27–30.

Wilson, Angelia R. 1997. "Somewhere Over the Rainbow: Queer Translating." In *Playing With Fire: Queer Politics, Queer Theories,* ed. Shane Phelan. New York: Routledge.

Young, Iris Marion. 1990. *Justice and the Politics of Difference.* Princeton, N.J.: Princeton University Press.

Zeller, Shawn. 2001. "A New GOP 'Tone' on Gay Rights?" *National Journal,* May 26, pp. 1582–83.

Index

The letter *t* after a page number indicates a table.